Parent Power!

from
Pam Fisher
2003

John K. Rosemond

Parent Power!

A Common-Sense Approach to Parenting in the '90s and Beyond

Andrews and McMeel
A Universal Press Syndicate Company
Kansas City

 For information write Andrews and McMeel, a Universal Press Syndicate Company, 4520 Main Street, Kansas City, Missouri 64111.

First edition published in 1981 by East Woods Press.

Designed by Edward King.

Illustration on page xix by Doug Dailer.

Library of Congress Cataloging-in-Publication Data

Rosemond, John K., 1947-
Parent Power! : a common-sense approach to parenting in the '90s and beyond. / by John K. Rosemond.
p. cm.
ISBN 0-8362-2808-1 : $9.95
1. Parenting—United States. 2. Child development—United States, I. Title.
HQ755.8.R665 1990
649'.1—dc20 90-28239
CIP

02 03 04 BAM 23 22 21 20 19 18

For Willie,
my love

Acknowledgments

The first edition of *Parent Power!*, published in 1981, would not have seen the light of day without the efforts and support of Anda Cochran, a good friend and colleague from whom I've learned much; Cathy Harvey, who brought my writing to the attention of the *Charlotte Observer* in 1978; Beth Resler Walters, my first editor at the *Observer,* who believed enough in what I was saying to recommend my column for syndication; Janet Johnson, Ph.D., for her comments on the manuscript; and Sally McMillan, Barbara Campbell, and Linda Benefield of East Woods Press, the original publisher.

I cannot adequately express my appreciation to all the good people at the *Charlotte Observer,* who've been so supportive and helpful over the years. Likewise, my thanks to the folks at the Knight-Ridder Wire and all the member and subscriber newspapers who think my ideas are worth sharing with the American public.

The current edition of *Parent Power!,* even better, in my highly prejudiced estimation, than the first, was nurtured into being through the efforts and commitment of Donna Martin, Dorothy O'Brien, Jean Lowe, Patti Dingus, Matt Lombardi, and Kathy Holder of Andrews and McMeel, my current and hopefully forever publisher. Thank you, squared.

Last, but not least, my thanks to Eric and Amy for providing me with such good material and such great stories and so much continuing good cheer and humor. I am one lucky daddy.

Contents

Read This First!!

Did I get your attention? Good, because there's a few things you should know before you read this book. I'll be brief.

Parent Power! was originally published in 1981 by East Woods Press and later, in 1983, released in a mass paperback edition by Pocket Books. In 1985, East Woods Press was acquired by a larger publishing house that subsequently decided it didn't want to spend time or energy pushing the one parenting book inherited in the buy-out. So, in 1987, it went out of print. Shortly thereafter, from all over the country, people began writing and calling to ask, "Where's *Parent Power!*?" I would shrug my shoulders and relate the sad tale of its premature demise.

Along came Andrews and McMeel, renowned in the publishing world for the success of such things as collections of The Far Side cartoons. They said they thought I'd be a compatible addition to their catalog and asked, "Will you write some books for us?" At first I thought, "What's this? *The Far Side of Parenting*?" But being a lover of irony, and needing some cash, I accepted their offer.

In 1989, they published *John Rosemond's Six-Point Plan for Raising Happy, Healthy Children. Esquire* magazine said it was "refreshingly reactionary." Tantalizing, eh? Anyway, it did (and continues to do) quite well. So, in 1990, Andrews and McMeel published *Ending the Homework Hassle.* Meanwhile, I wrangled the rights to *Parent Power!* away from its new owner and gave them to Andrews and McMeel, who agreed to publish it as the third book in their Rosemond Parenting Series, or something like that, but only if I'd revise and update it. So I did and here it is. For this edition, I've deleted stuff I was no longer comfortable with and added stuff I may not be comfortable with ten years from now. I've expanded the developmental section, "It's Only a Stage." I've added sections on Teenagers, Adoption, Divorce and Custody, and Bedtime Battles.

How is this book different from the other two? Good question! My *Six-Point Plan* is conceptual, controversial, and just a bit subversive. It's designed to shape—or *reshape* as the case may be—people's overall attitudes and perceptions of child rearing and themselves as parents. *Ending the Homework Hassle,* as the name implies, is about homework and the management of same. It's subtitled "Understanding, Preventing, and Solving School Performance Problems," which says it all. *Parent Power!* is, for the most part, developmental and problem-oriented. Its primary purpose is to help people understand the significance of each stage of a child's growth, anticipate the problems typical and not-so-typical to each stage, and provide practical advice for solving those problems.

Let's see . . . is there anything else you need to know? Oh, yes. If things work out, there are more *Far Side of Parenting* books to come. So stay tuned!

Introduction

This book had its beginning on the morning of January 22, 1969. As the first light of the sun cracked the winter sky, my first-born announced his arrival.

I was twenty-one, going on seventeen. My wife, Willie, was a much older and wiser woman of nineteen (going on twenty). We named our son Eric Brian because it conveyed a bold, authoritative feeling. He was, we were certain, destined for greatness. A name like Eric Brian was the least we could do to help him on his way.

At the time, I was midway through my senior year of undergraduate study and had been accepted by a graduate program in psychology. Yes, Eric Brian's daddy was going to become a psychologist. You know—predict the future, read minds, and know the question to every answer.

Raising Eric was going to be a snap. After all, my intentions were pure ("I will always give him the very best I have to give"), my ideals were lofty ("I will never treat him the way *my* parents treated me"), and besides, I was soon to know everything there was to know about human beings, birth to death, inside and out.

And then, there was Willie. She had grown up with five younger brothers and sisters and so knew all there was to know about the practical side of raising a child—feeding, changing, burping, bathing, and so on.

The Perfect Mother! The Perfect Father! Therefore, the Perfect, Problem-free Child!

Eric soon let us know how unimpressed he was with our perfection. For a few weeks, Willie breast-fed him (The Perfect Mother). Eric showed his disdain for her selfless generosity by screaming before and after every feeding. Willie concluded she didn't have enough milk (The Less-Than-Perfect Mother?), so she (now we) switched to bottle feeding. But Eric continued to scream.

Eric screamed if we put him down. So we rarely put him

down. If he was awake, which was most of the time, one of us was holding him . . . vertically. Horizontally would not do. Soon, even that wasn't enough. He required us to sit and bounce up and down with him before he would cease his howling. Not a gentle bounce, mind you, but a rather high-flying one. In no time the springs in both pieces of upholstered furniture were shot.

It wasn't long before Eric the Bold and Authoritative started screaming for us to walk around the house with him while constantly flexing up and down at the knees. Of course, we complied.

Sometimes he would sleep. But only during the day. At night, he screamed. Willie and I took turns pretending to be asleep. After several months of this we called the doctor.

"Eric screams an awful lot," we said. He told us to relax.

Several days later, we called him again. "Eric screams when we try to relax," we told him. He said it was only a stage.

"Do things get better?" we asked.

"In time," he assured us.

We held one or more of these existential conversations with the doctor every week. Nothing changed.

By the time Eric was 15 months old, he was talking. His screams became intelligible. Well, almost. A master of exposing our imperfections, he would scream for a cup of milk ("Mok! Mok!"). We'd bring him the mok. He'd take one look at it, knock it to the floor and scream for orange juice ("Ahn-doosh!"). We'd bring him ahn-doosh. He'd knock it to the floor and scream because it was in the wrong cup. The *mok* cup was the right cup. We were slow learners.

He ran everywhere and got into everything. Willie and I ran after him, putting things out of his reach. He learned to climb.

Looking back on those first few chaotic years, I realize that for the most part my education did not make parenthood any easier. In fact it was a handicap. Instead of helping me understand the difficulties we experienced as first-time parents, my graduate training contributed to my confusion. It taught me to think too much about too little.

Most parents, I think, are afflicted with this tendency to think too much. It is our undoing. We speculate about what we should do or should have done. We agonize over what we already did or didn't do. We worry about the elusive "Whatwillhappenif?" We search for some hidden meaning in our children's behavior. Think, think, think. The Perfect Parent is a Perfect Thinker, trying so hard to redo the past and see into the future that he loses touch with the all-important, all-there-is present.

Parents who contract this peculiar malady become so preoccupied with their children that they lose touch with themselves—so entangled with their children that it becomes virtually impossible to tell who's who. They think so much they forget how to act. Their spontaneity drowns in an overflow of worry and guilt. Eventually and inevitably, all trust in themselves—in their own feelings and in their common sense about what is and isn't right for them and for them alone—has vanished.

For the past fourteen years I have written a weekly newspaper column of comment and advice for parents (and anyone else with an interest in children and families). The column makes its first run in the *Charlotte Observer* and is distributed nationally by the Knight-Ridder News Wire. This book evolved from those writings (1976–90).

I want to change the way you think about your children and yourself in relation to them; I want to expand your options, to change the way you respond to your children; I want to pass along a practical understanding of childhood; I want to provoke you into reconsidering some of the ideas you may have taken for granted as absolute.

But more than anything, I want to help you improve the overall quality of your living with children.

The text begins with a tale, "Of Wizards and Kings and Living Things"—a children's story and an allegorical fantasy for adults. "Wizards" is the heart of this book.

What follows has been divided into four parts. Part One (Discipline: A Family Affair) focuses on broad issues involved in raising children. My aim here is to help you put your responsibilities into better perspective. I want you to realize that your child's success as a person, and your success with him, rests not on how many sacrifices you make, but on how well the overall needs of your family, particularly your marriage, are met.

In Part Two (It's Only a Stage) the theme is growth. These chapters describe some of the ways a child's growth is expressed during the first thirteen years of life. This section will help you understand these developmental challenges and support your child through them.

Part Three (So, What's *Your* Problem?) tackles common and not-so-common problems parents may encounter in raising a child, with specific advice on untangling little snarls before they become big ones.

Part Four (Uncommon Sense) examines a number of controversial issues. Be forewarned! To read this section is to risk having some of your sacred cows defiled.

It doesn't matter if you read the chapters out of sequence. I do suggest that you read "Of Wizards and Kings and Living Things" first.

Before we go any further together, a word of caution is in order: You cannot simply imitate my ideas and become a successful parent. If you follow only the *letter* of my advice, you may find that it flops as grandly for you as it has succeeded for me.

Instead, use my ideas as models for designing your *own* solutions and developing your *own* child-rearing style. To risk failure is also to risk success—*real* success. If you merely clone my approach, you risk nothing. And, ultimately, you will have gained nothing.

Ready to risk success? Turn the page.

Of Wizards and Kings and Living Things

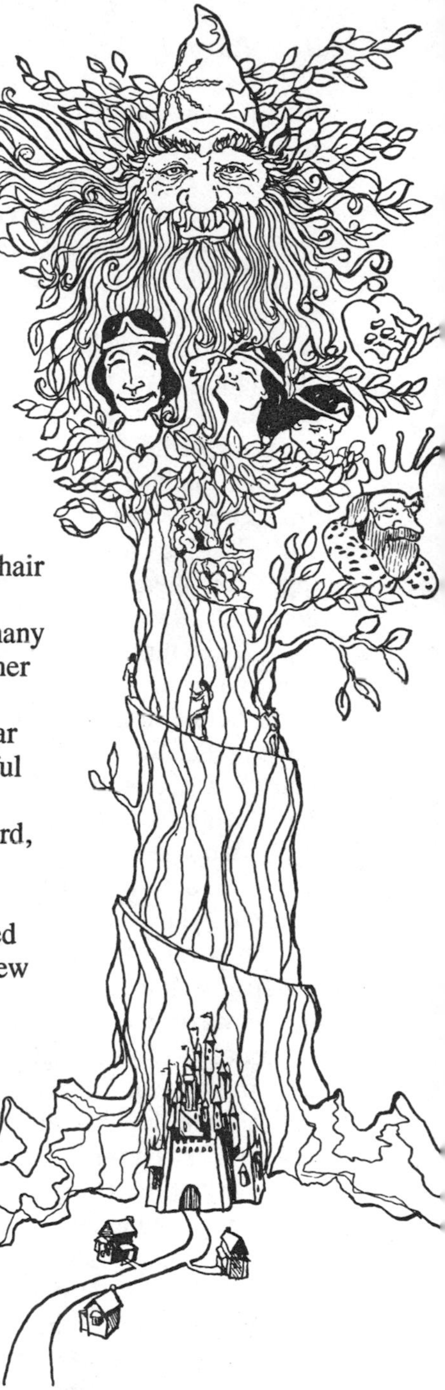

A long, long time ago, when magic was real, there lived a wizard. He wore silver hair to his shoulders and a beard almost to his knees, but it was impossible to tell how many years he had lived, since wizards are neither young nor old. They simply are.

This wizard lived alone in a cave near the top of a mountain high above a peaceful green valley. One narrow trail wound its way from the valley to the cave. The wizard, however, rarely came down (at least no one ever saw him come down), and it had been many years since anyone had climbed up to see him. Nevertheless, everyone knew he still was there, because on clear nights one could always look up and see wizard-light glowing like a star at the top of the mountain.

In the valley at the foot of the mountain lay a small kingdom ruled by a kind and gentle king who was loved and respected by all the valley people. The king was married to a beautiful queen, and they had three sons.

One day, the king called his sons before him and spoke: "Someday, one of you will take my place. Your mother and I have shared our love equally among you, but a kingdom cannot be shared. When I am gone, only one of you can sit on this throne, and he must be the one best suited to the task. I have given this much thought, but cannot choose between you. Therefore, I have asked the wizard for his help. The three of you must climb to his cave and do as he commands. Go at once, for it is impolite to keep a wizard waiting."

So the king's three sons climbed the narrow trail to the wizard's cave. When they reached the mountaintop, they found the wizard sitting cross-legged on a small rock ledge at the cave opening. From there he could look down upon the whole valley kingdom and out to where the land dipped below the sea.

As he turned toward the three young princes, his eyes twinkled and he smiled at the proud and graceful manner in which they stood before him. Then he held out his hand, saying, "Here are three seeds. Each one, when planted, will become a tree. This is your task. Go at once, for it is impolite to keep a tree waiting." Each son took a seed from the wizard's hand, and together they walked in silence down the mountain.

The oldest son planted his seed on top of a small round hill. Every day he brought it clear water from a nearby stream. In the winter, he laid straw around its base to keep the roots warm. When the spring storms came, he fashioned a shelter to protect it from the powerful winds. As the years passed, the tree grew so large and thick that no sunlight could pass through its many branches. The grass on the hill underneath began to wither and turn brown. All through the warmer months, the oldest son worked carrying bucket after bucket of spring water to the tree, for it refused to drink any other. During the fall, he toiled from sunrise to sunset every day, raking and hauling off the many thousands of leaves that fell from its branches.

The middle son planted his seed on another hill, not far away. To him, the shape of the tree was more important than its size. As it grew, he took great care to prune its branches, so they would not grow too thick. Using rope, he tied the trunk to wooden poles, making certain it would grow perfectly straight. He wired the branches so they would curve gracefully toward the sky. He inspected each twig and leaf and cut back those that did not please his eye. He spent nearly all of his time pruning, trimming, tying, and inspecting.

The youngest son planted his seed on yet a third hill, very near the other two. When his tree was a young sapling, he tied the main stalk to poles so that it would not bend and break in the wind. But as time passed, he removed the poles and let it stand on its own. He would bring his young tree water only when the weather was very hot and there had been no rain. He trimmed just enough to let the sunlight filter through. In the fall, he raked the leaves away so they would not smother the grass below. In the winter, he kept *himself* warm.

One night, after many years, the old king died in his sleep. The next day, a great storm blew down off the wizard's mountain. A mighty wind pushed sheets of rain across the valley. Streams became raging rivers, and ponds became lakes. Black clouds boiled across the sky. The storm raged on through the next two days and nights.

On the third morning after the king's death, the rain stopped and the skies cleared. As the valley people emerged from their homes into the morning sunlight, they looked toward the three hills.

The hill upon which the eldest son had planted his tree had been nearly washed away. The roots lay exposed, and it was leaning heavily to one side.

No tree stood upon the second hill. It had been uprooted in the storm and flung into a nearby field. Broken branches were everywhere.

The youngest son's tree was still standing, its wet leaves glistening in the sun. During the storm, it had swayed in the wind and trembled in the roaring thunder, but its branches had not broken.

That afternoon, the three brothers made their way once again up the mountain trail to the wizard's cave. He was sitting on the same rock ledge, his eyes fixed on the horizon. After a long moment, he turned his gaze to the oldest brother and began to speak: "You gave your tree love, but no guidance. It became selfish and demanding. It would not share the sun with the grass below, and so the grass died. Because the hill had no cover, it melted in the storm. You are not well-suited to be king, but your ability to love other things will not be wasted. To that, I add the gifts of knowledge and authority. You will become a great teacher, and the valley people will respect and honor you." The oldest son felt the wizard's touch upon his shoulder, and his eyes filled with tears of happiness.

To the middle son, the wizard then turned and said, "You gave your tree guidance, but showed it no affection. It had a fine and beautiful shape, but its roots were not deep and strong enough to hold it in the storm. You cannot take your father's place, but neither have you labored in vain. To you, I give the gift of love. You will go forth among your people as a great healer, and they will hold you in much reverence." The middle son felt the wizard's gentle touch, and his heart swelled with joy.

Then the wizard turned to the youngest son and said, "You have learned much in your few years and have earned your father's crown. You gave your tree the right proportions of love and guidance. Such is the way all living things must be cared for. Always remember that just as every living thing is a kingdom unto itself, so is every kingdom a living thing."

Then the wizard stood and spoke to all three of them, saying, "Go at once, for there is important work to be done, and it will not be finished in your lifetime." With that, he turned and walked back into his cave.

The three sons returned to the valley and went about the work assigned them by the wizard. The oldest son did become a great teacher, and before he died the valley people built a great university in his name. Just as the wizard had prophesied, the middle son became a great doctor, and he lived to see the valley people build a hospital in which to continue his work. During the time that the youngest son was king, he accomplished many great things, and ever since that time, the little valley kingdom has enjoyed peace and prosperity.

The wizard was never seen again, but to this day it is said that on a clear night one can sometimes still see wizard-light glowing like a star near the top of his mountain.

PART ONE

Discipline: A Family Affair

What follows is a collection of philosophical musings on the meaning and nature of parenthood. Taken together, they represent my concept *of what being a parent is all about. The emphasis is on the commonsensical, the practical, the down-to-earth. I do not care much for intellectual posturing or academic theorizing concerning the subject of raising children. Although I use it some, I do not even care much for the word "parenting," which reflects, I think, a change in child-rearing philosophy and method that began to occur in the immediate postwar years. The purpose behind this section is to put you, the reader, back in touch with a more traditional—old-fashioned, but hopefully not out-of-fashion—view of what the raising of a child is all about. I'm not saying anything new here. I'm just articulating what I consider some timeless truths in terms that speak to the modern ear. For a more in-depth treatment, I refer the reader to* John Rosemond's Six-Point Plan for Raising Happy, Healthy Children *(Andrews and McMeel, 1989), of which Willie and I have two.*

The Benevolent Dictatorship

I can still remember listening to one of my college professors—he was teaching a course in marriage and family relations—lecture on the difference between "democratic" and "autocratic" families.

In the democratic family, he said, everyone was regarded as an equal. Therefore, obedience (from the children) was not mandatory, and disagreements were resolved through discussion, negotiation, and compromise. Cooperation and harmony were the hallmarks of a democratic family. "How marvelous!" I thought, reflecting upon the way my parents had limited my freedom, kept me in a state of virtual servitude, and said things like, "Because I say so."

In contrast, the autocratic family was a hierarchy, with parents at the top. Children were punished if they disobeyed and were not allowed to make decisions for themselves. Compromise between parent and child was possible only on the parents' terms. Obedience, rather than joyous cooperation, was the bill of fare for children of autocratic parents.

"How nasty!" I said to myself, "just like when I was a child (with emphasis on the past tense)." I solemnly swore that when the time came, I would be a "democratic daddy."

Twenty-two years and two children put layers of dust on that promise. I tried my best, really I did. For the first three or four years after Eric was born, I regarded him as my equal. If he didn't like decisions I made, he rolled on the floor and I reconsidered. I thought it unfair to *make* him obey, so he didn't. The result of this exercise in democracy, however, was *not* harmony. The result was anarchy.

One night in a dream a wise-looking elderly gentleman appeared, calling himself the "Spirit of Rosemond's Future." In his hands he held a clear crystal orb, and while I gazed within, there appeared a vision of a slightly older Rosemond family, all of us trussed up nicely in stainless steel straitjackets.

I woke up screaming, bathed in sweat, and life with father has never been the same.

From that point on, our children obeyed us. We insisted upon it. They didn't enjoy the *right* to make any decisions for themselves. However, we allowed them the *privilege* of making *many* decisions, reserving, as *our right,* the option of taking this privilege away whenever it was abused or the potential consequences were not to our liking.

Compromise was possible—at *our* discretion. In short, we created a nasty old autocratic family, and Willie and I were dictators—"Benevolent Dictators," to be exact.

Benevolent Dictators are gentle authorities who understand that their power is the cornerstone of their children's sense of safety and security. Benevolent Dictators rule by virtue of natural authority. They know what's best for their children. They don't derive any pleasure out of bossing children around. They govern because they *must.* They prepare their children for the time when they must govern themselves and *their* children.

Benevolent Dictators do not need to instill fear in order to communicate their influence. They are authorities, but they are *not* authoritarian. They do not demand unquestioning obedience. They encourage questions, but make the final decisions. They restrict their children's freedom, but they are *not* tyrants. They restrict in order to protect and guide. They make rules which are fair and enforce them firmly. Life with a Benevolent Dictator is predictable and secure for children. That set of certainties guarantees more freedom than would be possible under any other circumstances.

Actually, whether they are willing to admit it or not, all parents are dictators of one sort or another. Some are more benevolent than others, and some are benevolent to a fault.

That may be somewhat difficult to accept, because we usually associate dictatorships with oppression and torture and people disappearing in the night. But a dictatorship is simply a system of government where one person is in control and is responsible for making decisions for a group of people who count on him or her to make good ones. And that's what parents do, isn't it? Like it or not, parents are dictators, preferably dictators of benevolent nature.

Some time back, I was speaking to a group of physicians, explaining my concept of the family as a "benevolent dictatorship." One of the group, looking disturbed, raised a challenge:

"I think you're throwing this idea out in too general a fashion. Your 'benevolent dictatorship' may work quite well when children are very young, but with teenagers especially, we must give them more freedom and more opportunities for making their own decisions."

"Yes!" I replied, "what you are saying is absolutely true and dovetails perfectly with my 'benevolent dictatorship.'

"You see," I went on, "the key in what you said was your use of the word 'give.' And I agree! Parents must be willing to *give* their children greater freedom and more choices as they grow older—even the freedom at selected times to make mistakes. But we must always retain control of the decision to give. We must *never,* as long as our children are dependent on us, hand complete control of their lives over to them."

There is no possibility of a democratic relationship between parents and children as long as children live at home and rely upon parents for legal protection and economic support.

Until a child leaves home, there can only be *exercises* in democracy which are carefully orchestrated by the parents.

Yes, increasing degrees of independence *must* be given as the child matures, but *given* from a secure position of authority.

It is parents' *right* to give the privilege and, likewise, their *right* to take it away. Within that framework, children learn the value of independence, not as something to be taken for granted, but as something to be worked for—and therefore something worth taking care of.

You are the boss. For *their* sake.

Your Marriage Comes First

Several years ago, at the beginning of a workshop I was conducting for about fifty working mothers, I wrote, "IN MY FAMILY, MY CHILDREN COME FIRST" on the blackboard. I asked if this was an accurate statement of their priorities. More than half of them raised their hands to acknowledge that it was. Since then, I've put several audiences through the same exercise and gotten the same results.

It seems we are our own undoing. "My children come first" is a one-way ticket to the place where parents worry about children who whine and fuss and won't do what they're told to do by parents who finally lose their patience and scream and then plunge headlong into that dark hole called *guilt.* It's a place where husbands come home to wives who complain because being a mother—working or not—takes so much energy they have none left to be wives. It's a place where people hurt, but hide the hurt behind "my children come first."

It's easy to understand how people get to this upside-down place. Most parents have been there—some to visit, some to stay.

From one perspective, our collective preoccupation with children and childhood is an offshoot of our infatuation with youthfulness in general. From another, it is an extension of the my-children-are-going-to-have-it-better-than-I-did thinking that was prevalent among parents of children born during the boom following World War II.

But whatever the roots of the problem, this fact emerges—we have created for our children a position of preeminence in the family. We have placed "The Child" on a pedestal and adopted a self-sacrificing reverence toward his "potential" and his "self-esteem." We have accepted into our vocabulary the phrases "child-centered family" and "democratic family," seeming not to realize that when a child is regarded as being central, or equal, to his parents' relationship, their relationship is in jeopardy.

There is but *one* proper place for children within a family—the backseat. Exclusive possession of the front seat belongs to the marriage.

The marriage is the bedrock upon which the family is built and *everyone* in the family depends. The marriage is "where it's at" and always will be. The marriage *precedes* the children and was meant to *succeed* them. But if you put your children first, if you plan your life around their presence, if you think that the meaning of "family" is synonymous with their existence, then the fabric of your relationship may not be able to endure the wear and tear of a life together.

The marriage is the nucleus of the family. It creates, defines, and sustains the family. It transcends the identities of the two people who created it, and yet a healthy marriage not only preserves those identities but also brings them to full flower.

To say that your commitment is to your marriage, rather than to your spouse, is to recognize that *you* are an equal partner. For the marriage to remain vital, you must take care of your *own* selves as well as you take care of each other—no more and no less.

But what about the children? Well . . . what about them?

Children's needs are met if the needs of the marriage are met. Children who experience their parents' relationship as an ever-present core of stability at the center of the family will feel as secure as they can possibly feel.

From their parents' example, they learn how to share, how to disagree in ways which don't compromise anyone's dignity, and they learn the human art of caring. They learn that their parents' relationship does not include them—and yet they eventually realize that they are protected and nurtured *because* of it.

Children discover who they are by first having it defined for them who *their parents* are, and who they are *not*. They discover their *own* place by first being told where it *cannot* be.

It is this clear sense of "separateness" that encourages the growth of autonomy and pushes children toward the fulfillment of their own promise.

There isn't a child on this earth who needs more than that.

Independent Parents

This chapter is about being single and raising children, but it is not for single parents only. It applies equally well to each of us, whether married or not, parent or not. It's about the traps we build for ourselves out of myths and pieces of broken fairy tales.

I'm thinking specifically about the myths that color our perceptions of the single parent (and the way single parents view themselves). There are many myths, but foremost among them is one that says raising a child (or children) is much more difficult if you are single than if you have a partner.

That is simply not the truth. Raising a child on your own is surely *different* from raising a child within an intact family, but it is only as *difficult* as the single parent thinks it is.

For every argument supporting the belief that raising children is a herculean task for one person, there is another, more optimistic interpretation of the evidence. Someone might point out, for instance, that single parents deserve sympathy because they are on the front lines all of the time, with no one to fall back on for emotional support. It can just as easily be said that single parenthood is relatively uncomplicated.

One single parent curses his isolation, saying, "I have to make *all* the decisions." Another rejoices at her independence, saying, "I get to make all the decisions." As with any other enterprise, there are, upon comparison, advantages and disadvantages. Select the perspective of your choice.

Whose point of view is right? Everybody's! If you believe that raising children on your own is an insurmountable hardship, it will be just that. If, on the other hand, you convince yourself that raising children independently is one of the greatest opportunities for creative living you've ever had, then you will use that positive force to create opportunity after opportunity for yourself and your children. Whatever we believe of ourselves we generally manage to prove right.

This attitude problem about single parenthood might not exist were it not for an even more insidious set of myths about marriage. These say, in essence, that marriage can do for us what we feel inadequate to do for ourselves—namely, it can make us complete, happy, and fulfilled. That delusion not only destroys many marriages, but scatters disillusionment and despair in its wake. In real life, marriage does not make someone happy, and divorce does not foreclose on the loan. In real life, we make ourselves happy, and we make ourselves unhappy (or angry or bitter or resentful or whatever).

Children from divided homes are swept into the melodrama. The prevailing view is that they are damaged, that there is something missing from their lives which handicaps them forever and ever, amen.

The myth says children must have two parents. The fact is that children need two parents who care for each other. The fact is that one parent who cares for them is preferable to two who don't really care for each other.

Those who accept the myth that single parents are playing at a loser's game have chosen to defeat themselves. Their feelings of helplessness, anger, isolation, and frustration are entirely self-imposed. For better or for worse, we are in control of ourselves.

If you are a single parent, you are as capable as any two parents of raising healthy, happy children. No, you can't be a mother and a father too, but you can be a whole, fulfilled person, with more than enough vitality to share with your children.

The job is never too big for one person, if the person is big enough for the job.

Do you want to believe it?

Respect Your Child: Another View

In the past thirty-five years or so, we have grown increasingly dependent upon experts to tell us how to raise our children. In the process, we have become more childlike in our unquestioning attitude toward their "expertness." Unfortunately, some of their advice has been more harmful than helpful.

The permissive school of child-raising experts advised us to "respect" our children. They have not been specific about what this involves, because we have not required specificity from them. They are, after all, the experts.

As they use the term, "respecting your child" implies that parents should treat their children democratically—as equals. Most of us agree that every human being is worthy of respect. Parents *should* respect their children—for what they are and are becoming, but *not* as equals.

Respect between parent and child is a two-way street, but the traffic going in each direction is different in *every way.*

Children respect their parents by obeying them. Parents, on the other hand, respect their children by insisting that they obey.

Parents who enforce obedience are caring for one of their children's most basic needs.

Unfortunately, many parents equate obedience with passivity. Not wanting to raise passive children, they find ways to avoid making them obey. These parents often fear that making their children obey will stifle the children's independence.

The opposite is true. Learning obedience *enhances* a child's independence.

Obedient children have parents who effectively describe and enforce limits. Within that clear framework, obedient children are free to be curious, to explore, to invent—in short, to be as independent as their maturity allows.

Contrast this type of respect with the "respect" demanded by the authoritarian parent, who usually equates respect with fear. Children who fear their parents don't obey—they submit. Children who are obedient are not fearful. They are self-confident and secure. They are even secure enough to indulge in a certain amount of rebellion.

Children who fear their parents often become deceptive—they learn to lie in order to escape their restrictions. Children who are obedient are more likely to be honest and forthright, because they have been treated honestly and in accord with what they *truly* need.

At the opposite extreme from authoritarian parents are those who require no respect. Children whose parents do not require obedience live in a world of constantly shifting limits. Now they see them, now they don't. Their parents' "agendas" are hidden, and the children are forced to search for them. Their searching is usually frantic and attracts disapproval. Consequently, they are called "disobedient." I maintain, however, that there are *no* disobedient children; there are only parents who fail to accept their responsibilities and children who are scapegoats.

Children who don't know their limits must depend on their parents to reward them whenever they discover part of their parents' secret. Obedience, however, is its own reward. To the extent that children accept and function responsibly within the limits their parents define, those limits should steadily expand. Eventually, the children no longer need someone else to define limits for them.

Obedience, then, paves the road to maturity.

Strictly Speaking

Few words in the parlance of "parenting" have been so generally misused and misunderstood as "strict." Not only has the term descended to the depths of disrepute, but its original meaning has been corrupted almost beyond recognition.

Nearly everyone today agrees that "strict" is synonymous with severe, authoritarian, inflexible, dictatorial, uncompromising, puritanical, dogmatic, heavy-handed, tyrannical.

Strict! It even *sounds* harsh, like the crack of a whip.

In this do-your-own-thing age, the strict parent is seen as a virtual Simon Legree, keeping one jaundiced eye open to what his children are doing (or even *thinking* of doing) wrong, and the other eye closed to what they are doing right. But none of this is true. Strict parents have been labeled and slandered by permissivists who would confuse our lives as easily as they confuse language.

To begin redeeming this much maligned adjective, let me point out that not too many years ago (before it became stylish to worship children and let them walk all over us), "strictness" in child rearing was considered a virtue. Way back when children were children and parents were the people in charge, to be strict meant defining rules clearly and enforcing obedience to them.

And what is wrong with that? Nothing at all. In fact, there is everything right and proper about being old-fashionedly strict.

Truly strict parents do their children a great service, in many ways:

• They communicate expectations clearly, leaving little room for misunderstanding.

• They are decisive. England may swing like a pendulum do (as that old song said), but they definitely don't. Their children, therefore, know where they stand.

• They teach their children to expect no more from a situation than they are willing to put into it. Gradually, their children distill a set of tried-and-true methods for living productive, satisfying lives.

• They know their children rely on parents to keep them on the right track, and they correct their children's inevitable wanderings with an even hand.

Strict parents must be disciplined themselves, practicing no less than they preach. Above all else, they understand the importance of rules.

Rules protect. They insure a child's physical and emotional well-being. Rules are the mainstay of order. They regulate and mediate a child's comings and goings in the world. Children are helpless without them. Paradoxically, a rule is both a constraint and a guarantee of freedom.

A rule which is ill-defined, not enforced, or enforced only sporadically, is not a rule. It is a fraud, a double cross, and under this kind of "rule" a child is a victim, a prisoner of uncertainty. On the other hand, a child who tests a rule (as children *always* will) and finds it a predictable quantity is then free to function constructively within its boundaries.

When he was age eleven, my son Eric and I had the following exchange: We were talking about a friend of his, and the conversation turned to her parents. I asked about his impression of them, and he answered, "They're very nice but, well, *strict,* ya know?"

Intrigued, I replied, "No, Eric, I don't know. I've never heard you use that word before. What does it mean to you?"

He thought for a moment. "It means," he said, "it means, well, like they don't let her get away with stuff she shouldn't do."

"I see. Well, Eric, do you think *I'm* strict?"

"Yes," he said, without hesitation, "but I think you *have to be* when you raise children."

Out of the mouths of babes.

The Sound of One Hand Clapping

As the occasion warranted, I spanked my children. I did so not because I had given it a lot of thought or believed that children *needed* to be spanked or had reached the end of my rope, but simply because I *felt* like it. I have learned, during twenty-two years of raising my own children, to trust my feelings.

You see, "to spank or not to spank" is *not* the question. The question, regardless of what you do or don't do, is simply this: "Does it work?"

Twelve years ago, I wrote in a newspaper column that spanking was not the big, bad thing it's been made out to be. It's not a big deal, but people who are obsessed with children find, in a spanking, the stuff that big deals are made of. After that column appeared, one such maker of big deals told me I had, in effect, endorsed child abuse. Another person said my attitude "disturbed" her because "it plays right into the hands (substitute switches or belts) of people with a 'spare the rod, spoil the child' mentality."

What really disturbed my critics was that I don't share their view of the world, part of which includes a myth that says children who are spanked (a) hate themselves for being such rotten kids, (b) learn to solve problems by hitting people, (c) will someday abuse their own children, (d) become violent criminals, or (e) all of the above.

I have good news. Those myths are wrong. The social, economic, political, and psychological factors that combine to produce criminals, child abusers, bullies, and emotional cripples are far too complex for even a computer to fathom. To suggest that spankings play a major role in shaping that kind of social behavior is ludicrous.

I have more good news. It is possible to spank a child *well,* to do it *right,* and to make it *work.* The problem with spanking is that most parents make a sorry mess of it.

The typical spanking scenario begins with a child doing something that is clearly out of bounds—let's say, leaping from a coffee table onto a sofa. Her parents react by jabbering, bobbing up and down at the waist, and flapping their arms. The child notices that, despite their agitated flutter, they have essentially done nothing. She files this valuable information away in a neuron bank marked "High Priority."

Fifteen minutes later, she climbs up on the coffee table and again propels herself onto the sofa. Her parents jabber, bob, and flap as they did before. And again, nothing happens. Remarkable! Fifteen minutes later, she does this leap again, but this time, before her parents stop flapping, one of them says, "If you do that again, I'll have to spank you! Do you understand?"

Of course she understands. She knows a challenge when she hears one.

Her parents, meanwhile, are becoming increasingly frustrated over her "disobedience" or "forgetfulness" or whatever term they use to avoid accepting responsibility for what's happening.

Five more times she leaps and five more times her parents bob, flap, and threaten. On the ninth try, she breaks an imported crystal bud vase. Her parents descend on her like furies, flapping their hands against her rear end, shouting, "We told you not to leap, and look what you did!" For several hours following the incident the home is wrapped in a mantle of gloom. No one talks; no one laughs. The child feels cheated. The parents feel guilty. All in all, it's a waste of time, energy, intelligence, and imported crystal.

But it wasn't the spanking that was wrong, it was the way it was done.

Rule Number One of a Well-done Spanking: *Don't wait.* For me, spanking is a first resort. This is not to say that I spank for everything or spank a lot. I seldom spank, but when I decide, quite arbitrarily, that the situation warrants it, I do it and that's the end of it.

Rule Number Two: *Don't threaten.* Why the dramatic build-up? A threat is nothing more than a pleading, apologetic way of asking a child to save you from doing "the bad thing." A threat is irresponsible and lazy. *Every* threat is empty.

Besides, the price of not acting is frustration, which builds steadily from threat to threat toward an almost inevitable, and worthless, explosion.

Rule Number Three: *Use your hand.* A spanking is a non-verbal expression of authority and disapproval from *you.* Make a direct connection, person-to-person.

Rule Number Four: *Don't hit and run.* A spanking is not the *end* of something—it is, or should be, the *beginning* of something. After you spank, it is important to talk. Don't offer apologies—just straight no-nonsense stuff: "Now that I have your undivided attention, let me tell you about life with Mommy."

Make a short, simple statement that sums up your feelings about what the child did and clearly marks the behavior as being against the rules. Don't ask for "I'll-be-good" promises or apologies. Say what you have to say, aim the child in a better direction, and let bygones be bygones.

The idea is *not* to cause the child pain, but to (1) quickly terminate undesirable behavior, (2) remind the child of your authority, (3) express, in a relatively low-key way, your anger, and (4) grab the child's attention for a moment of plain talk.

My children usually didn't know when they were going to feel my hand on their bottom. I didn't spank for any one thing in particular, so they couldn't predict when one was coming down the pike. In general, I spanked in response to open defiance, deliberate disobedience, or flagrant displays of disrespect. But a spanking was only *one* way I might have chosen to express myself under any of those circumstances. What matters is that I spanked long before I "had enough." That way, I never got there.

Plain Talk

"Because I said so!" was one of my father's favorite phrases. I argued with him a lot, and that was his stock way of shutting me down.

I was sixteen when I vowed upon a stack of rock 'n' roll

albums never to say "Because I said so" to my children. I wasn't going to be *that* kind of parent.

My children were going to be given *responsibility* and unlimited opportunity to make decisions. After all, these were the 1960s, and individual freedom was blowin' in the wind.

A son was born into those uncertain times.

Three years later, the times were no less uncertain for him. These were the 1970s, and tantrums were blowin' in the wind. It eventually became clear that Eric would never acquire enough self-control to make sensible decisions unless I was first willing to act decisively. So I brought the horse around to the front of the cart and moved into the driver's seat.

I still wince a little at the sound of "Because I said so," but I think Dad had the beginning of a sound idea: Young children (and here I refer to the under-five crowd) benefit immeasurably from being given reasons—if the reasons can be expressed in twenty-five one- and two-syllable words or less. But when the answer to "Why?" is lengthy, complex, or arbitrary, the child should hear a clear message that says, in effect, "I will take care of this situation."

The plain truth is, sometimes the most honest, straightforward, and authoritative (not to be confused with authoritarian) reason for making a decision or giving an instruction is "Because I said so."

The trouble with Dad was, he didn't know when to quit. I still heard "Because I said so" when I was in high school. But he taught me a valuable lesson: Never use fifty words when four will do.

So when my children wanted to know "Why," I sometimes answered, "Because I don't want you to," or "I have made the decision."

Son of "Because I said so."

The Games Parents Play

There is a game I call "Please?" that parents play with their children. "Please?" begins when a parent wants a child to do something. It's usually something simple, such as wanting the child to sit in the backseat of the car. But parents have the darnedest ways of making simple things complicated and even confusing.

To play "Please?" the parent acts indecisive, as though she doesn't know exactly what she *does* want the child to do. Therefore, she makes no imperative, commanding statements. Instead, she phrases all statements as questions and asks the questions in a small, pleading voice.

For example, rather than, "You are going to sit in the backseat," or "I want you in the backseat," the mother says, "Wouldn't you rather sit in the backseat so Mommy can sit up here?" This form and tone tells the child that Mommy needs his help in making this difficult decision. The child is glad to help: "No! I want to sit there. You sit in the back."

At this point, it's a jump ball, up for grabs to the quickest player. Often the parent commits a technical foul by changing the rules and becoming angry: "Look, I told you to sit in the backseat, now get there!" This is not true, since the parent never *told* the child anything. But the foul never gets called, unless the other parent is playing the role of referee.

More often "Please?" does not come to that abrupt an end. The parent usually negotiates a compromise in which the child gets what he wants, and the parent gets to be inconvenienced (having to hold the child on her lap).

Parents play "Please?" to avoid confrontations, showdowns, and embarrassment. And it works! But what they get in the bargain is no bowl of cherries. Children are quick to learn when their parents are afraid to assert their authority and can be relied upon to give in. When it comes to a question of "Who's the boss?" if parents won't run with the ball, children will.

There should never be any question about who's running the show in the first place. It is a child's inalienable right and privilege to be informed early in life that parent is boss. "When parent at a loss, child make bad boss."

Count the times you play "Please?" with your child today. Once is too many.

Parents need to tell children what to do and then stand prepared to enforce their authority (pick the child up and put him in the backseat). Don't ask questions if you don't really intend for the child to have a choice.

Children need to be told what to do by parents who aren't afraid or embarrassed by an occasional showdown. Children feel more secure and comfortable with parents who know where they stand (and where they want to sit).

She Hates Me, She Hates Me Not

This is a transcript of an actual conversation which took place in my house a number of years ago.

The speakers are my daughter, Amy, then 6 going on 16 (and making me feel 60), and her daddy—yours truly—a real tyrant, as you will see.

Daddy: Amy, I want you to set the table tonight.

Amy: I don't want to. Make Eric do it.

Daddy: I want *you* to do it. And right *now,* by the way.

Amy: I did it last night.

Daddy: Yes, and you did such a fine job that I want you to do it again tonight. And right *now,* by the way.

Amy: I *won't* do it. It's Eric's turn.

Daddy: Since you won't set the table, you will have to go to your room. You may come down when you decide to set the table.

Amy: What if I don't, and it's supper time?

Daddy: Then *I* will set the table and bring your supper to your room, where you will stay until morning.

Amy: I don't care.

Daddy: Well, I do.

Amy: Why?

Daddy: Because I want you to be able to eat supper with us.

Amy: Well, I *will* then, but I *won't* set the table.

Daddy: Amy, go to your room. Right *now.*

Amy: DADDY, IF YOU SEND ME TO MY ROOM, I'LL STAY THERE FOREVER!

Daddy: Either set the table or go to your room.

Amy: DADDY, I WON'T BE AROUND HERE MUCH LONGER! I'LL RUN AWAY!

Daddy: Either set the table or go to your room.

Amy: I HATE YOU! I'M NOT YOUR DAUGHTER ANYMORE! I BELONG TO SOMEONE ELSE!

This was followed by a volley of "YOU'LL BE SORRY!" and another chorus of "I HATE YOU!"

I'm sure there were times while she was growing up when she really did hate me, such as when I made her choose between two things she loathed, like setting the table or banishment to her room.

Feeling hate is predictable, genuine, and understandable for a six year old under those circumstances. Is she supposed to like it when I put her between a rock and a hard place? Heck, no!

It's not easy being a person with little power. On the other hand, it's even worse being a child who's been given, by default, a lot of power. Children want power, are frustrated by their lack of it, and don't know how to handle it when it lands in their laps.

So, where Amy was involved, I took firm hold of the reins, and there were times when she surely hated me for it.

She hated me when I parried her attempts to defy me and win. She hated me because when she tried to engage me in a power struggle, I refused to participate. Amy couldn't win a fight with me because I wouldn't fight with her—not if my authority was at stake.

If I *had* fought with her, I would have been encouraging the false idea that she was my equal. She was *not* my equal. She needed my protection and my resources. She is, at nineteen, soon to be my equal, and I nurture and cherish this transition.

As Amy was growing up, I held to the following basic understanding of our relationship: I will not compromise with her regarding my authority until she is more accepting of it. Our relationship is not democratic, and no amount of idealizing can make it so. Amy did not *choose* me for her daddy, and I do not come up for reelection every few years. Amy's voice in the running of the family and the management of her life is not equal to mine, and it will *not* be until she leaves home. Until then, I decide. I even decide when she *can* decide; then I tell her what the choices are. She has a right to hate me. It is, I hope, a measure of the basic openness and frankness in our relationship that she feels able to tell me so.

By the way, Amy *did* set the table. The spoons were on the left, and my place mat was turned at a ninety-degree angle. Oh, well.

The "Three R's"

Have you taught your children their three "R's"? No, not Reading, 'Riting, and 'Rithmetic, but Rules, Routines, and Responsibilities.

If you haven't, you'd better, and time's a 'wastin'!

Twenty-one years of clinical experience and twenty-two years of parenthood have convinced me that most, if not all, childhood behavior problems result from deficiencies in one or more of these three essential "R's."

The reason for this is really quite simple. Parental authority consists of nothing more than establishing and enforcing rules, routines, and responsibilities. These three are the essence of discipline, and discipline is one of the two primary cornerstones of security, the other being love. The child who is as well disciplined as he or she is loved is a secure child.

Security is the foundation upon which a child builds self-esteem. A child cannot develop a sense of unqualified worth unless his parents go before him, making his way straight and secure. With self-esteem goes a sense of purpose, and with purpose comes such things as initiative, motivation, resourcefulness, and perseverance. Since all these things amount to growth, it follows that security is the pad from which a child launches his growing.

It is plain to see that without rules, routines, and responsibilities, a child cannot be fully secure, cannot have complete self-esteem, and is not therefore free to become all that he can be.

A child so handicapped will compensate by misbehaving. Misbehavior attracts attention, puts the child center-stage, and gives him a measure of control over certain aspects of his life. In other words, misbehavior enables the insecure child to experience a fleeting, hollow facsimile of how it feels to be secure and have self-esteem. Self-defeating, yes, but powerfully addictive.

The secure child, on the other hand, has no compulsion to misbehave, no neurotic need to attract attention to himself for the mere sake of attention. He is secure not only because his parents love him, but also because they discipline him well. And their discipline consists of nothing more than a consistent regimen of rules, routines, and responsibilities.

The three "R's." Together, they organize, stabilize, and energize the child's life. They provide for consistency and predictability. They bring order to potential chaos. They give the child a sense of direction and purpose, and they are the framework in which his life takes form and substance. Without them, the child is sure to flounder.

The bad news is that many among the present generation of children are foundering in their own disobedience, petulance, laziness, and self-centeredness precisely because there aren't enough "R's" in their lives. The good news is that rules, routines, and responsibilities cure misbehavior as quickly as their absence causes it.

If you have a child who compulsively misbehaves, the antidote is as simple as A-B-C, or I should say, R-R-R. First, define for the child the difference between the way you want him to behave and the way he is behaving. Then, make rules that describe that difference as well as consequences for the misbehaviors in question. Next, assign the child a set of household chores. In addition to responsibilities within his or her own "area," the child should have chores in common areas of the home. Third, establish routines that define when the chores are to be performed. When you have this structure in place, enforce it!

Security and self-esteem are every child's birthright. It is, therefore, every child's birthright to have parents who provide the three "R's." If it sounds like I'm advocating a "Back to Basics" approach to child rearing, you're right!

Commitment: More Than Just a Try

Not long ago, a young woman asked me about a problem she had with her five-year-old daughter. The problem was not anything unusual, but it had hung on in this family for two years, draining lots of energy and wasting everyone's time.

After I listened to this mother's exasperated description of the goings on and asked a few questions, I told her what I thought could be done to settle the issue once and for all.

When I finished, she gave a slight shrug and said, "Well, I'll give it a try."

"Well," I replied, "Giving it a try won't make it work."

"What do you mean?" she asked, coming to life again.

"Excuse me for being so frank, but at best, the most watertight of all possible solutions to your problem won't make change happen if all you're going to give it is (and I shrugged) 'a try.' "

She is by no means alone. Plenty of parents never get past "trying." And that is why so many of them lose control of their children—and themselves in the process.

"I'll give it a try" is another way of saying, "I can't." It is a statement of defeat, surrender, and personal ineffectiveness.

That brings us to the point: When you deal with a problem involving a child, more importantly than *what* you do is the act of *doing*.

Because of my professional credentials and my reputation, parents ask me a lot of questions. Most of them begin with the phrase, "*What* should I do when . . ." (the italics are mine). This manner of asking a question reflects a fundamental, widely held misunderstanding: For every specific problem, there is one equally specific, "best" solution.

Not so. For every specific problem there are countless effective solutions. It doesn't matter which one you select—you can even invent a new one—because for *any* and *all* problems the *real* solution has nothing to do with technique or method.

It's called commitment, or determination, or resolve. It's the sense of purpose you invest in the method of your choice (or invention). The difference between method and commitment, the *what* and the *doing*, is the difference between form and substance. Method is nothing more than a vehicle. Without commitment that vehicle is doomed to stall. Without commitment your method is impotent.

The difference between method and commitment is the difference between saying "I'll give it a try," and "This is the way it's going to be."

Commitment is the backbone of whatever you do. Commitment is the energy of change. Believe me, your children will know immediately when you are "giving it a try." They will sense your ambivalence and your lack of determination, and *they will not cooperate with you because you will have given them no substantial reason to cooperate.*

When a child tests you, she is doing precisely that—she is

testing *you.* Not the form, but the substance. And when, in response, you demonstrate your own sense of purpose in what you are doing, you demonstrate also your commitment to *her.* When she is convinced of *that,* she will cooperate with you.

No question about it.

What's a "Fair"?

"It's not fair!"

I heard that a lot in my day. In fact, I listened to variations on the same theme, delivered in sundry ways, from statement to scream, for most of Amy's childhood.

Poor Amy, she must have arrived before her appointed time, because the world was not prepared. The news of her arrival didn't even make a big splash in the media—just a blurred picture and two or three lines to distinguish her from the other infant mug shots in the lineup.

Ever since then, Amy tried to convince us that a mistake was made. This time around, she was scheduled to do time as a princess. She had, no doubt, paid her dues as a serving wench, a peasant—you know, the usual stuff we all endure before getting to the big time. This fling was to have been different. But something went wrong.

What a disappointment it must have been.

Her mother and I couldn't even buy her everything she wanted. She didn't understand about mortgages and car payments. After all, the castle was supposed to have been paid for along with a villa on the Mediterranean.

But the worst of the worst, the supreme insult, was that there was another child in the family before her. His name is Eric.

The problem, as Amy saw it, was that Eric was sometimes given things before she was, or that he got something bigger or two of something to her one. Dad might have even taken Eric to the store and bought him something and come home empty-handed for Amy.

"It's not fair!"

"But Amy," I would say, "sometimes you and I go to the store and get something just for you. Why, don't you remember that we bought you a new coat and a pair of shoes yesterday? Eric didn't get anything then."

"It's not fair!"

Come to think of it, she was right. "What is fair?" I ask myself. It's a vague concept that is nothing short of impossible to achieve.

What would satisfy children is not for us to be "fair," but for us to give them everything they want. "Fair" means "me first" with the biggest and the best.

When there is more than one child in the family, there is no avoiding explosions over who gets what and whose is the best and the brightest and on and on.

So what are we to do? Should we try to spend the same amount of money on both children or buy the same number of things for each? Should we have bought Amy something whenever we took Eric to the store?

No. It would not have been in Amy's best interest for us to encourage the idea that the world could be relied upon to deliver to her an equal measure of whatever she saw someone else getting. Children with this idea are popularly called "spoiled," and spoiled children, when they grow up, are likely to be extremely frustrated and unhappy because the fairy tale *never* comes true.

I usually tried something like this:

"It may not seem fair that Mommy and Daddy have given something to Eric and not to you. But you and Eric are different people, and we treat you differently. You will have trips to the store of your very own."

Sometimes the explanation didn't sit well, and she went into her dying swan routine. I walked away, refusing to get involved in the drama. Eventually she got over it.

It's not a question of fair. It's a question of balance.

In Defense of Inconsistency

The solution to any problem simply changes the nature of the problem. I can't recall where I heard that, but it came to mind as I began writing about consistency.

Few people would deny that consistency is a cornerstone of

successful child rearing. But I would, because it isn't. It's just another brick.

I used to talk about the importance of consistency as if it were the One True Way. I don't anymore. These days, I'm more likely to say, "There's a time for being consistent and a time for being inconsistent," and then talk about the benefits of inconsistency.

Although it has had extremely bad press, inconsistency has little to do with the problems parents have raising children. If anything, the idea that parents *must* be consistent to be successful has contributed to at least as many problems as it may have solved.

The commandment to *be consistent above all else* has been handed down by well-meaning professionals who, like me, are inclined to be more than a little compulsive. The belief that predictability and routine are what makes people-systems run well is the model they use to guide their own personal and professional lives. Since it works for them, they prescribe it for everyone.

And, to a certain extent, they are correct. Consistency is as essential to the maintenance of our existence as oil is to the smooth functioning of an internal combustion engine.

I'm certain we would all be candidates for the loony bin were we not able to reduce confusion and uncertainty by organizing our lives around a network of routines. But in our enthusiasm, we social scientists have oversold the notion that consistency is the oil that tunes our social engines. And the public has overconsumed the idea in like proportion. The resulting overdose has fouled our plugs and blown sludge into our carburetors.

Yes, children need routine. It simplifies their lives, promotes security, and provides a stable framework within which freedom is possible.

Yes, every child needs parents who agree on the rules and boundaries that guide the child's growing.

No, parents do *not* have to agree on how those rules are enforced. To the extent that parents feel they *must* agree on this, they will have problems.

It is unrealistic to expect that two fundamentally different people, who come into a marriage with different ideas about children, can agree on a single set of tools with which to regulate a child's behavior.

Each parent's toolbox is different, and each feels familiar

and skilled with his or her own set of tools. Mom is inclined to sit Junior in his least-favorite chair when he disobeys, while Dad is likely to whack Junior's behind parts. So what? There is no conflict here and there need not be disagreement. That Mom and Dad use different means of enforcing the rule is only superficially relevant.

What counts in maintaining harmony in the family is that Mom and Dad agree on the importance of the rule—Do What We Tell You to Do—and are both quick to act when Junior gets out of line. Mom and Dad are acting consistently, even though *differently,* to reinforce the rule.

But parents can get so hung up on the need to be consistent that they begin fighting over their stylistic differences. Meanwhile, as the forest is increasingly obscured by the trees, the rule itself begins to gather dust, and it dawns on Junior that there is no rule at all—sometimes he can disobey and sometimes he can't.

It isn't even necessary for either parent, acting alone, to respond in the same manner every time a rule is violated.

Mom *prefers* to put Junior in the "thinking-chair" when he's a "rebel without a cause," but she is not required to do that *every* time. Sometimes she says he can't go outside, sometimes she sends him to his room, sometimes she simply repeats herself with more emphasis and sometimes she reaches over into Dad's toolbox and pops Junior's behind.

And Dad may not always spank. There are times when he has a man-to-man talk with Junior. Sometimes he takes something away, and sometimes he sits him in Mom's favorite chair.

But no matter what Mom and Dad do when Junior disobeys, the *rule* is there. It is being consistently enforced by a variety of means, but the end is the same. Furthermore, Mom and Dad's reactions are consistent with how each *feels* at the moment a transgression occurs.

There is even something to be said for being unpredictable in the way you enforce rules. Messages lose their impact when they are stated repetitiously. Being too consistent can evolve into boredom and rigidity.

Too much consistency also prevents parents from seeing changes in their children and adapting to those changes. Too much consistency restricts growth. Too much consistency promotes a simplistic view of life.

Consistency may be the oil, but variety is the spice of living. Don't limit your options by subscribing too literally to *any* single idea. Agree on the rules and agree to disagree over how each parent chooses to enforce them. Appreciate and support one another's differences and let your children know that, yes, Mom has her way of doing things, and Dad has his.

That's consistent with the way the rest of the world turns.

Worry: The Future Game

We influence the future in the way we anticipate it. In this respect, we are all, to some degree, fortune-tellers.

This is not whimsy, but a documented principle of human psychology called "the self-fulfilling prophecy." It's the lesson we learned as children from the story of the little engine that could: If you think you *can,* you probably *will.* If you think you *can't,* you probably *won't.*

We not only affect our *own* future in the way we anticipate it, but, in like manner, we influence the lives of others. The stronger the bond between two people, the stronger the potential effect.

Between parents and children, parents wield the most potent influence. On the constructive side are influences such as commitment and optimism. Parents who are not only hopeful, but optimistically *certain* that their children will be all right, seem blessed with children who, by and large, turn out well.

On the destructive side are guilt and worry. Both are forms of negative energy which not only prevent parents from paying adequate attention to the here-and-now, but are also self-fulfilling. Parents who worry about their children always seem to have something to worry about.

Billy-Bob is three years old. He has been tossed out of two preschool programs and is working on being expelled from his third. Few children in his neighborhood are allowed to play with him. Billy-Bob bites.

Billy-Bob is an only child whose middle-class parents want him to grow up without any emotional problems. They have read countless books and articles about raising children. They want desperately to do it right, but something has gone wrong.

They search the past for a reason for Billy-Bob's biting.

"What did we do to cause it?" they ask, needing a hook on which to hang their guilt. The more they search, the more they ask, the more Billy-Bob bites.

Billy-Bob bit his mother when he was thirteen months old. He was in the throes of a frenzied tantrum which began when his mother took a photograph away from him. The bite set off a guilt-quake inside his mother. It was so big, even Billy-Bob knew something extraordinary had happened. So he bit her again.

Three months later, after sufficient practice on his mother, he bit the next-door neighbor's child. When he was eighteen months old, his parents enrolled him in a day-care program, hoping that his being around more children would help. He lasted two months.

Billy-Bob's parents worry so much about what he will be like in ten minutes, ten days, or ten years that they don't notice what he's doing *right now.* Whenever he's around other children, they are consumed with anxiety. Billy-Bob can feel their tension and knows just what he's expected to do. So he does. And the more he bites, the more his parents worry.

It's usually impossible to determine, in such situations, whether the worry or the subject being worried about came first. The more parents worry, the more the subject comes up, the bigger it gets, and the more they worry. Until the cycle is broken, there is no resolution, only repetition. And the more the cycle is repeated, the more indelible its imprint on the family.

Worriers cannot be spontaneous, because they are not dealing with things as they happen. Their concerns are scattered somewhere up ahead, in the future, where they will *never* be. The more parents worry, the more they ignore the *real* problem. Meanwhile, the child bears the present-tense weight of the issue on *his* shoulders.

When, and if, Billy-Bob's parents decide to do something about his biting, they might begin by telling him, "Billy-Bob, you have been biting other children, and now you are going to stop. We are going to help you stop, because that's what mommies and daddies are for. Whenever you forget and bite someone, here's what's going to happen, every single time."

It won't matter much *what* they do. What will matter is that his parents will be doing *something.*

Billy-Bob will be *very* relieved, believe me.

Spare the Rod, But Not the Rule

Rules are social boundaries. They outline the limits of acceptable behavior and preserve the stability of human environments. Rules knit society together; they are as essential to our survival as water is to the life of a fish.

For children, rules are an extension of parental authority. Rules are as necessary to healthy development as are stimulation, good nutrition, and sunshine. Rods can be spared; rules cannot.

Rules can be communicated to children in a number of ways. A direction or instruction is a rule. A task assigned to a child is a rule. Any decision defining what a child may or may not do or have is a rule.

When the rules of a game are clear, the players know what moves are available and can predict with some degree of certainty what moves the other players will make. Rules organize the game. They reduce uncertainty and anxiety.

And so it is with children. When rules are present, a child knows what is and is not allowed and is able to predict his parents' behavior. Rules are fundamental to feelings of security.

When rules are unclear or enforced sporadically, children can't predict what their parents will do next. Under these circumstances, children become anxious, insecure, and sometimes even physically sick.

I do not advocate rules for the sake of rules. Bad rules, or too many rules, can be as detrimental to a child's well-being as poor nutrition. Good rules should meet four basic requirements:

(1) *All rules should be stated clearly.* No dressing or garnish is necessary, nor is a complicated explanation. Preschool children will have difficulty understanding even the best explanation of why a rule is necessary. If you must explain, make the explanation brief and to the point: twenty-five words or less.

Older children understand reasons and like to argue about them. If parents argue back, the basic issue—that parents set rules and children abide by them—becomes confused. If a child wants to argue, say, "I will not argue. You will have to do as you are told."

Some parents feel guilty about making straightforward demands on their children. So they disguise their demands as requests which require "yes" as the only acceptable answer. "Will you take out the garbage?" is really a rule if the child has no choice but to take out the garbage. Phrased as a question, however, the rule is unclear. The garbage sits in the kitchen, the parents become upset, and the child gets increasingly confused.

(2) *Rules should be clearly defined.* What is meant by "clean up your room"? Parents think their children know, but a child's idea of clean is *never* the same as a parent's. Only Sylvia's mother knows exactly what she wants when she tells Sylvia to clean up her room. To reduce uncertainty and confusion, define tasks specifically, as in, "You must make up your bed, fold your clothes, put them in your dresser, and put your books back on the shelf before you can go outside." If a chore must be done every day, making a list of the steps involved will eliminate many unnecessary arguments. When a rule is defined clearly, it is easier to enforce.

(3) *Rules should be reasonable when they refer to chores.* A child's day should not be filled with chores. There should be plenty of time for rest, study, and play. Before assigning a *chore,* be sure the child is able to do *it.* If she's capable, but needs some initial guidance, break the task down into small steps and teach her one step at a time.

For instance, most five-year-olds don't know how to make beds, but they can be taught. First, have Sylvia watch you make the bed while you describe each step. Then have her help you. Over several days, let her do more and more of the job until she does it alone.

(4) *Parents should only make rules that they CAN and WILL enforce.* When rules are made, children will break them. *That is a rule.* Children *must* break new rules to be sure that they *are* rules. If their parents fail to enforce them, they are *not* rules. If this happens enough, the relationship between parent and child becomes tense and uncomfortable. Parents often become angry at children for breaking rules, not realizing that every child breaks every rule that is ever made. When parents say, "I've tried everything and nothing works," they really mean rules have not been enforced.

Some parents attempt to enforce too many rules. These parents are usually found in hectic pursuit of their children, making up "don'ts" while the child tries desperately to escape.

Don't invent rules on the run. Concentrate on enforcing only two or three at a time. You will be surprised at how quickly other things seem to fall into place once this is accomplished.

We live by rules because without them there would be no freedom. When parents make good rules and enforce them, they create a relaxed emotional climate in which their children are free to be O.K.

Rewards and Incentives

"O.K., Junior, I know you don't want to take out the trash, but if you do, I'll give you a dime. How's that sound?" Sounds pretty good, huh Junior?

The notion that children need to be rewarded for obedience has become popular, with some unfortunate consequences. Foremost among these is the idea that children perform better when they are promised tangible rewards, such as candy, a toy, or a special privilege.

In part, this is true. If you want a child to do something mundane, such as cleaning up his room, offer him a piece of his favorite candy, a new toy, or a trip to the neighborhood ice-cream parlor. And then, the next time you want him to clean up his room, be prepared to make the same offer. If you're lucky, the child will only expect more of the same. If luck isn't standing on your side of the street that day, however, he'll want something even better. Yesterday, an ice-cream cone; tomorrow, a super-deluxe Bicentennial hot marshmallow cream sundae!

Children are impressionable, and nothing impresses them more than stuff for their mouths or hands. (Unfortunately, many adults have the same trait.) It's the "what's in it for me?" syndrome, as much the new American way as Mom's factory-made, frozen apple pie.

Accuse me of being an Adult Chauvinist Swine (ACS), but I subscribe to a double standard—what's tolerable in an adult is not always tolerable in a child.

When a child learns to expect something in return every time he puts out a little effort for someone besides himself, it's obnoxious, but it's not his fault. The child is the addict, but we big people are the pushers. We adults tend to look for the most expedient way to accomplish things, the shortest distance between two points. When we want cooperation from a child, we know that offering some "goody" is likely to get the job done fast. In the child's mind, however, cooperation and the performance of certain tasks or chores become hooked to the promise of special rewards.

This can quickly become a revolving door situation that traps both parent and child. Parent wants the work done without having to deal with the child's excuses . . . child wants the handout and has learned that if he stalls long enough, parent will come through with the goods.

Children need certain tools to meet the challenges of adult life. Extremely important among these are the virtues of industry, initiative, and responsibility. All three involve being willing to work, even when the payoff may be intangible or in the uncertain future. Feelings of pride and a sense of accomplishment are the best rewards of all.

"All right then, I won't ever again offer my child a bribe to get him to cooperate with one of my requests. And he won't ever again lift a finger around here to help me! Now, whose move is it?"

Well, I'm glad you asked. It's *your* move and the sooner you make it, the better. You must play Brer Rabbit and outfox your young Brer Fox.

Begin by listing some privileges your child enjoys and now takes for granted. Any activity which is available to him regularly, but which has not been earned, can be defined as a privilege. The list might include having friends over, riding a bicycle, going out to play after supper, or being allowed to stay up later than usual.

Make another list of the chores and responsibilities Brer Fox avoids so cleverly. This list might include putting away his toys, taking his bath, doing his homework, emptying the trash, and walking the dog.

Now you have made two lists, and he still hasn't lifted a finger. Don't get excited. The next step is to look at each item on the lists and ask yourself the musical question, "When?" For the first list, for example, ask, "When does he like to ride his bike?" For the second list, ask, "When do I want him to take his bath?"

Put the lists side by side and there you have it! By connecting the items accordingly, you can make rules such as, "Before you can play your stereo (list 1 item) in the evening, you must take your bath (list 2 item)." Or, "Before you can ride your bicycle after school, you must change your clothes and take the dog out for a walk." Put only one item from the list of privileges into each rule. You can include more than one item from your second list if that seems reasonable. For instance, one rule at our house when Eric was twelve years old was that he had to take a bath, do his homework, and straighten his room before he worked on his models in the evening. It didn't matter to us exactly when he did the chores or in what order. We didn't remind him, but we checked to see that his chores were done and sometimes applied a little "quality control" before he was allowed to play.

So make some rules, because rules are a parent's most indispensable tools. This is also known as the "Godfather Game," because you are making your child an offer he can't refuse.

Or, *can* he? Sure, he can, and he *will. Every* child will test *every* rule ever made. Like chemists trying to discover what solution a substance will dissolve in, children will put rules to every conceivable test, but there is one substance in which no rule will dissolve, and that is . . . consistency.

By consistency I mean enforcing rules under all but the most unusual circumstances. I do not mean that a rule must be enforced in the same way every time (see In Defense of Inconsistency, page 23). If a rule has many exceptions, if a child discovers that a rule does not withstand the "stress tests," then it is not a rule, but simply a wish.

Also involved here is the issue of trust. If you establish rules and then fail to enforce them, can you be depended on in other ways?

These methods may not yield the kind of instant results that bribes do, and they require patience, a rather old-fashioned virtue. But, as Brer Rabbit said, "I never promised you a briar patch."

Painless Punishment

Even before they become parents, most people have fairly fixed ideas about punishment. One of these is the notion that punishment must involve a certain degree of discomfort. Extending this idea, many people seem to believe that, within certain limits, as the discomfort increases, so does the strength of the message to the child—ten slaps on the rear will go further toward eliminating undesirable behavior than two slaps; three weeks under "house arrest" will produce more of a lasting change for the better than three days; and so on.

This philosophy has probably filtered down from days of old when "badness" was thought to be a symptom of demonic possession. In those enlightened times, demons were persistent rascals. Once they set up housekeeping inside someone, they would move out only if the person were made to endure intense, and often fatal, scourging.

It is this reputation that causes us so much confusion when the need to punish arises. But punishment does *not* have to be painful. In fact, it is probably better for all if it causes as little discomfort as possible.

We should punish to make two things clear to a child: "I don't like what you did," and "I am in control here." It isn't necessary to say those words. Whether you spank, send the child to her room, or takc away a privilege, those are the ideas you communicate.

Furthermore, it is not important that you cause pain in the process. In fact, the more painful the experience is for the child, the *less* likely it is that she will hear the message.

So, let's set the record straight. If a child is "bad," bad things do *not* have to happen to her. Punishment should not be regarded as retribution. It does not have to induce suffering, guilt, or remorse. In fact, punishment should, and can, be "good"—for all concerned.

Consider, for example, the act of setting a two-year-old in a chair after she has committed some dark deed (throwing Jell-O on the wall). Believe it or not, it is irrelevant whether the chair is wooden or upholstered in soft velvet. It does not have to be straight-backed, nor must it face a corner.

It also makes no real difference whether the child sits for two minutes or twenty, except that a two-year-old forgets why she's sitting after two minutes. Finally, attempts at extracting apologies or promises of "I'll be good" before commuting her sentence are meaningless.

The act of putting the child in the chair says all that needs to be said. Where she is put and for how long have little bearing on whether the child will "do it again." *Every* two-year-old will do it again. Count on it.

What matters is the parent's willingness to take action and be assertive (as distinguished from aggressive). When the child throws Jell-O on the wall, you respond immediately by putting her in a chair. This communicates strength and authority in a firm, yet gentle, way.

If you invest your energy in trying to keep the child in the chair for any particular length of time, you have missed your own point. Even if the child gets out of the chair immediately, you have still said what you needed to say. If you fight with the child over how long she must sit, you are then saying, "I'm not sure who is in control here, you or me."

By the time she gets out of the chair, you should be facing in some other direction. If you are lucky and she waits for you to give her permission to get down, wait no longer than two minutes. If she looks ready to get down before then, say, "You may get down." Stay one step ahead of the game. If you consistently take the lead, she will learn to look to you for guidance.

A Parent's Best Friend

(Q) What are kitchen timers for?
(A) They alert the cook when the food is done.

Wrong! This simple machine was not designed with the kitchen in mind at all. The so-called kitchen timer is actually a parent's best friend, an indispensable aid in the proper raising of children.

This was known in biblical times, but the knowledge was lost because of a slight error in interpreting an oft-quoted passage from the Good Book. I'm referring, of course, to "spare the rod, spoil the child."

It is now known that "the rod" was an ancient clock. A rod some three feet long was set in the ground, and its shadow was measured at intervals to calculate the passage of time—hence, a timer. The actual meaning of this passage is clear: The author was exhorting parents to use a timer when things get rotten.

Kitchen timers, the portable kind, should be standard issue

to all parents. There is not a more versatile and handy tool for raising children.

A kitchen timer can be used to organize activities. It helps young children understand the concept of time. It will, upon demand, establish routines and define limits. It supplements, enhances, and reinforces the parents' authority and helps everyone detour around power struggles.

Last, but not least, it is a virtually infallible way of communicating when "time's up." In other words, a timer can help with all those tasks parents try to accomplish using words alone—the "in-one-ear-and-out-the-other" method, which has never proven reliable, especially not with preschoolers.

The timer makes unnecessary that repetition of oneself *ad nauseam* that has come to be called the "nag"—another way of putting the cart before the horse.

Below are seven suggested uses for timers. Come down off the wall, moms and dads, your troubles are over. Well . . . almost.

(1) Use a timer to signal "when." For instance when the child can go outside. Take the timer on trips to serve as an audio-visual answer to, "When are we gonna be there?" Instead of repeating "in just a little while," set the timer and let the ringer do the talking.

(2) Timers are an excellent way of defining how much time you will spend playing with your child before going back to your chores or taking a much-needed break. Mom or Dad says, "I'll play blocks with you until the bell rings. Then I have to stop and go back to my work."

(3) Is there a struggle in your house every morning to get your child dressed and out of the house on time? Play "Beat the Bell!" Lay out his clothes the night before, set the timer when you wake him up in the morning, and make a game of getting dressed before the bell rings. If more encouragement is needed, make him an offer he can't refuse: "If you have all your clothes on before the bell rings, you may ride your bike when you come home." The "prize" should not be something extra special or out of the ordinary. Just a privilege that has been, up until now, taken for granted.

(4) The timer will answer the question, "Can I come out of my room now?" which the child usually begins asking within

thirty seconds of being sent there. Stop playing warden. Set the timer when he goes in (five to ten minutes will suffice for most infractions), and tell him that he may come out when the bell goes off. Use the time to call a friend on the phone. After all, how many opportunities do you have for five minutes of uninterrupted conversation?

(5) Use the timer as a prompt for getting chores done. Before: "I've told you twenty thousand times to pick up your toys and take them to your room! If I have to tell you one more time I'm going to do something irrational!" After: "I want to see if you can pick up your toys and have them put away in your room before the bell rings."

(6) The timer can answer how-much-longer questions, such as, "How much longer can I stay in the tub, play outside, bounce on my bed, play in the toilet, drive you crazy?" For example, my daughter liked to read in bed before going off to sleep. "Yes, Amy," we'd tell her, "but you must turn off your light when you hear the bell."

(7) The best use of all is when Mom or Dad (or both) want a little time to be alone (together?). This is known as Mother's (or Father's) Time-Out and is easily set aside with the help of a timer. "Now it is quiet-time for everybody in this house. I want you to play in your room until the timer says you can come out. You may take a nap if you want to (very sneaky)." Nothing compares with a few moments of peace and quiet in the middle of an otherwise hectic day.

Some timers give a barely audible "ding." I'd recommend purchasing what's known in the industry as a "long-ring" model. They're more than worth the slight increase in price. Remember, "A *watched* (timed) tot never spoils."

A Matter of Timing

Of all our many responsibilities as parents, the most demanding is the job of teaching our children the distinction between acceptable and unacceptable behavior. Learning this distinction is, likewise, the most difficult task of childhood. There are no options here—the child *must* learn, and we *must* teach.

Praise and punishment are the two sides of this coin. Praise is good stuff. It feels as good to give as it does to get. Punishment, however, is generally thought of as a negative event, so it often ends up feeling as *bad* to give as it does to get. No one likes to punish, but sometimes it must be done. We muddle through a myriad of approaches (or avoidances) as we grapple with this problem. We reason, threaten, take away privileges, yell, ignore, give menacing looks, spank, confine the child to a chair or room, assign unpleasant tasks, criticize, plead, and cry. Each approach works sometimes; none works every time. Our hearts are just not in it.

I would like, therefore, to propose an alternative called Time-out. Time-out is painless, so you need not feel guilty about invoking it. Time-out can be used without fear of damaging a child's self-esteem. Most important, Time-out works! It works for the parent (it teaches!), it works for the child (who doesn't really want or like to misbehave) and it takes the pressure off of everyone.

First, select a safe (child-proofed) place where a child can be isolated for a short (three to five minutes) period. The placc itsclf must not be threatening (dark) or painful (hot, stuffy). Consider half baths, an out-of-the-way chair, the child's room, or any other convenient space.

Use a kitchen timer (portable) to define the period of isolation. This relieves you of playing "warden."

Third, draw up a list of misbehaviors, and post it on the refrigerator door or some other easily visible place (it is irrelevant whether the child can read). The items on the list should be stated concisely and concretely. For example, *"Saying 'No' when you are told to do something."* as opposed to *"being disobedient"* or *"not listening."* Start with no more than five items. You can always add to the list later, if need be.

Explain Time-out to the child as simply, specifically, and briefly as possible. The explanation must not be punishing. Present Time-out as "the way it's going to be," rather than "the last straw" or "you're in for it now." Go over the list, explaining that when one of the behaviors occurs, she will be taken (or sent) to the "Time-out place," to stay until she hears the bell. She may come out any time after the bell rings.

Then, when a list-behavior happens, say, "Running in the house is on the list. You must go to your room for Time-out."

Disregard apologies, changes of heart ("O.K., I'll pick 'em up"), verbal abuse, promises ("I won't do it again"), tantrums, or physical resistance. If the child needs your "help," *take* her to Time-out—firmly but gently.

Disengage yourself from the problem once the door is closed and the timer is set. Do *not* respond to pleading, tantrums, running water, flushing toilets, or deathly silence (but don't forget to child-proof). If she opens the door before the bell rings, reset the timer and close it.

After the bell rings, the child may open the door *when she wants to.* Don't position yourself outside, ready to confront or comfort, and do *not* engage in long conversations about the misbehavior.

Remember: no reminders, warnings, or second chances. Do not refer to Time-out as though it were something to be dreaded. It is a constructive way of communicating limits and authority to a child.

As is the case with many other things, it's all a matter of timing.

PART TWO

It's Only a Stage

This is the "ages and stages" section of the book, where I trace the development history of the child from birth through the teen years. In 1981, when I was writing the first edition of this book, Eric was going on thirteen. So having had no experience living *with a teenager, I did not feel qualified to say much about teens. Therefore, the original* Parent Power! *had next to nothing in it about children of those years. When people asked me if and when I would ever write a book on teens, I told them it would have to wait until my kids were beyond those years. Eric is now twenty-two and in his third year of college (as distinguished from his* junior *year) at N.C. State. Amy is a freshperson at U.N.C.-Chapel Hill. Over the last ten years, I have collected material for a book on teens—anecdotes about my own and other people's children, observations, statistics, and so on. All with the intent of writing that book. But I've decided not to, after all. You see, in order to write it, I would have to relive the entire experience. Once is enough. To satisfy the thrill-seekers among you, I've added a chapter on teens in this section of this edition of* Parent Power! *That will have to do.*

Birth to Eight Months: Infancy

"The first eight months of a baby's life . . . are probably the easiest of all times for parents," Burton White says in *The First Three Years of Life*. "If they provide the baby with a normal amount of love, attention, and physical care," he adds, "nature will pretty much take care of the rest. . . . Nature, almost as if it had anticipated the uncertainties that beset new parents, has done its best to make the first six to eight months as problem-free as possible."

Dr. White certainly makes it sound easy, doesn't he? Still, some infants are "easier" than others. Researchers who study newborns have found vast differences in temperament, activity levels, how much and how loudly they cry, their reactions to different forms of stimulation, how much and how soundly they sleep, and how "sensitive" they are to the environment.

While more generalizations can be made about infants than about children at any other age, their differences far outweigh and are, in the long run, more significant than their similarities.

Every infant applies himself in different ways and at different times to the many facets of growth and development. One baby may develop a true social smile sooner than another. But the baby who was slower to smile may be quicker to crawl. He may still be crawling when the early smiler gets up and walks. In fact, by the time a baby is six months old, it often looks as if he has "chosen" one or two particular areas of his development to concentrate on. Put three six-month-old children in a room together and you are apt to see one working diligently on learning how to creep, another spending most of her time experimenting with sounds, while the third is working intently to develop his finger dexterity and eye-hand coordination. While each baby's timetable may vary considerably, however, the *sequence* of development is fairly predictable.

Personality traits emerge sooner than many parents expect. For instance, by the middle of the second month, babies express definite likes and dislikes, particularly in terms of what they enjoy looking at, how they want to be held, and how much stimulation they need and can tolerate.

In short, each and every human infant is fascinating in his own right. He begins to define who he is and what he wants from you during the first few weeks of his life.

The following topics are of special interest and concern to parents of infants during the first eight months of life.

Pacifiers

There are two schools of thought regarding the use of pacifiers. On the one hand (usually the right) is the pro-thumb school (Thumbers), a group of purists who promote the thumb as a natural, built-in tranquilizer. The thumb, they say, is more convenient than a pacifier, and babies who suck this digit practice independence and self-control. Thumbers maintain that pacifiers are artificial and warn that children can become dependent on them.

Proponents of the pacifier (Pacifists), point out that a pacifier can be taken from a child after a certain age. Furthermore, pacifiers do not push against the roof of the mouth and upper gum as thumbs often do.

Both points of view seem reasonable, and each has its merits. There are two reasons for giving a pacifier serious consideration: First, it can supplement an infant's sucking needs, and second, it can quiet the "fussies."

During the first months of life, the need to suck dominates the infant's limited behavioral repertoire. Beginning as a survival-oriented reflex, the need to suck comes increasingly under voluntary control after the second month of life and gradually diminishes in strength over the next ten to sixteen months. In most cases, it disappears completely by age eighteen months.

The sucking instinct is definitely stronger in some infants than in others. Most infants quickly discover the hand-to-mouth connection and by their second month spend a significant portion of their waking time mouthing various parts of their hands. By this time, they also attempt to put anything they grasp into their mouths.

Except when a child's safety is involved, there is no reason to interfere. An infant's need to suck should never be denied or obstructed, unless, of course, the object to be sucked constitutes a threat to the infant's safety. For an infant whose sucking need is especially powerful, a pacifier can be a worthwhile supplement to her hand, her mother's breast, or the bottle.

Until she is six to eight weeks old, baby may have some difficulty keeping the pacifier in her mouth. And some infants, regardless of how fussy they are or however strong their need to suck, refuse to accept pacifiers altogether.

With all this in mind, I offer the following recommendations:

• If your baby discovers her thumb (or fingers), don't interfere and don't attempt to substitute a pacifier. In the first place, it will probably be rejected. Keep in mind that when an infant is sucking on part of her hand, two parts of her body—mouth *and* hand—are pleasurably stimulated. When she sucks on a pacifier, only *one* part of her body—her mouth—is pleasured. Once an infant experiences the added benefit of hand-sucking, she's not likely to settle for less.

• If your baby has periodic bouts of the "fussies," she may be signaling a need for additional sucking time. If she doesn't make the hand-to-mouth connection, try introducing a pacifier.

• Use pacifiers sparingly, perhaps only during baby's fussiest part of the day (this usually occurs in the late afternoon or early evening). The conservative approach will diminish the odds that she will develop a prolonged dependence on it.

• Don't use a pacifier to "hold off" your baby's next feeding. If she's hungry, feed her.

• If your baby isn't particularly fussy, doesn't find her thumb, and seems content with the amount of sucking she's getting during feedings, then there's no reason to offer a pacifier. Lucky you.

• By no means should a pacifier be used *every time* a baby cries between feedings. If your baby is obviously uncomfortable or bored, pick her up and comfort her. Pacifiers are not a substitute for cuddling.

Crying

Some babies cry a lot. Some cry very little. But all babies cry. Sometimes fussiness is caused by a readily identifiable source of discomfort: the baby's hungry, has stomach cramps, or is in an uncomfortable position and needs rearranging. Other crying is unrelated to physical discomfort and seems to be an attempt at self-stimulation—a way of asking for attention. Some crying can't be explained in terms of discomfort or deficiency. Sometimes babies cry for the sake of crying, for the "just because" of it all. Perhaps this is baby's way of reminding himself of his existence—talking to himself, so to speak.

By the end of the third month, most mothers have become quite sensitive to their babies' crying language and can identify the differences in tone and volume that mean "I'm hungry," as opposed to, for example, "I'm bored."

Most babies have regular periods of fussy crying, often in the late afternoon or evening. This daily upsurge in crying usually wanes by the fifth or sixth month.

Here are some suggestions for calming a fussy baby:

• Holding and gently rocking a crying baby will calm all babies some of the time and some babies all of the time. Every baby has his definite likes and dislikes, and you may have to experiment with different positions, rhythms, and rocking techniques until you find the right combination for your little one. Music often has a calming effect. If you don't have any recorded music handy, or if you happen to feel creative, sing to your baby while you rock him (singing, because it enhances language development, is actually preferable).

I find that most infants like to be held upright so they can look over your shoulder. Sometimes it's easier for them to fall asleep in that position, too.

If you don't have a rocking chair, or if a gentle back and forth motion doesn't seem to do the trick, sit on the edge of a bed and bounce gently up and down. Both of my children preferred this to the motion of a rocking chair.

• Swaddling, or wrapping baby snugly in a blanket, may help him relax. Some infants, however, don't like being physically restricted. Others are soothed by swaddling as long as they are held and rocked at the same time.

• Pacifiers can be helpful with some babies (see Pacifiers, page 42).

• Burping. If no gas is released, try again in three to five minutes. A howling baby tends to swallow air, adding to his discomfort.

• One of the most useful baby-care products I have tried is called a Snug-Li. Snug-Li is a cross between a knapsack and the traditional Indian papoose carrier. In a Snug-Li, baby can be carried either in front or back. Either way, it leaves the adult with both hands free. Unlike most other backpack carriers or slings, Snug-Li supports even the tiniest head. In addition, Snug-Li grows with the baby (to enlarge the pack, you just take out some of the tucks in the soft, washable corduroy) and can be used comfortably until the baby is eighteen months old or so.

Having used Snug-Li with both of our children, Willie and I know that it's pleasant and satisfying for both parent and child. By the way, the fear that too much cuddling and physical closeness encourages overdependence is groundless. The opposite is true: the more secure a child feels as an infant, the more readily he will move away from his parents when the time comes.

Snug-Li is sold in many infant stores and can be ordered by mail. Write Snug-Li, 12520 Grant Drive, Denver, Colorado, 80241. This has been an unsolicited testimonial.

Meet Baby's Needs as Well as Your Own

Throughout the book I will use a question-and-answer format such as what follows to elaborate on typical problems parents may encounter.

(Q) The host of a local television show recently interviewed a pediatrician who has just written a book on fussy babies. His description of what he called a "high-need baby" fit my six-month-old to a *T.* He is very active, alert, and requires a great deal of stimulation and attention. I must hold and entertain him almost constantly to prevent him from becoming upset. If I put him down and leave the room, he begins screaming. So, I carry him around with me all the time. I feel I no longer have a life of my own and find myself beginning to resent the demands of motherhood. This doctor's solution to the problems that come with a high-need baby like ours was to "wear the baby like a sweater." When the interviewer pointed out that this leaves no room for other responsibilities, he replied that meeting the baby's needs was more important than doing housework or anything else. He made it sound like our son would achieve independence sooner if we put his needs first; nevertheless, his advice left me with a rather hopeless feeling. Do you agree with him? If not, what other advice would you have for me?

(A) I agree with the doctor's description of "high-need infants." It's also true that if you repeatedly frustrate an infant's need for closeness and attention, you're going to delay the baby's independence and create other potentially serious problems.

I *don't* agree, however, with the doctor's statement that parents of high-need babies should "wear them like a sweater." That's similar to, "You can't spoil an infant," which, while essentially true, is usually taken to mean that parents should pick up a baby every time he cries. That advice is not only impractical, especially with a fussy baby, but also unnecessary.

Meeting your baby's needs involves meeting your own as well. Stated differently, you can't take care of someone else unless you also take care of yourself.

Parents who feel that they must devote themselves exclusively to their babies and forget about themselves begin to develop feelings of frustration and resentment. If there's one thing a baby doesn't need, it's parents who feel that parenthood is a burden.

Somewhere between the doctor's injunction that you should wear your baby like a sweater and a state of unselfish neglect, there's a point of balance where it's possible for you to meet both your needs *and* your child's.

There is no getting around the fact that fussy, high-need infants require more attention and physical closeness than the norm. And, for the most part, it's good practice to respond to an infant's cries shortly after they begin.

However, there's no harm in putting your baby down for a few minutes to take care of something you can't do with him in your arms, even if he cries during that time.

In other words, if it's practical for you to "wear him like a sweater," do so. But if it's not practical, put him down and do what you must. If you leave the room, call to him every ten seconds or so. The sound of your voice isn't going to stop him from crying, but at least he'll know he's not been abandoned.

A couple of things are going to happen within the next few months that are going to make life with your baby a whole lot easier

First, he's going to become increasingly mobile. At the moment, his intense need to explore is frustrated by the fact that he can't get around on his own. So, you do his exploring for him. You bring things to him, thus feeding his curiosity.

You have to do a lot of "entertaining," because a high-need baby doesn't stay interested in any one thing for very long. The more mobile he gets, however, the less he's going to depend on you for stimulation, and the more time you'll have for yourself.

Second, around age eight months, he's going to develop what is called "object permanence." Right now, in his mind, if something vanishes from sight, it no longer exists. That includes you. In a few months, however, he'll realize that you're here to stay, and he'll be able to tolerate your being out of sight for longer and longer periods of time.

Until then, feel free to put your baby down and go to the bathroom, brush your teeth, wash your face, fix yourself something to eat, or just sit and pull your wits together for a few minutes without fear of causing permanent psychological scars. I hardly think your child's long-term emotional health rests on such simplistic circumstances.

Fathers

With the exception of breast-feeding, there is nothing mothers do that fathers cannot do just as well (take it from me). The obsolete notion that mothers can better fulfill their babies' needs has encouraged mothers to feel more responsible for their children than they actually are, while it has caused fathers to feel insignificant and excluded. Without a doubt, there are differences in the ways mothers and fathers interact with their children. Each parent brings a unique set of personality factors into the child-rearing situation, and each contributes invaluable, though differently, to the child's growth and development.

Several studies have shown, for instance, that babies show no innate preference for one parent over the other (with the exception of breast-fed babies). Other research shows that babies whose fathers are actively involved in their upbringing tend to be more outgoing, less fearful of strangers and new situations, more willing to accept challenges, and generally more assertive. I suspect these findings have less to do with fathers *per se* than with the fact that it's more stimulating and enriching to have two actively involved parents than just one.

Since males have not generally been brought up to think of themselves in the primary parent role, many fathers feel awkward and inept around their children at first. But a father who *chooses* to be relatively uninvolved, or whose wife discounts his significance, usually ends up feeling as though he is on the outside looking in at the mother-child relationship. Almost inevitably, this father develops jealousy and resentment toward the child. Often his reaction is to put even more distance between himself and his family by becoming increasingly involved in his occupation.

The other side of this coin is the mother who feels overly protective of her role as primary parent. It is usually easier to get a somewhat reluctant father involved with his child than it is to get a possessive mother to loosen her grip. The overprotective mother generally ends up feeling as though she is raising her child in a goldfish bowl—she feels trapped, helpless, isolated, overly responsible, and usually ineffective. Suffice it to say that both an uninvolved father and an overly involved mother interfere with a child's overall growth and development.

Postpartum Blues

It's not uncommon for new mothers to experience a sense of letdown and depression soon after the birth of a child. The "blues" may come and go in the form of mild, infrequent bouts of uneasiness and anxiety, or they may be frequent and intense enough to require professional help.

The postpartum "blues" are probably a combination of several factors including:

• *Disappointment* at discovering that motherhood isn't the earth-shaking, consciousness-raising event it is sometimes cracked up to be. Maybe Mom is a little shocked at her baby's wrinkled, rather flabby appearance, having expected her baby to look for all the world as though she stepped out of a baby-powder commercial.

• *Fatigue* at being wakened one or more times night after night and being constantly on call for another human being who is not only helpless but seems to have a talent for making messes.

• *Adjusting to a new life-style,* new routines, and new priorities (including the fact that her own interests seem to be moving further and further to the back of the bus).

• *Changes occurring in her relationship with her husband.* Perceptions and expectations of one another are modified. Consequently Mom may experience a sense of loss and feel that "things will never be the same."

• *Doubts* about whether she is really cut out to be a mother or whether parenthood is what she wants for herself. Almost every new mother goes through a stage in which she feels somewhat resentful toward her baby.

Any or all of these, combined with the rather helpless realization that "there ain't no turning back," can be temporarily unsettling to a woman's self-esteem.

In addition to getting as much rest as you can and saving time for yourself and your marriage, new mothers should talk to other mothers. Express your feelings. You'll be surprised at how comforting and reassuring it is to find that other women experience similar emotional upheavals.

And here's some advice for the new father: Get involved! Pitch in! Offer to help with changing, bathing, feeding, and everything else that goes into taking care of the baby. If your wife seems reluctant to accept your help, it's probably because she feels she should be "all things at all times" to her child. If that's the case, gently point out to her that the two of you are in this thing together. If you must, insist that she let you help and even at times take over. Her reluctance may also be a way of testing your continued commitment to her. When the baby wakes up in the middle of the night, get up with your mate and talk softly with her while she feeds the baby. If the baby is bottle-fed, take a regular turn at the "night shift."

The more involved you are with the baby, and the more supportive you are of your wife, the less isolated she will feel and the more resistant she will be to the postpartum "blues." Therefore, the more involved she will be with you. How about that?

Can You Spoil an Infant?

Not a chance. There is no such thing as too much closeness (except in cases where a mother's anxious overinvolvement with the baby dominates her life to the exclusion of husband, interests, friends, and so on).

Most experts agree that you can't spoil an infant, but I'm afraid that many parents, and mothers in particular, have taken this to mean that a baby must be picked up and comforted every time he cries. This just isn't so. There are definitely times when baby will cry (see Crying, page 43), not because he is uncomfortable or needs attention, but simply for the sake of crying. When this seems to be the case, it is perfectly all right to let him fuss by himself for a while.

It won't take much time for you to know, from the sound of your baby's cry, what, if anything, he needs from you. If the cry is an attempt at communication, then he should not be left to "cry it out." You should attend to him and make every reasonable effort to comfort him. Your responsiveness to his needs helps him develop a trusting attitude toward the world and toward you in particular. A sense of trust and protectedness gives him the freedom to be curious, explore the world, and become assertively independent.

Most babies cry themselves to sleep, at least for a time. Crying at bedtime helps them dispose of tensions that might disrupt the transition from waking to sleeping. There is no reason to interfere with this type of crying either. For your own peace of mind, though, you may want to look in on a crying baby every five minutes or so from the time you put him in his crib until he is asleep. If his crying becomes more insistent, pick him up immediately.

On occasions when you're not sure whether your baby is crying for you or not, always give him the benefit of the doubt. Studies have shown that babies whose parents respond quickly to their cries for attention feel more secure and, consequently, cry less and less with the passage of time. They also tend to be less demanding and more self-sufficient as they get older.

Feeding

Most newborns require a feeding every three to five hours. Initially, baby's tummy won't discriminate between daytime and nighttime, but somewhere toward the middle or end of her second month, she may suddenly give up her three A.M. feeding and sleep from around eleven P.M. till nearly six the next morning. Don't count on it, though. She may not sleep through the night for many months to come.

Feed your baby when she's hungry. Although some pediatricians continue to favor a strict four-hour feeding schedule, most child development experts agree the so-called demand schedule makes more sense. Actually, the term "demand" hardly fits. Infants don't make demands. When they are hungry, they cry, simply because that's their way of expressing physical tension. Being made to wait until someone else decides it's "time" for them to be hungry only makes them feel frustrated and insecure.

Your baby's internal feeding schedule will be fairly well established by the end of the second month. She will still have her off days, however, and you will need to stay flexible.

Between baby's fourth and sixth months, your pediatrician will probably advise you to introduce solid foods into her diet. Some babies take quickly to solid food at this age and seem to enjoy experimenting with new tastes and textures. Other babies, particularly breast-feeders, reject solid food at this age and possibly for several weeks and even months to come.

Don't ever force feed an infant. Even at this early age, the attitudes you have about food will be communicated to your baby. If mealtime becomes associated with tension, and if questions of *how much* or *what* baby eats become issues, she will acquire a negative attitude toward meals. If this happens, I can virtually guarantee that the family dinner hour will become more and more of a battleground as she grows older.

Introduce new foods one at a time. Baby is less likely to resist a new taste if you offer it near the beginning of a meal, when she is hungriest. Small portions help her get used to a new taste more gradually.

By the time she is six months old, baby will take great pleasure in feeding herself "finger foods" during part of her meal. At this age food is a sensory adventure, and baby will experiment on almost everything you give her to eat—mashing, smearing, crumbling, and hurling it to the floor.

Bottle-fed babies are usually able to hold their bottles by the time they are six or seven months old. But even though baby will prefer to hold it herself (and should be allowed to most of the time), it isn't a good idea to let her take a bottle to bed at night or at nap time. Mealtime is for eating and bedtime is for learning how to go to sleep. Babies who take bottles to bed quickly develop a dependence on them which can persist well into the second and even third year of life. In addition, the milk from a bedtime bottle can more easily adhere to baby's teeth, resulting in a form of tooth decay know as "nursing bottle syndrome." Finally, closeness between parent and child at mealtime is important throughout the first year of life.

Breast or Bottle?

Before your baby is born you will decide whether to breast- or bottle-feed. In making this decision, don't be taken in by the myth that breast-fed babies are more secure and happy than bottle-fed babies. The quality of the mother-infant relationship is enhanced when breast-feeding is successful, but nursing is *not* essential to this interaction. No evidence supports claims by advocates of breast-feeding that nursing provides a more secure foundation for healthy psychological development. If a woman would rather not breast-feed but feels that she *must* in order to be a good mother, she won't do herself or her baby any favors. Furthermore, this unreasonable pressure reduces her chance of successful breast-feeding.

In my estimation the advantages of breast-feeding are purely practical. It is more convenient. It requires no preparation or paraphernalia. Breast-feeding is a lot less time-consuming. Breast milk is preheated to an ideal temperature; you never have to worry about storage, and breasts don't require sterilization. Breast milk is free and replenishes itself. Breast milk is nonallergenic; some physicians believe that breast milk may prevent later allergic reactions to cow's-milk products.

Here are answers to some frequently asked questions about breast-feeding:

(Q) Is breast milk healthier than commercial formulas?
(A) Commercial formulas attempt to duplicate the composition of human milk, and overall the similarities outweigh the differences. The differences, though subtle, do favor mother's milk.

(Q) Are breast-fed babies more resistant to disease?
(A) Apparently so. Until an infant builds up his own defenses against infection, he relies heavily on antibodies from his mother for protection. Many of these antibodies are present in colostrum—the yellowish, protein-rich substance secreted from the breasts for the first few days after birth—as well as in breast milk itself. These protective factors temporarily immunize the baby against a broad range of infectious agents.

Breast-fed babies suffer milder and less frequent episodes of diarrhea and have fewer respiratory and gastrointestinal illnesses than bottle-fed babies. These effects are more pronounced in babies who have been nursed for more than five months.

(Q) Do bottle-fed babies gain more weight than breast-fed babies?
(A) On the average, bottle-fed babies are larger and heavier at one year than breast-fed babies. This is sometimes seen as a sign of good health; actually, bottle-fed babies gain weight more quickly than they grow in length. In breast-fed babies, the two measures tend to be in better proportion. In brief, bottle-fed babies are more likely to be overweight.

Breast-fed babies have more control over the feeding process. When they stop sucking, the mother stops nursing. On the other hand, bottle-fed babies may be encouraged to continue drinking even after their hunger has been satisfied. Bottle-fed babies are usually started on solid foods much earlier than breast-fed babies. Introducing solids prematurely can also contribute to excessive weight gain.

Bottles should *never* be used as pacifiers. Babies should be fed *only* when they are hungry, and not necessarily every time they cry. Having a fat baby is neither cute nor desirable. Excess weight can slow a baby's developmental progress. An overweight baby is more likely to become an overweight child, and later, an overweight adult. Being overweight is not healthy for humans at any age.

(Q) Are there any other dangers in bottle-feeding?
(A) Bottle-feeding can be extremely dangerous when the water supply is unclear, refrigeration is inadequate, or preparation of the formula is not carried out under sanitary conditions. If the formula becomes contaminated, the baby is exposed to serious infection.

Diluting the formula to save money can result in malnutrition. Mothers who bottle-feed need to be cautious about overfeeding and refrain from adding solids to the diet prematurely. There is nothing *inherently* dangerous about bottle-feeding. In fact, modern formulas are quite close in composition to human milk and promote healthy development.

(Q) Are there women who should not breast-feed?
(A) Women with active tuberculosis or chronic infectious diseases should not nurse. A nursing mother should consult her physician before taking any kind of medication. Women who commonly use alcohol, marijuana, cigarettes, or coffee should ask their doctors whether these substances might have adverse effects on a nursing infant.

Some mothers (*very* few) have an inadequate milk supply, making nursing difficult or impossible. The most common causes of milk shortage, however, are depression, anxiety, and fear of failure. All can inhibit the flow of milk. As I said before, a woman who pressures herself into nursing, but who would rather not, is stacking the deck against success. Don't let your ego get involved in this decision. Do what you feel most comfortable doing.

(Q) I have breast-fed our first child six months. Sara takes a feeding around seven P.M. and then wakes for a slightly smaller one at ten, after which she sleeps the night. Since she won't take a bottle yet, my husband I haven't been out in the evening without her since she was born. Naturally, we would like to have some time to ourselves, but I'm in somewhat of a conflict about introducing the bottle this early, since the breast-feeding arrangement is so convenient and satisfying for both of us. Any suggestions?
(A) It's not too early to begin supplementing Sara with either a bottle or solids, and if your approach is conservative, neither should disrupt the breast-feeding arrangement. At her seven P.M. feeding, try giving Sara one or two teaspoons of cereal, mixed thinly with formula or extracted breast milk and perhaps a small amount of baby fruit (check with your pediatrician beforehand). The added substance may help push her late-evening wake-up time to around midnight, which would give you and your husband five continuous hours of freedom.

Now, about bottles and breast-fed babies: A breast-fed baby

expects only the very best from Mom, so you may have more difficulty getting Sara to accept a bottle than either your husband or sitter. The fact that she rejects a bottle from you is no indication she'll reject it from someone else, as long as that someone is patient and has experience caring for babies. If you decide to let someone else try offering Sara a bottle, it might be best if you leave the room or even the house. She might not accept a bottle from anyone if she knows that you're nearby.

Your concern that success with a supplementary bottle will put an end to breast-feeding is unwarranted. Should Sara warm to an occasional bottle, she will continue to prefer your breast at least until she can hold a bottle herself. My wife and I introduced an evening bottle to our daughter at five months for exactly the same reasons. Amy accepted bottles from both myself and baby-sitters long before she would take one from my wife and continued to be a breast-fed baby for another eight months.

Whether or not you decide to begin the cereal supplement, and whether or not it extends the evening nap, hire an experienced baby-sitter and give her instructions to offer your daughter a bottle of formula or extracted breast milk when and if she wakes at ten.

Take a chance! If things don't work the first time, try, try again.

For additional information about nursing, contact your local La Leche League. There are quite a few good books on breast-feeding, including *Nursing Your Baby,* by Karen Pryor, and *The Womanly Art of Breast Feeding,* published by the La Leche League.

Sleeping

Sometime toward the middle or end of her second month, your baby will probably begin sleeping through the night, much to your delight. In most cases, she will still require an eleven P.M. feeding, after which she may sleep until five or six o'clock the next morning. The first time this happens, you will probably wake up in the middle of the night wondering why you haven't heard from her. Check on her, if it will make you feel better, but don't *under any circumstances,* wake her up.

There is *no* need to whisper or walk on tiptoes while baby sleeps. Your baby will sleep quite soundly and restfully while life goes on at a normal volume in your household. In fact it's more important to turn down the level of stimulation while baby is *awake*. An excess of noise and visual activity can provoke distress in an infant and even overwhelm her defenses, making her irritable and disrupting her schedule. If baby is constantly or frequently exposed to a high level of stimulation, she may fail to settle into a routine.

By four weeks of age, the tonic neck reflex (TNR) becomes established. The TNR, or "fencer's pose," is a characteristic posture of all babies and is in evidence until sometime around the fourth month. When on her back, the baby will turn her head to a preferred side (85 percent turn to the right) and extend the same-side arm outward. Her opposite arm will be bent, with the hand usually resting on or near the chest. Thus, the "fencer's pose."

In addition to preferring that her head be turned to a particular side, your baby will also show definite preferences in sleeping positions. With some experimentation, you should be able to determine whether she prefers sleeping on her stomach or her back. In either case, it is best to satisfy her natural inclinations. There is absolutely no substance to the idea that babies are more likely to choke when on their backs or smother when on their stomachs.

By the end of the third month, your baby may have eliminated her eleven P.M. feeding and be sleeping about ten hours a night. *Now is the time to begin using a consistent bedtime.* A routine will not only help your baby anticipate when bedtime is coming, but will also give her an opportunity to wind down from the activity of the day. Then she is more likely to accept bedtime when it arrives.

With or without a routine, your baby may cry after you put her in her crib. It's not unusual for babies to cry themselves to sleep, and many seem to sleep more soundly if they are allowed to cry for ten or fifteen minutes after being put to bed. You need not interfere with this unless her cry is obviously distressed.

Many babies continue, even after the third month, to waken for short periods during the night and fuss or make noises. These semi-waking periods are part of a normal sleep cycle. Baby requires no attention during these times, and left to her own devices, she will find her way back to sleep in short order. On the other hand, you can condition your baby to wake up completely and repeatedly in the middle of the night by handling or feeding her every time she does.

If your baby hasn't started sleeping through the night by this time, don't try and force the issue by keeping her up as long as you can in the evening. The best way to encourage a long sound period of sleep at night is to put her to bed in the evening at the first sign of fatigue. When a baby is kept up past the time when she should have been put to bed, she will have more difficulty falling asleep, her sleep will be fitful, and she will be more irritable when she wakes up.

At four months your baby will still take two or three naps during the day. By the fifth month, however, there may be days when she takes only one nap. Even so, it is best to put her down for a second rest period, even if she doesn't actually fall asleep. You will certainly need it and an additional quiet time won't do her any harm either.

By the eighth month most babies sleep twelve hours a night and take just one nap during the day. (Some babies, however, take two naps until they are nearly one and a half.) Around the eighth month, many babies, regardless of how cooperative they have been in the past, begin protesting at bedtime. By this time, baby crawls, sits well without support, and pulls herself to a standing position. Her mobility stimulates her interest in exploring the environment. This is an exciting time for baby, and she may be unwilling to cease all activity when you call an end to her day. In addition, eight-month-olds are more likely than either six- or twelve-month-olds to become upset when separated from their mothers, so you may have some problems at bedtime.

This is a time for gentle firmness. Adhere to the bedtime routine you have established, and regardless of her protests, let baby know that bedtime is an irreversible fact of her daily life. Your decisiveness, your firm resolve, and the control you demonstrate in this situation will be an ultimate source of comfort and security for your baby.

(Q) We just spent a week of "vacation" with my parents, during which my mother and I got into it over the way I put our three-month-old first child to sleep.

I insist that the house get quiet fifteen minutes before I put him down and that it stay that way for at least one hour, until he is completely under. At that point, I only ask that people not make any sudden, loud noises. My mother called me a "worry-wart" because of what she termed my "neurotic attitude" about putting Josh to sleep.

She says that when putting a baby to sleep, the noise level in the house should stay right where it is during any other time of the day. I say noise disturbs Josh's sleep. She says Josh will get used to it.

She also says I'm already too concerned about Josh, and that if I don't get over my constant worrying about him, he'll be in control of the family by the time he's two years old. Who's right, me or my mother?

(A) Your mother's right. She's tactless, but she's right.

Like yourself, most new parents believe that a house must be deathly quiet while a baby is going off to sleep. No so. Life in the family should go on at its normal volume. The baby will quickly accommodate to whatever noise level is normal for the household and will only be disturbed if there's a sudden and significant increase from this "baseline."

I don't think any studies have been done to verify what I'm about to say, but I would speculate that babies who get used to going to sleep in quiet homes sleep much less deeply than babies who go to sleep in homes that are relatively noisy. It's just a guess, mind you, but it makes sense that if the "noise baseline" is initially low, it will take less noise to disturb the baby than if the baseline is established at a normal level.

It seemed to work that way for our children. When they were babies, there was loud rock 'n' roll on the stereo almost constantly, sometimes until well into the wee hours of the morning. They slept right through it, I think because it was a normal part of their noise environment from day one. They are both, to this day, sound sleepers, for which my wife and I were always thankful.

They also have great senses of rhythm.

Contrast this with my two-year-old nephew, whose mother insists that everyone tiptoe around and whisper after he's put to bed. Not only does it take him upwards of an hour to fall asleep, but he wakes up at the slightest noise. Come to think of it, he also controls his family. Everything revolves around him, from the time he gets up in the morning until well past his bedtime.

Concerning your mother's warning to the same effect, I don't have a crystal ball, so I don't know what will be going on in your family twenty-one months from now. I *do* know, however, that you are already setting certain precedents with Josh that once set, will be hard, but not impossible, to undo.

A family should revolve around the parents, and its lifestyle should be defined by their tastes. It goes without saying that raising children requires that one make certain changes and compromises, but a family should never revolve around a child's presence.

For all these reasons, I think you would be better to heed your mother's tactlessly given advice and get Josh used to the fact that life goes on normally around him and normally without him.

(Q) Our first child, a girl, was born six weeks ago. As yet, we haven't been able to get her on a good bedtime routine and were wondering if you might have any advice for us. Initially, we were putting her to bed at eight o'clock, immediately after her last nursing. This went well for about a week, then she started crying as soon as we put her in her crib. One of us would rock her back to sleep, but when we'd put her back in her crib, she'd wake and start crying again. Thinking that perhaps she wasn't ready for sleep at eight, we tried keeping her up later, but the later we kept her up, the crankier she got and the longer it took to get her down. As it stands, we are "playing it by ear," trying to catch her when she's most ready, but this doesn't seem to be working well either. We've heard that you can't spoil an infant, but this is ridiculous!

(A) When our son and firstborn, Eric, made his triumphant entrance into the world, he was greeted by two young, anxious parents who picked him up every time he cried, day or night.

Bedtime quickly became a circus, with Eric holding out and his parents holding on. No one had ever told us most babies cry for a short period before falling off to sleep. Left to our own ignorance, we decided that crying was his way of telling us that we hadn't done something right—rocked him long enough, given him enough milk—so we picked him up and tried again.

On a good night, Eric fell asleep around ten only to be up again two or three hours later. This kept up, off and on, all night long. Looking back on all this, it seems we were trying to create a perfect, pain-free world for Eric. The more we tried to protect him from discomfort, however, the lower his tolerance for discomfort became, so that by the time he was eighteen months old, he could not handle any frustration whatsoever. When he was two and a half, he slept through the night for the first time.

Amy, born three and a half years after Eric, had no such luck. Several weeks before the blessed event, Willie looked me in the eye and said, with complete conviction, "*This* one's going to have a bedtime." And so she did. At eight P.M., Amy was nursed, burped, and put in her crib. She usually cried for about five or ten minutes, then fell asleep.

If her crying suddenly became intense or lasted much longer than ten minutes, one of us would check. More often than not, finding nothing amiss, we rubbed her back for a minute or so to let her know we were there, and left. Amy slept through the night when she was two weeks old.

Most contemporary authorities, including Dr. Burton White, author of *The First Three Years of Life*, maintain it's impossible to spoil an infant. This may be, but it is definitely possible to respond to an infant's crying such that you are sure to have a thoroughly spoiled toddler on your hands.

While I agree with White that letting infants "cry it out" is an undesirable practice, I disagree with his recommendation that parents respond promptly to an infant's every call for attention. As I said earlier, most babies cry some at bedtime. This is not necessarily an indication of discomfort, but may be a natural way of discharging tension and thus making the transition between waking and sleeping.

Rushing in every time an infant cries is just as extreme as making him always "cry it out." A moderate approach, such as we took with Army, is the most sensible alternative.

(Q) My son did not sleep through the night until he was almost five months old. Shortly after that, we moved to a new house. He seemed slightly upset by the move and began waking periodically through the night again. On the advice of our pediatrician, we gave him a chance to get used to the new house and then stopped picking him up. Instead of crying himself back to sleep, he cried every night for one to three hours for nearly a month. We finally gave up and started picking him up again. Now, at nine months, he wakes up every hour on the hour throughout the night. As soon as we pick him up, he falls back to sleep for another hour. During the day, his naps never last longer than thirty minutes. What should we do?

(A) To begin with, your pediatrician's advice was inappropriate for a six-month-old infant. He should not have advised you to let your baby "cry it out" at bedtime or when he woke up during the night. Separation anxieties are common enough at this age without compounding them with insecurities associated with sleeping.

If an infant needs reassurance, give it to him. The more available you are during the first year of life, the more secure he will feel and the better able he will be to move toward increasing degrees of independence.

Your baby is becoming overly fatigued during the day because his insecurities are overriding his need for sleep. This is another factor preventing him from settling into a restful night's sleep.

First, establish a morning and afternoon quiet period for his nap. If he wakes up prematurely (less than one hour), try encouraging him to fall back to sleep. If he doesn't cooperate, discontinue this effort and let him out of bed.

Then begin putting him to bed at 7:30 P.M., preceded by a "winding down" ritual beginning at seven. This could include a bath, a short story, a tucking-in ceremony and whatever else you want to throw in.

When he wakes up in the night, respond *immediately* to him and do whatever is necessary to get him back to sleep as quickly as possible. You might want to move his crib back into your room until he's sleeping more restfully.

In short, let him know that your presence is not a questionable thing. Within a couple of months, he should be back on track.

Day Care

(Q) I took a leave of absence from my job to have my first baby and be totally available to her for the first three months of her life. Now people—including both sets of grandparents—are telling me I shouldn't go back to work until Kristin is at least three years old.

That will mean starting over in my career, which is very important to me.

I feel torn between my responsibilities to my baby, who means everything to me, and all the things I've worked for over the past ten years. Will putting Kristin in day care cause problems with her development or our relationship?

(A) That depends upon the day care and how much you are otherwise available to her.

Despite the warnings of experts such as psychologist Burton White, author of *The First Three Years of Life* (Prentice-Hall), who advises against any day care before age three, most research indicates problems can be minimized, if not eliminated, if the day care responds to the infant's needs.

For infants, I recommend a family home in which the caregiver is looking after no more than two or three children. A small-scale home setting all but guarantees that each child will receive enough individual attention.

Because there is no staff rotation or turnover in a home setting, an infant can form a more secure attachment to the caregiver. Fewer children also means the caregiver can accommodate varied sleep, feeding, and activity schedules.

A family day care also gives the parents greater communication with the caregiver, who can more easily respond to parents' requests concerning how the baby should be held or fed or put to sleep than is generally possible in a larger group.

Since most states inspect and license or register day-care homes, the first question to ask a prospective home-caregiver is, "Are you licensed?" Although a license doesn't necessarily mean better care, it at least guarantees the home meets minimum standards.

After starting day care, an infant will go through a period of adjustment to the environment and the new caregiver. During this transition, the baby may feel stress and express it by increased crying, general irritability, and disturbed sleep.

An initial stress reaction that doesn't begin to abate after a couple of weeks can indicate problems. It may be the child and provider are a poor match, in which case another setting might work out better.

It may be, however, that the child isn't ready for any day care at all. In either case, if a baby needs to be removed from care, parents should wait a few weeks before attempting another placement.

If the care you find for Kristin is of adequate quality and you are otherwise sufficiently involved with and responsive to her, there's little, if any, reason for concern.

In fact, day care can help the mother-child relationship by giving a mother a chance to feel adequate outside the home. The self-fulfillment a mother such as you derives from a satisfying career will, in all likelihood, have a positive effect on her baby.

A final word of advice: Don't wait until the last minute to find day care for your baby. Take the time to look and compare, so that you find the best setting available. Don't choose strictly on the basis of cost or convenience. The extra time and extra money you may have to spend for truly good care will pay off handsomely.

In her book, *Tips for Working Parents: Creative Solutions to Everyday Problems* (Storey/Garden Way), Kathleen McBride gives excellent advice on choosing a family day-care provider. Contact the child-care referral agency in your community for a list of day-care homes.

(Q) Being the mother of a three-month-old girl, I read your recent article on infant day care with interest. My leave of absence from my job is almost over, and I've been trying to find suitable care for my daughter for the past few weeks. The family day-care homes in our area are currently full, so I have no choice but to put her in group care, at least until something opens up. What should I look for in group care?

(A) Parents who are locked into group care or, for whatever reasons, prefer group care, should consider the following factors:

- Staff/child ratio: How many infants are there per full-time staff person? The lower the ratio, the more likely it is that each infant will receive sufficient individual attention. For infants, the ratio should be no higher than one caregiver per five babies.
- Rotation and turnover: Consistency of care allows the infant to form a secure attachment to the caregiver. Are the same staff persons in the infant room throughout the entire day, or do they change shifts in the afternoon? If so, at what point is the change made? How long has the present infant-care staff been at the cen-

ter? Lots of turnover in staff probably means the center isn't a very good place to work. If it isn't a good place to work, it's probably not a good place to leave a baby.

• Experience and training: How and how often are staff persons trained, which certificates do they hold, and how much experience does each have working exclusively with infants?

• Environment: The infant room should be bright and airy, with no door. An open floor-play area for the crawlers that's fenced or divided from the remainder of the room and either carpeted or covered in mats is preferable to having three or four individual playpens. The crawling area should contain a few chewable playthings that encourage exploration and stimulate motor development as well as one or two relatively large, soft cushions or tunnels the babies can crawl over and through.

• Cribs: Although so-called "stacking" cribs are less visually appealing, they do offer more floor space. Are the infants allowed ample time on the floor or confined for most of the day to their cribs or individual playpens? If the center uses traditional cribs, there should be plenty of space between them. Each crib should contain no more than one or two crib toys to occupy babies who are waking up or needing a little quiet time.

• Equipment: Look for such things as one or two baby swings, adequate changing table facilities, and tables with built-in chairs for the babies who are eating solid food. Make sure that babies are always held and talked or sung to when drinking from bottles, as opposed to having bottles "propped" into their mouths.

• Staff: How and how quickly do the caregivers respond to crying? How actively involved are they with the babies? Do they only pay attention when a baby is crying or are they calmly busy almost all the time? Is their tone soothing? Do they handle the babies gently or somewhat abruptly? Most important, do they enjoy their jobs?

Finally, do the director and staff seem interested in you, the parent, and are they sensitive to the anxieties you feel about putting your baby in day care? Are they warm, patient, and reassuring? Do you feel you'll be able to communicate effectively with them? You may not know it yet, but their relationship with you is every bit as important as their relationship with your baby.

Eight to Eighteen Months: The Toddler

For children between eight and eighteen months old, the world is changing rapidly.

By his eighth month, a typical infant sits upright on his own, crawls, pulls himself to a standing position, and may even side-step around the perimeter of things (cruising).

Improvements in eye-hand coordination and finger dexterity also take place. For instance, it is now possible for him to pick up small objects (buttons, crumbs, and so on) between his thumb and index finger (pincer grasp). This stimulates his interest in the world of tiny things and correspondingly increases the risk of injury.

During these ten months the child makes tremendous gains in motor, communication, and intellectual skills. It is a period of "tooling," when the infant outfits himself with the skills and information he will need to begin mastering the environment.

These maturational events are truly groundbreaking. They are the seedlings of self-sufficiency. For the first time in his life, the child can do a significant number of things on his own.

Driven by an insatiable appetite for discovery, he propels himself from place to place, putting the pieces of the puzzle together into a coherent "picture" of the world as he knows it. He has become an explorer, a collector of information, an active participant in the overall scheme of things. His one all-consuming purpose is to *know,* to penetrate the mysteries of the universe. Why? Because it's there!

Shrinking Violets

This new freedom, as always, has its price. At the same time the child is experiencing this acceleration in motor, perceptual, and intellectual skills, her mother is probably calling the pediatrician asking why her baby is so reluctant to separate from her in the presence of other people. And why, her parents ask, does baby constantly check on them, as if she were afraid they will vanish at any moment.

There are several reasons (or one reason in several parts) why children this age seem so eager to try their wings one moment and so fearful of venturing away from their parents the next.

For starters, the ability to explore the world on their own rearranges their priorities. The qualities of *things*—their texture, taste, and movement patterns—are of prime importance to them now. In the short span of several weeks, the world becomes a radically different place, and the prospect of venturing out by themselves into this alien landscape is both exciting and frightening. It's exciting because of the exhilarating sense of accomplishment that goes with opening a new door; it's frightening because taking those first steps into unknown territory is risky. A child of this age wants to take those steps, but not until she makes certain that her primary security figures are still there. That's you, Mom and Dad. You are her insurance policy!

Up until now, most of what she has seen, heard, or touched has been courtesy of her primary caretaker (usually mother) who carried her, brought things to her, moved objects within her grasp, played with her, and so on.

Mother has been synonymous with gratification of the infant's needs for food, comfort, and stimulation. And, from the child's egocentric point of view, their identities have been blended. She has not distinguished "ma-ma" from "me."

As the infant discovers that she can do things on her own, a sense of separateness from mother begins to develop. This is the first stirring of a sense of identity—the beginning of self-consciousness.

For the first time in her life, the infant has a *choice*. Now that she can, to a certain degree, control the distance between herself and her mother, she must decide how close she needs to be. She must balance her need for security and the urge to become ever more independent.

The child is pulled in two directions simultaneously. One voice says, "Hey, kid, you can do it yourself!" If she answers that call, she gives up some of the security that goes with having Mom right there to do everything for her.

The other voice pleads, "No! Not yet! It's too much to deal with all by yourself! Get Mom over here before she slips away forever!"

How well the child resolves this conflict depends on the answer to one critical question: *How responsive and supportive is the environment to the child's explorations and inquiries?* Is her primary experience exhilarating or frustrating? Are her discoveries joyous or painful? Do her caretakers *assist* or *obstruct* her in her playful work? Is her environment stimulating or boring? Her future is in *her* hands. How often are they slapped?

For a time, the child seeks to restore her equilibrium by gravitating closer to her mother. She seems to intuit that her link with her mother is vital, that mother's presence is essential to her continued security.

Not surprisingly, other people become one of the most threatening elements of the child's universe. They tend to move in on her before she has a chance to size them up, and they often want to snatch her out of her mother's arms and into their own. Her only protection is to cling and scream.

Unfortunately, because few adults understand the reason behind these rebuffs, grandparents often feel hurt, fathers often feel angry, and mothers frequently feel responsible for everyone else's hurt feelings.

The following questions and answers illustrate the clinging-toddler phase.

(Q) I am the mother of a delightful but very mother-oriented one-year-old. He gets upset sometimes if I just leave the room. He won't let anyone else hold him, if I am in sight. Sometimes, not even his daddy. Needless to say, this gets very frustrating for me at times. I nursed him until he gradually weaned himself at eleven months, and I wonder if this contributed to his being so clingy. I thought letting him nurse for as long as he wanted would promote independence.

(A) When you leave the room, panic sets in because *he* is not controlling the separation. It's one thing for him to crawl away from you; another entirely for you to walk away from him.

And yes, breast-feeding can promote the growth of an independent spirit, but so can bottle-feeding and being held and comforted and so on. But, before a child can take those first tentative steps toward independence, there must be no question, no lingering doubt whatsoever in his mind, about whether you will remain close at hand. He must reassure himself that you will stay there until he doesn't need you to be there any longer.

If he wants to cling, let him cling . . . if he wants only you to hold him, *you* hold him. The more receptive you are to his expressions of need, the shorter this phase will last.

The evidence clearly shows that the harder the child has to work to keep Mommy close, the more clinging he will ultimately become. This does not mean that putting a child in day care or leaving him with a sitter must be traumatic. At those times it is best for Mommy to hand him over quickly. The longer Mom hangs on and hangs around, the worse things become.

If, instead of closing in on him with outstretched arms, people will just sit and wait, he will eventually get around to approaching them. If they make no sudden movements, he might hang around long enough to make friends. At this somewhat fragile time in his life, he will feel most comfortable when closeness happens on *his* terms.

(Q) I have my ten-month-old son in a Mother's Morning Out program one morning a week. He cries almost the entire four hours unless one of the teachers is holding him.

In the program, there are ten children, ranging from six to eighteen months, and three teachers. Ricky has attended since he was three months old, but the problem didn't begin until a couple of months ago. He's also doing the same thing at church nursery.

He's an otherwise secure child. At home, Ricky will play by himself for more than an hour at a time. He enjoys his familiar baby-sitters and going to other people's homes when only one or two other children are present.

He is an only child, and I do have a lot of time to spend with him. I sometimes feel guilty about taking him to Mother's Morning Out, but I also feel I need a few hours a week to myself. Am I wrong to continue taking him? Will he outgrow this stage?

(A) The problem is twofold:

First, Ricky is right in the midst of the first of two separation crises that occur during early childhood. This one started on schedule around his eighth month and will probably last until his first birthday, or thereabouts. The second has its onset around eighteen months and lasts for several months thereafter.

Second, Ricky is made even more anxious by the fact that in both Mother's Morning Out and church nursery, there is a noisy gaggle of children, some of whom are much older, much more active, much more aggressive, and therefore much more threatening. Comparing Ricky's reaction to Mother's Morning Out with his reaction to being with one other child his own age is like comparing apples to watermelons.

Console yourself with the fact things could be much worse. At least Ricky is content to play alone for long periods of time when he knows you're there. He also can tolerate being left with a sitter. Many children this age cling tenaciously to their mothers, refusing to let even fathers or grandparents hold them.

Infants can't tell us why they feel and act the way they do, so developmental psychologists have to make educated guesses when it comes to explaining much infant behavior.

Ricky's anxiety over separation probably has a lot to do with his rapidly expanding ability to move around in and explore the environment. Previously, his moving about was done courtesy of you and your husband, mostly you.

Like most other human beings, Ricky wants to have his cake and eat it, too. He wants to move around on his own, but he also wants to make darn sure you're not going to slip away while he's not looking. Somewhat paradoxically, he doesn't need you quite as much, but seems to *want* you that much more.

The evidence clearly shows that the more upsetting separation is to a child of this age, the longer this phase will last. In other words, it will probably pay in the long run for you to avoid, at least temporarily, situations that cause Ricky great separation distress.

Instead of leaving him in Mother's Morning Out, hire a sitter to come into your home one morning a week. In a lot of cities, there are "Rent-A-Granny" services that provide child care of this sort.

If you can't arrange for a sitter on Sunday morning, it might pay for you and your husband to alternate staying home from church until Ricky is older and feels more secure in a group of small children. Wait a couple of months after he starts walking and try again.

Magical Mischievous Tour

Sometime between eight and fifteen months, a child discovers that the world is full of magic and that she is one of its foremost magicians. When a child becomes a magician, the old saying that "The hand is quicker than the eye" is never more true.

Around this time, parents find cryptic messages scrawled on the walls in lipstick, pages torn out of the family Bible, the contents of the toilet in the tub, all the books out of the bookshelf, all the clothes out of the dresser, and the kitten in the refrigerator. The magician's quick hand is, of course, the child's. The slow eye belongs to the parent.

Parents don't seem to mind at first. They laugh and praise the young magician for her tricks. "Isn't she cute?" they say.

Then they become jealous because the child's magic is better than their own. They make their faces go red, their eyes grow cold, and begin applying the old quick-hand to the slow-rear, just to prove they haven't lost their touch. "Isn't she awful!" they say.

The young magician tries in vain to make the old ones understand. She invents more tricks, pulls more pranks, performs more and better feats of legerdemain, only to be reminded of her slow-rear. The young magician learns fear, and this is her Waterloo. Fear will slow the best hand down. The old tricks stop working. In years to come, when all magic is forgotten and the eyes get slow, she will be ready to become a parent herself.

Toddlers and parents live in different worlds. Toddlers live in a wonderland of enchantment, where every sight, sound, and touch is new. Everything that happens in a toddler's world happens for the first time ever. And it all happens just for her, and no one else.

The small child does not have words enough to explain the amazing things that happen in her world: no words to tell why paper shreds and glass breaks. There are no reasons for anything except "just because." No wonder children believe in magic.

The Cookie Tree, a children's book by J. Williams (out-of-print, Parent's Magazine Books), should be required reading for all parents. It begins:

> The village of Owlgate was quiet, and tidy, and nothing surprising ever happened there. Everything had a place, and everything was in its place. Everybody knew why things happened, and everything happened just as it was supposed to. Nothing surprising ever happened because nothing surprising was *allowed* to happen. "That way," said the people of Owlgate with satisfaction, "you always know where you are."

Parents live in Owlgate. They have reasons and places for everything. They work hard all day long giving reasons and finding places and making sure things stay put. Words have taken the place of wonder, and if something cannot be explained, then it isn't there.

When an egg falls on the floor, a twelve-month-old may see a piece of the sun spill out. A parent sees a mess. Tiny fingers reach for things that come apart or fall and bounce and break or splatter and spread out in all directions. In Wonderland, it's magic. In Owlgate, it's mischief, and mischief is the reason for messes. But in mischief, there is also the thrill of discovery, and therein is the reason for Learning, with a capital "L."

The young child does not have enough language to understand the "Whys" and "Why Nots" of things in Owlgate. She discovers the world by experiencing it directly. The splat, bounce, and break of things are defined by the child's own action, and it is through action that she discovers all the different things the world is made of, how it comes apart, what's inside, what happens to what, and when, and how, and so on. She must experience *all* of this before she can ever make sense of the words we use to describe the "Why." And so, messy, magical mischief is also the reason for Language, with another capital "L."

Children who are allowed to roam about being mischievous learn that words can also be used in magical ways. They learn language quickly, and they learn to use it well. Mischief also flowers into imagination and creativity. A scientist is, after all, nothing but a grown-up magician, making the mischief of progress.

The mischievous nature of a child's curiosity is the force

underlying all learning and accomplishment. At the same time, it is also the source of many childhood accidents.

During this critical developmental phase, it is essential that certain physical boundaries be established, both to insure the youngster's safety and to provide an environment which encourages exploration, learning, and creativity.

The toddler cannot predict what objects and situations in her surroundings could be harmful, nor is she able to appreciate the value of irreplaceable or expensive household objects. Her nature *demands* that she touch, feel, and taste everything within reach. Powered by an insatiable appetite for discovery, she is most alert when in motion, exploring for novelty everywhere.

At some point, it is inevitable that this exploratory drive will aim her toward fragile ceramic figurines, antique glassware, the African violet collection, and everything else within reach.

By far the easiest, least expensive, and most sensible way to reduce the obvious risk is to put treasures well out of her grasp, as soon as she is able to reach them. By child-proofing your house in this way, the boundary between "can touch" and "don't touch" is established by the child's own physical limitations. Parents who fail, or refuse, to child-proof must constantly watch where their toddlers are and what they are doing. These parents never have a moment's rest, and their children cry a lot.

I can hear you now: "But Michelle has to learn what she can't have, and besides, it took me years to collect all these things." You have a point. A child must eventually be taught the difference between what she *can* have and what is out of bounds. But the connection between reaching for a certain object and a slap on the hand or a loud "No!" is established (maybe) only at great cost to the parent's peace of mind and the child's sense of confidence and capacity for learning.

Protect your valuables and breakables by putting them up and away. Chasing a child around the house, frantically trying to cover all the bases, is a losing proposition. You cannot win, because a child has more energy and determination.

Relax and enjoy your parenthood. Feed your child's curiosity, but not with African violets. Provide her with a variety of objects around the house of different colors, shapes, and textures (but not a lot of toys). Let her "discover" things that are unbreakable. When she finds them, teach her to play "put-and-take" with you. Play *with* her, not *against* her.

Before you visit friends or relatives, call and ask if they would help make the visit a more relaxed and pleasant one for all concerned by gathering up their treasures and closing off certain rooms. "Please don't think me rude, but I'd so much rather talk with you than worry what Michelle is doing behind my back."

Child-proofing is even more essential when objects and substances that are potentially harmful to children are involved. Cleaning fluids, paint, medicine, pins, glass bottles, plastic bags, aerosol sprays, and tools must be out of child's reach. Electric sockets can be fitted with childproof plates. A lock on the door to the basement steps is a deterrent to broken bones and concussions. Lower cabinets can be fitted with childproof latches or cleaned out and made safe and fascinating to crawl into.

Playpens

Playpens have their pros and cons. Used wisely and sparingly, a playpen can perform a service for parents and provide baby with a safe place to play. If misused, however, a playpen can be an obstacle to normal development. When left unattended in playpens for long periods, children become bored and frustrated and even depressed.

Use of a playpen after a child is old enough to walk is even more damaging. There is evidence suggesting that children who spend lots of time confined in cribs or playpens suffer delayed speech and are less coordinated. A handicap imposed on a child in this way is not easily undone.

As your child grows, use the playpen less often and for shorter periods. When he begins crawling, give him plenty of free time to roam and explore. The more a child is able to exercise his curiosity, the more intelligent and creative he will become. If you use the playpen while ironing, washing, or cooking, set it up near you and talk to your child while you work. This keeps him alert and stimulates language development.

Protect your child's health by providing a safe environment for him to explore without having to experience frequent frustration, boredom, or punishment. By establishing these physical boundaries in a loving, sensible way, you not only insure his safety, but promote his development and provide a more relaxed atmosphere for yourself.

(Q) My son is eight months old. I've kept him in a playpen for short periods during the day ever since he was three months old. Until recently, he occupied himself quietly until I returned, but those days seem gone. Lately, as soon as I put him down in the playpen, he screams bloody murder and doesn't stop until I pick him up. This poses a dilemma. I can't be with him every minute of the day. There are times when I'm busy and can't give him any direct supervision, which he definitely requires since he's already pulling himself to a standing position and sidestepping around furniture. In other words, I can't leave him alone, and I can't *not* leave him alone, but he hates the playpen, so what can I do?

(A) Before we go any further, you need to understand that playpens aren't for play, not in the real sense of the term. They're boring. Boredom is about all that's possible in a fenced-in area no larger than twenty square feet. The more stuff a parent heaps in to occupy the child, the more cluttered the pen becomes, further restricting the child's ability to play.

Before they begin crawling, most children will endure the relative isolation of a playpen for brief periods during the day. Crawling, however, stimulates an infant's desire to explore the world. Once a child discovers what constant excitement there is to be had by moving from one place to another and then another, getting his hands in the stuff of what's happening, he's not likely to sit quietly in the confinement of a playpen. Add to his curiosity the fact that a young toddler (between eight and twelve months) isn't at all clear on how much closeness he wants with his mother. This business of getting around on his own is a barrel of monkeys, but it also takes him further away from the one he loves most.

So this age child is caught in his *own* dilemma. He wants to be with you and he wants to be away from you, doing his own thing. He feels a bit better if he's in control of how much distance there is between you and when separation happens. If *you* walk away, he yells, but if *he* crawls off, it's goodbye. Just to make sure you haven't vaporized while he wasn't looking, he checks on you every few minutes. If a stranger's about, he makes straight for you. When you put him in a playpen, his anxiety level goes up. Not only is he not controlling the separation, but he can't get to you.

Now, I'd like to digress a moment and tell you a true story about baby ducks. Several days after they hatch, a brood of ducklings will line up behind their mother and follow her wherever she goes. This is called *imprinting*. After a few weeks of parading about in this fashion, they break away. Ethologist Nikolaas Tinbergen wanted to see what would happen if imprinting was tampered with. Small barriers were placed around a controlled course the mother duck walked. The baby ducks had to scramble over the barriers. The result: these frustrated ducklings persisted in following their mothers long after other ducklings had moved off on their own.

Before a child can begin making motions of independence, he must know, beyond any shadow of a doubt, that his mother will be easily accessible in times of need. Playpens frustrate the newly mobile child in the same way Tinbergen's barriers frustrated the ducklings. Frustration makes a child all the more determined to keep his mother close.

So, by using a playpen to get away (for whatever reason) from a child who is moving under his own steam, you increase the likelihood that he will cling to you long after most children are becoming more self-sufficient.

One of the nicest gifts you can give you and your child once he begins crawling is a child-proofed living area where he can crawl and putter and get into safe, unbreakable things to his heart's content while you relax, knowing he's all right. He'll experience the same insecurities as other post-crawlers, but instead of getting stuck, he'll go right on through them.

The rule is a simple one:

> After crawling, don't confine,
> Child-proof for your peace of mind,
> Allow your child to freely roam,
> In the safety of his home.

Biting

During the first year of life, biting is almost exclusively exploratory in nature. An infant's mouth is as primary an organ of discovery as her eyes and hands. Furthermore, the sensations that arise from using her mouth to explore things are extremely pleasurable, so nearly everything gets put in there.

An infant learns to discriminate tastes, textures, and temperatures with her mouth. She finds out what is food and what isn't by chewing on everything from ashtrays to zwieback.

She finds answers to the same questions about people: "I wonder what Mommy tastes like. Uhmmmmm. Not bad! Hey, she does interesting things and makes new sounds when I do that. Wonder if she can do that again?" As an added bonus, infants discover that biting relieves teething pain and feels plain ol' fashioned good (by gum!).

Sometime close to the beginning of an infant's second year, biting becomes a way of being playful and affectionate. It's a way of saying, "Hey! I love you! Wanna play?" Biting continues to feel extremely pleasant and the child doesn't know that you are not sharing her ecstasy.

As your toddler grows into her second year, she encounters an ever-increasing number of frustrating situations. She may well make the discovery that by biting down very hard on something, she can release the tension she builds up in these encounters. A likely target is the someone most closely associated with her frustration.

Here's the tale of a typical biter and my advice to the bitee:

(Q) I have a fourteen-month-old son who bites me several times a day. Sometimes he is clearly frustrated at me, but sometimes he bites for no reason whatsoever that I can see. This has been going on for the past three months and is getting worse. I have tried spanking, putting him in his crib, and biting him back (on the advice of my pediatrician), but nothing seems to get the message across. He only bites *me,* and I don't understand what I could be doing to cause it. What should I do?

(A) Don't take it so personally. He's not biting you because he hates you or because you deserve it—he bites you because you're *there.* You are the person most available to him. You frustrate him more than anyone else because you share more time with him than anyone else does. Throw in the fact that toddlers are easily frustrated, have no self-control, and love to sink their chops into things, and you have a typical fourteen-month-old biting his typical mother.

Your son bites you at different times for different reasons, but he continues to bite because you have never insisted that he stop. Thinking about what you might be doing to "cause" his biting has prevented you from acting on the biting itself.

Put yourself squarely in the present tense and *do* something about it. As much as possible, prevent his toothy attacks, even playful ones. Surely you can tell when one is on the way. Every time he tries to bite you, regardless of whether he succeeds, face him and say "No!" Then pick him up, turn him around so he faces away from you, and take him to his room. Put him down on the floor (*not* in his crib), and walk away, leaving the door slightly ajar as you go. He will "hear" the message clearly.

When he emerges, he will probably come straight to you. If he wants the reassurance of being held, hold him, but do not talk about the incident. If he is still agitated and tries to bite you again, repeat the sequence.

When he learns that you are not a willing victim, he may try biting someone else. Again, whether or not you are able to prevent that from happening, say "No!" and put him in his room. If you aren't at home, improvise with an out-of-the-way chair.

By the way, biting a child back sometimes works, but more often it makes the problem worse. I don't recommend it because it confuses the child, puts parents in the position of modeling the behavior they want eliminated, and is likely to start a lets-see-who-bites-harder contest.

This method should bring noticeable improvement within two or three weeks. As usual, commitment is the key. And that, my friends, is the honest tooth.

Weaning

(Q) I'm having trouble getting my fifteen-month-old son to give up drinking from a bottle. He drinks from a cup during meals but cries for his bottle whenever he is upset or sleepy. Should I refuse to give it to him?

(A) There is much to lose and nothing to be gained by struggling with your son over a bottle. When we make issues out of things like bottles and thumbs and security blankets, children are likely to become more desperate in their attachment to them.

Allow your son to drink from a bottle whenever he expresses a need for that source of comfort. Insist, though, that he follow your lead and drink from a cup during meals.

I strongly advise against filling a bottle with milk or any sugar-sweetened liquid, such as iced tea or fruit punch. The sugar in these drinks greatly increases the risk of tooth decay. As his parent, the decision regarding what goes in the bottle is yours. Fill the bottle with unsweetened (strained) fruit juices or water only, and stand firm on this decision.

Your son will probably lose interest in the bottle quickly if you begin to water down the juice and gradually (over several weeks time) increase the proportion of water until you have eliminated the juice altogether. During this process, leave the bottle, filled with water or the water-juice mix, where he can reach it without asking for your help. He will eventually forget about the bottle, and so will you.

Just the other day, I read an article by a pediatrician which dealt with weaning. His opinion was that continued use of a bottle beyond the twelfth month will almost surely "stunt" (my translation) a child's social and emotional growth. Consequently, he said, the child might continue to "baby talk," require diapers long after the time for potty training was due, or indulge in some other infantile fixation.

This is malarkey, genuine and undiluted. There is no clinical evidence to support such a claim, and the doctor's statements will ultimately create more problems than they pretend to solve.

That these statements were made in a national publication by a man of medicine virtually assures their acceptance by the average reader as fact. Chances are that readers who are parents of toddlers who still suck an occasional bottle will become scared that the bottle is warping the child's psyche.

Thereafter, when the child wants a bottle, the parents will become anxious. They will fabricate excuses, diversions, and persuasions, all to little avail. Having met with no success, they may become upset. At this point, the child will become upset too, because his parents' behavior is confusing. Lacking the words to express his confusion and frustration, he may well have a tantrum. Predictably, his parents will feel guilty and give him a bottle. The end result: nervous, insecure parent . . . confused, screaming child . . . and an issue that will continue to cause distress in their relationship.

By no means should a child who is capable of drinking from a cup be encouraged to continue drinking from a bottle. Nor should parents offer a bottle as a pacifier. Allow a child access to the bottle, simply and naturally. As with so many things, the more of a problem you make of it, the more troublesome it will become.

Strange Fruit

At this age, everything in the environment is fascinating; everything must be explored. Infants will touch everything they can, and anything that passes inspection by the hands goes to the mouth. After being tasted, chewed, and mashed, if the tongue says, "Yes!" then it's swallowed.

(Q) My daughter, thirteen months old, has begun playing with her b.m.'s. If I don't catch her in time, she scoops it out of her diaper and smears it all over herself. What is most upsetting, however, is that she also manages to eat some of it. The word "aakey" usually keeps her from putting certain things in her mouth but hasn't worked with this. I try to keep my cool, but I'm just about at my wits' end. What can I do?

(A) Given the opportunity, most children will play in their bowel movements, just as they will play in the dirt from your potted plants, the sugar bowl, oatmeal, or whatever. To an infant, b.m. is no different, except she made it! How delightful! Another bit of magic from the world's greatest magician.

Rest assured, however, that there is nothing abnormal about this behavior (at this age), and nothing is wrong with your child. Furthermore, aside from what we might *think,* there is nothing dirty or unhealthy in what she is doing. Granted, it's a mess, but no more than a rather exasperating example of recycling.

Nor is there anything especially significant about this behavior. The trap, however, is that we big people have an outstandingly negative reaction to it. We are repulsed, disgusted, and infuriated at having to "swab the decks" afterward. No matter how we try to keep cool, it's difficult not to let our true colors show, thereby tipping the child off to how significant the whole business is to us.

Make a big deal out of something, and it will become a big deal. Any exaggerated reaction on your part (spanking, screaming, fainting, throwing up) is probably going to set the stage for a repeat performance.

I would suggest that you maintain as much cool as you possibly can and wash her up without any special to-do. If you need a break to recover, then put her back in her crib and "take five" (or fifteen).

Bedlam at Bedtime

(Q) We can't seem to get our fifteen-month-old daughter to go peacefully to sleep at night. We've even tried keeping her up until she's absolutely exhausted, but no matter when we put her down, the moment she hits the crib mattress, she starts to wail. And wail. And wail. Don't tell us to let her "cry it out," because we just can't. Besides, she's already proven she can scream nonstop for almost an hour. The only thing that seems to work is rocking her to sleep, which takes about twenty minutes, then staying in there and rubbing her back for another ten or fifteen minutes once we put her in her crib. The added problem is, if she goes down crying, she almost always wakes up screaming in the middle of the night. There must be a better way! What is it?

(A) Indeed, there is a better way to put an infant to sleep. Known as "J.R.'s Guaranteed No Mo' Sleepless Nights," it involves three easy steps to permanent bliss, while, at the same time, answering forever the question, "How do you keep 'em down in the bed, after they've seen the alternative?"

Here are the steps to take:

• Set a definite bedtime and stick to it. Do not, I repeat, do not try to wear an infant down by keeping her up long after reasonable people have gone to bed. Contrary to popular belief, the later you keep an infant up, the more agitated she will become and the more difficult bedtime, when it finally arrives, will be. Instead of waiting for a signal from your daughter that she's ready for sleep, make the decision for her. Somewhere between 7:30 and 9 P.M. is probably reasonable.

Thirty minutes prior to bed, start putting her through the preliminaries, which might include a bath, a snack, and a story. When the appointed hour arrives, put her down with a brief tucking-in ceremony and promptly leave the room, screams not withstanding.

• Assuming the child screams, go back into her room every five minutes and repeat the tucking-in ceremony. If you must, lay her back down, reassure her that the world as she knows it still exists, kiss her, and exit, stage left. Do not pick her up and do not stay longer than one minute. Five minutes later, if she's still at it, go back in and repeat the procedure.

Sooner or later, she will begin to tire of this foolishness and her screams will turn to whimpers. At this point, you should extend the interval to ten minutes, or whatever your common sense and intuition advises. If, however, she goes back to full-throttle, return to the five-minute plan.

True, she may scream for a couple of hours at first, but after several nights of this, she will scream less and less until, after a few weeks, she will scream for only a few minutes, if any at all.

Look at it this way: At present, you spend approximately forty-five minutes getting her to sleep, more if you count the fact that you are keeping her up much too late to begin with. With this method, if she screams for two hours, you will have gone in twenty-four times at less than a minute each for a total of around twenty minutes.

• Should she wake up in the middle of the night, which is likely for a week or so, repeat step two.

Lest you have lingering doubts, I've been pushing this plan for at least ten years, and it's yet to fail. Just call me "The Sandman."

Eighteen to Thirty-six Months: The Terrific! Twos

The "Terrible Twos." I have this image of children screaming, throwing things, playing in make-up, eating soap, breaking china figurines, saying "No!" to everything—running amok while Mommy and Daddy chase, grab, spank, yell, scream, and run amok.

To be honest, it's not exactly an image. It's a vivid memory starring the inimitable, one-and-only Eric!

To live with Eric at twelve was to wonder if this was the same child who didn't sleep through the night until he was two-and-a-half years old. Could he have been the same child who was dubbed "Mr. Mad" or "Mr. Tough," depending on his mood, by two of our best friends? Twenty years ago no one could have convinced me Eric would be sane when he grew up, much less the mellow, thoughtful, delightful person he is today.

It took me several years and another child to learn that two-year-olds can be terrific. There's no question about it, their reputation for terrible-ness has, to some extent, been earned. But the difference—terrible or terrific—is not primarily a matter of child. It's a matter of parents.

The most dramatic and significant transition in the development of an individual occurs between eighteen and thirty-six months. It is a revolution, involving sweeping changes in the child's experience of both himself and the world. Naturally his behavior takes some dramatic turns as well.

It can be one of the two most stressful periods in the overall life of a family (the other being pre- and early adolescence). *But it doesn't have to be.* As with most endeavors, the key is understanding, which can help make the "Terrible Twos" *terrific.*

"I'm a Me!"

Infancy is a time of almost total dependency: Infants must rely on parents and other people to feed, bathe, dress, change, and even move them from place to place. Between eight and eighteen months, children make rapid gains in cognitive (problem-solving), motor, and communication skills. They begin to experiment with cause-and-effect relationships, discovering in the process that they can manipulate the environment. Children between eight and eighteen months old are collectors of information. They are constantly on the move, harvesting information with their hands, eyes, and mouths. At this stage the process is random. The child has no blueprint—just an irresistible urge to know everything there is to know about every "thing."

Throughout her meanderings, the toddler absorbs an incredible amount of information without, however, knowing how to *use* it. Then sometime around her eighteenth month she realizes she can act upon the world to *make things happen.* At this point, her guidance systems switch from automatic to autonomous pilot. Before she was an explorer; now she is an *experimenter,* an alchemist, out to create history—her own, at the very least.

From this moment on, things will happen the way *she* wants them to happen, and people will do what *she* wants them to. Full speed ahead and damn the torpedos!

As the "sense" of her environment is revealed, the toddler begins interacting with it to *solve problems.*

A fourteen-month-old, seeing a jar of cookies on the kitchen counter, will reach in vain and point and yell until someone comes along to lend a hand. Several months later, this same child pushes a chair to the counter, climbs up, and gets the cookies for herself.

As her mind expands, so does the world. In no time she is consumed with excitement, with no way to express her exhilaration except through activity. She is "on the go" constantly, "getting into everything," climbing up on counters and bookshelves, climbing down out of her crib and car seat, always one step ahead of you. She won't take "No" for an answer. After all, what does "No" amount to when everything else around and inside her says "Yes!"

One of the limitations nature has imposed on two-year-olds is a gap between physical and intellectual development, favoring the latter. Their bodies have not caught up with their minds. They may be able to "see" the solution to a problem but may *not* be able to make their bodies perform the movements required to carry it out.

For example, a child may know that a certain shape fits into one certain space in a puzzle but be unable to make her fingers work well enough to maneuver it in.

This frustrating disparity is often expressed in sudden, violent, and sometimes destructive tantrums. If someone tries to lend a helping hand, the child usually becomes more enraged. She would rather do it herself and fail than watch you succeed. That's understandable. Whose growth is this, anyway?

Sometime around the middle of her second year, a child realizes, in one relatively sudden, insightful moment, that "I'm a Me!" It's the flowering of individuality, of self-consciousness. It's the biggest "Aha!" of all.

For the next eighteen months or so, the child is absorbed in defining who "Me" is and establishing clear title to that psychological territory. Much to her dismay, she also has to accept that her boundaries are not all-encompassing. She is not the only "Me" in the world, but one of many.

At this age, children must learn that independence means less than being able to do as they please. Just as the task of the child is to establish her autonomy, her parents' task is to begin the process of socialization, of communicating and enforcing boundaries, limits, and rules governing the child's expressions of independence.

It gradually dawns on the child that in order to become a separate, independent person, she must give up a corresponding measure of her attachment to her parents, Mommy in particular. These sacrifices and disappointments can be overwhelming. For all these reasons, the third year of life is a relatively uncertain time with few dull moments.

Dominated by the central question of whether it is more advantageous "to be or not to be (independent)" the child is a study in paradox: clinging and cuddly one minute, demanding and defiant the next. She wants the best of both worlds and slowly, painfully realizes that there is no middle ground.

This is the second time the infant has had to deal with issues of separation, the first time having occurred between eight and twelve months (see Shrinking Violets, page 65).

"Don't Leave Me!"

It isn't unusual for 18- to 24-month-olds to respond to the temporary uncertainty of this internal revolution by demanding more visual, physical, and verbal contact with their parents. For a short time they may need someone to hold on to, a port in the storm.

If parents are fairly tolerant of the child's determined clinging, the child will, within several weeks or months, gain all the reassurance he needs to move through this metamorphosis.

(Q) My son is twenty months old. He has been a delightful baby, but has recently started clinging to me somewhat more than before. He follows me around the house and wants to be held a lot. How should I handle this?

(A) His need to cling expresses, paradoxically, the realization that he is a person in his own right. He has made the discrimination between "me" and "you." He now knows you are not a blend: you are *two* people, and that fact places "psychological space" between you. This distance allows him to begin testing his wings—to move further away from you and into the environment.

This metamorphosis, however, carries with it a certain degree of uncertainty at first. You no longer seem as available and accessible as before. He doesn't know how great the distance between the two of you will become. He wants to fly, but he does *not* want to give you up. He doesn't have the words to express his anxieties, so he follows you from room to room, reassuring himself that this change is not the beginning of some disappearing act. In other words, before he can take one giant step forward, he must take one baby step back. In this game of "Mother May I?" your answer must be, "Yes, you may." If he wants to be held, hold him. If he wants to follow, let him. The fewer obstacles in his path, the less disruptive this transition will be for everyone in the family.

The Roots of Rivalry

The birth of another child into the family during this period of transition can be very disruptive. The older child often acts as if the new baby were a tiny trespasser who sneaked into the picture while her back was turned. Feeling that this small someone will take her coveted place next to Mommy and not yet fully committed to giving it up, she rushes back to close the gap.

(Q) We have a two-and-a-half-year-old daughter and a six-month-old son. Off and on, ever since the baby was born, the oldest has asked us to rock her at bedtime. She has also asked to have her bottle back. We have *not,* in spite of several tantrums, given into these requests, but now there's an additional problem. We began our daughter's toilet training about five weeks ago, with success at first. A couple of weeks ago, however, she began refusing to go if prompted and now she has more accidents than not. They seem to be almost deliberate, and this disturbs us. She now says she wants to be put back in diapers. Should we stop for a while, put her back in diapers, and try again later?
(A) One thing your daughter does *not* need, regardless of what she asks for, is permission to backslide.

The problems you describe are typical of what can happen when less than three years separates one child from the next in a family. When the second child was born, your daughter's position in the family shifted, creating anxiety and distracting her from the basic task of growing up. The reasons for this kind of developmental stall are not at all mysterious, and such problems are generally short-lived. The arrival of the baby reminded your daughter, at an inopportune time, of how wonderful it was to be carried and rocked to sleep and bottle-fed and have Mommy change her diapers.

Your task is to reassure her that her place in the family, while different and changing, is still secure and protected. And you must convince her, firmly but gently, that she has no choice in the matter.

The time for bottles, being rocked to sleep, and wearing diapers has passed. She is obviously ready for training, and it should proceed. Keep her in training pants, except at night. She probably won't stay dry at night for another year. *Do not* follow her around asking her if she needs to use the potty. When she gets up in the morning, take her into the bathroom, point to her potty and say, "Remember to put your wee-wee and poo-poo in here today. If you want Mommy to help you, just call me." If she asks to be put in diapers, tell her that she is a big girl who wears pants during the day and diapers only at night. If she has an accident, change her without fuss. Then take her into the bathroom and remind her once again where to put her business in the future.

Continue, even in the face of resistance, to relate your expectations to her in a clear, calm voice. I've said it before, but it deserves repeating: the more effectively authoritative the parents, the more successfully autonomous the child.

(Q) We have two boys: one has just turned three and the other is sixteen months. My problem is with the older one. He wants my attention almost constantly throughout the day—hold me, read to me, play with me, help me. If I can't go to him immediately, he whines and cries until I do. He's been this way since shortly before our second child was born, but it seems to be getting worse. It is extremely frustrating for us all. What could be the problem, and what can be done about it?

(A) It sounds as though his demands are beginning to dominate the family. It is everyone's best interest, including his, for you to act, before the problem gets firmly rooted in your lives.

Set aside two specific times during the day: a time with him and a time without him. Perhaps your time with him could be during the younger child's nap. In any case, set aside at least thirty minutes to spend totally with him, doing what *he* wants to do. Take the phone off the hook, and don't answer the door.

For your time away from him—at least thirty minutes—stay out of his sight and relatively inaccessible to him (it may help to have another adult take over during this time). Go to your room and lock the door. Take a drive or a walk. Mom's time out—just for Mom.

The rest of the time let common sense tell you whether to comply with his requests for attention. If you can give him your attention without interrupting something else, fine. But if giving him attention means stopping what you are doing, say, "No," (assuming he's not in dire straits). If he acts as though he can't live with that, take him to his room with the suggestion that he "cry here."

I suppose it's the need parents have to be all things to our children that works us into holes like this. "Good" mommies don't make their children cry. "Good" mommies sacrifice everything for their children. Those are the sort of whips we flog ourselves with. But there is a difference between being a "good mommy" and being a slave.

As you dismantle his present set of expectations and start to build new ones, he will yell. He has learned that sobbing brings you around in short order. His crying also means he senses a change in the rules and rituals that govern his relationship with you. The uncertainty of not knowing what's going on or where you are headed will stimulate a healthy amount of distress.

Nonetheless, the best way to help him deal with his discomfort is to chart your course and stay confidently on it.

You might also consider finding a preschool program for him to attend several mornings a week. The break from one another would do you both good.

James Dean

As the second birthday approaches, the child's personality clamors even more persistently for recognition. Young children have little, if any, appreciation for the virtue of moderation. They tend toward extremes in their behavior, so when the self is discovered, it emerges in exasperating ways.

"I don' wan' to! . . . No!"

Rebellion is nothing less than an expression of the toddler's need to be a separate person and assert her flowering identity to its utmost. It is important for parents to realize that this behavior, in its many manifestations, has a definite place in the overall scheme of things. However infuriating, it is an exclamation of growth and becoming.

If all this is put in its proper perspective, parents are less likely to overreact. Keep in mind, parents run the show, regardless of the child's protests and contrariness. It is our responsibility to establish limits and enforce them in firm, yet gentle ways. When we respond to these small mutinies out of fear or anger, we have, in essence, lost control of ourselves. This not only increases a child's anxiety, but feeds the fantasy that she is more powerful than we are. The power struggle that inevitably ensues leads nowhere.

The patterns established at this early stage in the parent-child relationship will tend to endure, and as the mold sets, it becomes more and more difficult to break.

(Q) My two-year-old has recently started ignoring and testing me whenever I ask her to do something. Can you tell me anything about handling this behavior?

(A) What you describe is typical of two-year-olds. In fact, rebellion is a healthy ingredient in any child's developmental process.

Encourage your daughter to recognize your authority and cooperate with the limits you set by using more than just your voice when giving directions. For instance, if she ignores you when you ask that she come away from the television set, move her away gently. At the same time, repeat your request and give her something else to do, such as, "Sit down here, and I will get you some pots and pans to play with."

This "show and tell" technique can even be used with commands such as "Pick up your toys." A child's resistance can be overcome by gently moving her through the paces, as though you were physically teaching her what you expect.

Aggression

Two-year-olds are extremely territorial. The space immediately in front of them, and everything in it, is "mine!" Intrusions into that territory threaten the child's self-concept and, therefore, provoke distress. The more passive child cries, while the more assertive child strikes out in some way. Brief, but intense, clashes over space and toys are commonplace in a group of toddler-twos.

As if that weren't enough, they are virtually oblivious to one another, insensitive to each other's feelings, and incapable of remorse. A two-year-old can give and take on a limited basis with adults and older children, but has a difficult time doing the same with another two-year-old. Put two or more children of this age together and you have all the makin's for a good fight. But this is nothing to lose sleep over. In a way, their willingness to tangle reflects healthy, expressive personalities.

(Q) We are best friends, writing to you about our children, two girls, ages twenty months and two years. Both children are fairly easygoing—until they are in the same place at the same time, that is. When they get together, which is almost every day, they fight constantly. It looks as though they dislike each other. They pull hair, snatch toys away from each other, hit, scratch, and refuse to share. This is all the more puzzling because with other children they get along fine most of the time. What's going on, and what can we do to stop it?

(A) You have inadvertently stumbled upon the recipe for Instant Tot-bash: Take two toddlers between eighteen and thirty-six months old. Blend them together for two or more hours almost every day. Sit back. Watch them bash each other. (Warning! This mixture is highly volatile and will, in almost every instance, undergo spontaneous combustion.)

The level of aggression you describe is not only typical, but heralds the flowering of two healthy, demonstrative personalities.

The most important thing to keep in mind is your friendship. It is the catalyst to the conflict: The friendship brings the youngsters together frequently. The more children this age are together, the more likely they are to do battle. It is actually better, when pairing two-year-olds, to select ones with similar temperamental characteristics. Two passives or two actives will mix far more compatibly than an active and a passive.

Don't let the friendship be an obstacle to letting the problem solve itself, which it eventually will do. Both of you have an investment in the children's liking one another. Their relationship, had it been affectionate, would have affirmed and strengthened your own bond. But if you want their relationship to be an extension of your own, then their conflict may become threatening to you.

Use your friendship as a way of coping with their rude interruptions. As much as possible, let them have enough space and time to work things out for themselves. At the same time, give each other permission to intervene whenever the warfare seems to be getting out of hand. Two-year-olds can, and will, hurt each other without ever "intending" to.

When a toy is snatched, gently take the toy away from the snatcher and give it back to the snatchee. Then keep the screaming snatcher away from the snatchee. If need be, remove her to another place until she calms down. If they both go bonkers at the same time, separate them until they relax.

Above all else, keep your sense of humor about you, and be an example of harmony for the children to follow.

(Q) When my two-year-old has a friend over to play, they fight over toys almost constantly. Today he pushed a little girl down for no reason. I spanked him and sent him in the house. Did I do the wrong thing?
(A) I was intrigued with your use of the phrase "for no reason," because it illustrates how we big people often misunderstand the behavior of children.

When your son pushed the little girl down, he did so for no reason of ours, but just "because." That is the way toddlers are. They fight over toys because they want everything *right now,* and there is only one way to skin a cat, and there are no rules—just things to want—and waiting is not fun at all. That is why at this age, and in this situation, neither a spanking nor any other form of punishment will make any connection. "Reasoning" won't complete any circuits either.

Take time to comfort both the pushee and the pusher. They are both upset, so reassure them that their world is still safe. Then, involve yourself in their play, showing them, with your own actions, how to play side-by-side without a battle. Be a facilitator, a moderator, a Henry Kissinger of the sandbox. Remember, however, that the game is *theirs,* not yours. If things flare up, hold them both on your lap and say soft things.

Will this solve the problem? Not today. But, in time, they will learn moderation and reason. Meanwhile, remember that you are the only one with patience, and use it.

(Q) We have two girls, who are four years and eighteen months old. I've heard that the second born is more aggressive, but this is ridiculous! I actually have to intervene to keep the baby from hurting Audrey, our oldest. If Audrey is playing with something and will not give it up when Molly wants it, Molly will kick and bite and throw things at her. I know that an eighteen-month-old has very little self-control, but what can I allow Audrey to do in her own defense?
(A) It sounds as though Audrey is very tolerant, patient, and gentle with Molly, especially in light of the abuse she takes from her. Molly is entering her "first adolescence." During this stage, chil-

dren tend to be extremely demanding and rebellious and, when frustrated, will often react with a tantrum or some form of aggression. So the situation you describe is not at all unusual.

You are, in some ways, fortunate that Audrey is not younger. If that were the case, both children's self-centered territorial instincts would clash dramatically, and you would be having an even more difficult time.

From this point on, Molly needs, as much as anything else you can give her, the constant presence of a firm, yet gentle, hand. It is time for her to begin learning who is the proper authority in her life and what is appropriate behavior with you, older adults, peers, and Audrey.

Audrey should *not* be made responsible for protecting herself against a toddler who knows little about restraint. As much as possible, however, allow the children to work out their own arrangement concerning toys and other things. Tell Audrey that you do *not* want her to strike back when Molly attacks, but that she should protect herself by first getting away from Molly, and second, asking for your help in resolving the conflict.

When a toy is involved, see that Audrey gets it back and attempt to substitute something for Molly. This will not always sit well with her. If she throws a tantrum, take her to her bed or crib (with the side down), or put her on the floor (if carpeted), and walk out of the room. By doing this you will let her know that there are definite, constant rules concerning expressions of frustration that occur when the world does not turn according to her whim.

"The Dracula Syndrome"

Biting, relatively common to toddlers and two-year-olds, strikes an especially dissonant chord among adults. It is, from our civilized perspective, irrational and barbaric.

When there's a biter in a group, we tend to lose sight of other aggression that might be taking place. The biting becomes the focus of attention and the child who bites becomes a scapegoat. If another child begins to bite, the blame falls on the original biter, who must have "infected" him.

If the biting takes place in a nursery, as is often the case, parents may develop the mistaken idea that the teacher, through neglect or ineptitude, "allows" children to bite. What we need to realize is that toddlers give no warning when they are about to attack—they just attack.

Not long ago, for example, I was asked into a day-care center to observe an eighteen-month-old "biter." There were five toddlers in the group. I had been in the classroom for about forty-five minutes when this child did his "thing." There were three adults in the room at the time. None of us could have anticipated his attack, and we were not able to prevent it.

The child's parents can't do anything about what takes place in the classroom either. In fact, the more responsible the parents feel, the more likely that biting will be talked about in the home and during the ride to and from the center. This attention only increases the odds of his biting again and again.

There is nothing "wrong" with a toddler who bites. He simply has learned, probably through a chance combination of instinct and accident, that his teeth are an effective weapon. Now he must be taught to restrain this impulse—one of many lessons in self-control.

(Q) I am the director of a day-care center and would like your comments on a situation in our toddler classroom, in which there are six energetic and assertive children, ranging in age from seventeen to twenty-four months. Three months ago, one of the children began biting occasionally, usually when another child was trying to take a toy away from him. Despite our efforts to stop him, he still bites once or twice a day, generally when the activity level of the group is high. The biting has triggered a reaction from this group of parents that has been difficult to handle. All of them are up in arms over this and insist that we do something to stop him. He is not an unusually aggressive child in other ways and is not the only child in the room who has bitten. Both the teacher and his mother are beginning to feel defensive. Can you offer any suggestions?

(A) His parents must not talk about biting with him or around him (unless, of course it also takes place at home). It is not even necessary to keep them informed of incidents in the classroom. The less they know, the less fuel they bring to the fire.

Biting is more likely to occur during periods of general

excitement, so separate the biter from the group when the activity level goes up. Provide him with a less active alternative until things settle down. When he does bite, or even *tries* to bite, the teacher should face him immediately with a firm "No," then sit him in a chair facing the group. She must do this as quickly as possible, *before* tending to the wounded child. The biter may be allowed out of the chair after the victim is calm and has returned to the group.

Tantrums

I will now demonstrate my truly remarkable ability to encompass past, present, and future, all in one ordinary vision. As I close my eyes and concentrate, the message rises slowly through the murky waters of time, revealing itself in a burst of clear light . . . Yes! It is revealed! The Spirit speaks!

"Two-year-olds throw tantrums. This has been so since time began and will be forever . . . so what's the big deal, anyway?"

That's a good question, Spirit. Parents tend to exaggerate the significance of tantrums. Suffice it to say that when adults make mountains out of a child's molehills, the child will learn to build mountains.

For instance, some parents feel that tantrums occur because they have made some mistake in dealing with the child's demands (which they mistakenly interpret to be expressions of need). It stands to reason, if they *are* to blame for the child's tantrum, then they must right the wrong as quickly as possible. So, having said "No," they say, "Yes." Or having spanked, they then give the child more than she originally demanded, to keep their guilt at bay.

These maneuvers work. The tantrum stops, the parent is relieved, and the child learns that tantrums are a successful means of obtaining anything she wants. So she throws more and better ones.

Other parents react to tantrums with anger rather than guilt. To them, the tantrum is evidence that the child does not accept their authority. They see the tantrum as a mutiny and react by demonstrating their authority on the child's rear end.

The paradox is that a spanking, in this situation, is *not* an expression of authority. It is a display of fear, panic, and desperation. Parents who are truly in control and secure in their feelings of authority are aware that an occasional tantrum is normal for any young child. If spanking stopped tantrums, the tantrums would stop. But they don't; both continue, more and more often.

Between eighteen and thirty-six months, tantrums are almost a reflex response to anything that is frustrating. And two-year-olds are easily frustrated. They want more than their stomachs can hold or their arms can carry. In fact, an occasional tantrum is a healthy expression of the child's need to experiment with being a rebel.

Keep tantrums occasional by reacting to them calmly and matter-of-factly, in the manner of an authority who is in control.

When a child of one or two makes a tantrum, simply pick her up and carry her to her bedroom. Deposit her in her bed. If she still sleeps in a crib, leave the side down so she can get out. If she can't get out, put her on the floor. Then leave, because there is nothing to discuss. If you *must* say something, say, "You may have your tantrum in here."

As you leave, pull the door partly closed. If she comes out before her frenzy has subsided, gently put her back in. When she is quiet and comes out, do not mention the tantrum. It's not important.

It's neat and simple. Do this whenever a tantrum occurs, and they will never become major issue. Parent is still boss. Child is still child. Molehills are molehills.

Jaws II

(Q) My two-year-old occasionally bites himself when he is mad because he can't have his way. What can I do to stop him? Does this mean he is insecure, or that something is troubling him emotionally?

(A) To your first question, my answer is, do nothing. Children of this age are largely uncivilized, and the ways they express their anger are, likewise, quite primitive. They scream, throw things, roll on the floor, strike out at objects or people nearby . . . and sometimes they bite. Their targets include toys, furniture, parents, other children, and themselves. It is possible to "cure" a toddler of biting other people, but virtually impossible to prevent him from biting himself. In the first place, you can't predict when it's going to happen. It is somewhat like lightning, except this bolt will often strike more than once in the same place (usually the arms or hands).

Parents become alarmed and confused by self-biting and generally respond with one form or another of uncivilized panic. They shriek, run for help, struggle to separate "Jaws" from arm, or faint. They are also likely to feel guilt at having "caused" the child to bite himself, in which case the child ends up being held and pampered.

All those reactions send this message from parent to child: "I lose control when you bite yourself." Biting becomes an issue of great significance, and the child capitalizes on the issue as a source of power and reinforcement. Giving a child attention for biting himself makes it more likely to happen again.

So do nothing. Pretend to be busy with something else. If your child shows you the bite marks, tell him how sorry you are that he hurt himself and go about your business. If he breaks the skin, calmly help him wash and apply antiseptic to the area. If there is any doubt about his being adequately protected from infection, call your pediatrician. Watch the wound for festering or failure to heal. By reacting calmly, you lessen the chance that it will happen again.

The answer to your second question is no, he is probably not insecure or emotionally troubled. Many children bite themselves (more than parents are willing to admit). Two-year-olds "teethe" on themselves purely to play and test your reaction. There are many superstitions about the meaning of "odd" behavior, but often the behavior occurs initially because children are simply children. It continues because parents overreact.

On the other hand, if you live with an older child who has developed this practice into a habit that occurs whenever he is frustrated, or a child who bites himself more than occasionally, I recommend a talk with a therapist.

The Bedtime Blues

(Q) We have an eighteen-month-old girl who has, until lately, always gone to bed (at nine o'clock) very pleasantly, fallen asleep quickly, and slept through the night. In the past several weeks, she has become a monster at bedtime. She screams, becomes rigid, and goes into a rage when we leave the room. I have always rocked her for several minutes before putting her down. Now, the moment I stop rocking, she starts yelling. This went on for three-and-a-half hours last night, as we did everything we could think of. Finally she wore herself out in my arms. She has also been waking up briefly in the middle of the night. What have I done to cause this, and what can be done to stop it?

(A) You haven't done anything to cause her screams. Her Jekyll to Hyde transformation at bedtime is the first stage of a revolution commonly called the "Terrible Twos."

Gone are the days when she would smile and coo pleasantly as Mommy and Daddy put her to bed. Cribs are confining and not compatible with her new way of thinking. Gone are the days when a few minutes of rocking was enough. What right does Mom have to stop rocking? None!

She has also figured out that life goes on in the house after the lights go out in her bedroom. It's a trick! How dare you!

To make bedtime go more smoothly, you must first rid yourself of the paralyzing idea that she screams because you have done something wrong. She screams because *you* have done something to *her,* and she will not stand (or lie) for it. There may be no way, short of letting her sleep with you (*don't* do that!), to put her to bed without screams for a while.

Next, keep it firmly in mind that her bedtime exists solely for *your* sake. The importance of putting a child to bed is so daddies and mommies can be husbands and wives again. Bedtime is an exercise in learning how to separate the child from the marriage (see Bedtime Is for Parents, page 233). With that in mind, I recommend that you move bedtime back to eight o'clock. Between 7:45 and 8:00, move her through the preliminaries. Then put her in her crib and, screams or no screams, leave the room. Remember that "in hesitation, all is lost."

I realize how difficult it is to forget you are parents when there's a child screaming in the house. So put yourselves on a schedule. Take turns "checking in" with her every ten minutes. Walk with feigned casualness into her room, say a brief something about going to sleep, lay her back down, give her rigid body a kiss, and walk out. As she begins to get the message, you can extend the time between checks to fifteen or twenty minutes.

While she rages, you and your husband can talk, play backgammon, read, or do whatever you enjoy doing together. Support one another and help one another make the transition from parent to spouse. Real people again! Now *that's* something to look forward to.

(Q) Our twenty-month-old son is putting us through some changes. He is becoming more active and refuses to take an afternoon nap. In addition, he has learned how to climb out of his crib. Bedtime is becoming a battle. What can we do?
(A) Before you do anything, you need to understand how important these changes are to your son's growth and development. On the surface, this behavior may appear to be symptoms of rebelliousness, so it's no surprise that you've engaged him in "battle."

But there's more going on here than meets the eye. The transformation taking place is more accurately described in terms of an underlying process—the fertile soil from which this "rebellious" behavior grows.

The metamorphosis from caterpillar to butterfly has begun. Caterpillars fly and babies climb from their cribs. As your son's sense of himself expands, so does his view of the world. Everything takes on new and exciting dimensions, stimulating his wonder *and* his activity level. Who can blame him for not wanting to stay in a crib?

The not-so-simple act of climbing out of the crib is much more than an athletic event. It requires and expresses a feeling of trust, an irrepressible confidence in his ability to accomplish new things (scale new heights, so to speak). Most of all, it acknowledges that he has given himself permission—and he senses you have, too—to begin uncoupling from you and becoming independent. He no longer has to stay put just because you put him there.

Take the path of least resistance. Instead of trying to make him stay where he is determined not to, begin a gradual changeover from crib to bed. Dismantle the crib (let him help) and put the mattress on the floor. Let him sleep there until he learns the boundaries of the mattress and no longer rolls out in his sleep. Then move him to a regular bed.

You might want to put up a childproof gate at his doorway, especially if you live in a two-story house. The gate will secure him in his room after you put him to bed, but will allow him to roam within reasonable boundaries until he's ready to sleep. In this way you aren't forcing him to lie down, but you are setting limits on his activity after bedtime. If he stands at the gate and screams, return to his room at regular, lengthening intervals (begin with ten minutes) to calm him down and tuck him in with a firm message about going to sleep. This will take some effort for several days but will eventually pay off.

The best solution to his increasing activity level is to child-proof your home, if you haven't done so already. This not only guarantees the child's safety, but your peace of mind as well.

As for nap time, trying to make him sleep is a losing proposition. You can still require that he remain in his room for one hour every afternoon, though. Continue putting him to bed for a nap as part of his daily routine. If you must, use the gate to keep him in his room. Once he gets accustomed to this regular down time, he will probably start napping again. Whether he sleeps or not, use the time for yourself. For the next few years, in fact, the more time you can make for just *you,* the better off *he* will be.

Einstein Didn't Talk Until He Was Three

(Q) We are the parents of an active and alert twenty-month-old boy who doesn't talk. He has a limited, single-word vocabulary which includes "ma-ma," "da-da," and "bye," but whenever he wants to say something to us, he acts it out with gestures. He has no trouble understanding anything we say to him, but we wonder if he has a problem. Up until now, we've put no pressure on him to talk, but it has been suggested to us that we not do things for him unless he uses words to tell us what he wants. What are your thoughts on this?

(A) A three-word vocabulary at twenty months is not cause for concern. In one sense, you son's vocabulary sounds fairly extensive.

We all have two vocabularies: one active, or expressive; the other passive, or receptive. Our active vocabulary consists of words we use when we talk (or write), while our passive vocabulary includes all the words we understand. We generally understand more words than we use, and in children the difference is marked. You son's passive vocabulary is probably the more accurate reflection, at his age, of how well he is progressing in language development. From this point of view, he is obviously doing fine.

Well, then, why doesn't he talk more? Probably for several reasons, all having to do with his age.

He stands on the threshold of the "Terrible Twos," a traumatic eighteen months in the lives of most children. It is the agony and ecstasy of childhood—and parenthood as well. The child who is almost two views and acts on his world as though he were the center of all experience. He also takes his first, tentative steps toward independence. And tentative they are, since his need to be cuddly and close is still powerful. His need to feel independent is satisfied by being in control of situations—and people. His continued dependency needs are met through involvement with you, his parents. All these needs are, paradoxically, satisfied by not talking. He is able to control certain situations, prolong your involvement with him, and receive plenty of attention in the bargain. Isn't he clever?

So cooperate with him, casually and matter-of-factly. Don't try to force him to talk by ignoring his pantomimed requests. That would create a useless and frustrating power struggle. He is, after all, becoming adept at gestural language, an art which will enhance his overall communication skills in the long run.

Talk to him, but don't require him to talk back. When he's ready and has found other ways to satisfy his need for attention, he will no doubt discover that talking works better than charades.

When a child is twenty-four months old, a speech and hearing evaluation might be appropriate if several of the following indicators are present:

- The child uses less than a twenty-word expressive vocabulary.
- His expressive vocabulary is not increasing, or he shows no interest in talking.
- The child is becoming increasingly dependent on gestures.
- He is becoming visibly frustrated in his attempts to communicate.

• He does not respond when spoken to nor seems to understand simple directions.

• The child does not show an understanding of what you want him to do when you show him a picture and say, "Point to the puppy," "Show me the ball," or "Where's the hat?"

Three-Year-Olds

A child's growth, like that of every other living thing, proceeds through a sequence of stages. Each stage, or phase, is defined by new ways of interacting with the environment, and each successive theme is an extension and elaboration on previous ones.

A three-year-old begins to build a sense of initiative, or purposeful self-confidence, upon the trust and autonomy acquired during the "Wonderful Ones" and "Terrible Twos."

During the eighteen months prior to her third birthday, the child was busy forging a clear sense of who she is. As you might expect, her young self-image is fragile, like a clay pot that hasn't yet dried.

The omnipotence she felt as a two-year-old has turned inside-out. Once upon a time, she ruled the world. Now all she can lay claim to are a few toys and a vague, shifting sense of her identity, and even that small territory is a struggle to maintain. Is it any wonder, then, that three-year-olds are so easily threatened by such things as the dark, loud noises, and bumps on the head?

Owies

Physical injuries, no matter how minor, strike too close to home for the three-year-old's comfort. Even the slightest pain from a tiny scratch can dislodge the tentative grasp he has on the "me" he feels he must guard so carefully, lest it slip away as mysteriously as it came.

Furthermore, a three-year-old has no way of knowing that wounds heal, which inflates his fear and feeling of helplessness.

(Q) Our usually easygoing three-year-old has recently started acting more sensitive to pain than he used to be. He gets almost hysterical over a little scratch or scraped knee. I won't even attempt to describe his reaction to a cut. We have tried to get him to realize that his injuries aren't that bad, but it doesn't help. We don't know what more we can do. What suggestions do you have?

(A) Threes (and young fours) have a reputation for overreacting to mild pain in the manner you describe.

It will do no good to try to persuade your son that his perception of these traumatic events is inaccurate. There are some things only time can teach. The more you do, the more you talk, the more exaggerated his reaction is likely to become. Simply tend to his wound, put your arms around him, and sit quietly until he calms down. Your being there is all he needs to restore his misplaced sense of "togetherness."

Isn't it nice to know we don't always have to talk so much?

Fears

Fears are common to three-year-olds. Leading the list are fear of the dark, of being left along, and of "things that go bump in the night."

Three-year-olds often misinterpret ordinary events as threatening because of the interaction of three characteristics:

(1) Their need to protect their recently acquired and still fragile sense of identity. As children grow in self-sufficiency, they must come to grips with the anxiety associated with letting go of their parents. Fears dramatize this process. They are symbolic, fantasy-laden expressions of the young child's feeling of vulnerability.

(2) The flowering of imaginative thought. Threes have the ability to conjure up mental images of things real and unreal, but lack the ability to control the process.

(3) Their inability to separate *word* from *thing*. If there is a word for something, then it *must* exist. Threes can't separate fact from fiction because both are represented in the same medium—language.

Parents often misinterpret a child's fearfulness as a symptom of insecurity or upcoming emotional problems. They react as if the fear were the child's way of saying, "You guys aren't taking care of me." They feel responsible for the child's anxiety, so they try to protect him from it. Unfortunately, the parents communicate their anxieties to the child and actually *increase* his sense of helplessness.

Trying to reason the fear away usually doesn't work either. The rational explanation and the imaginative fear are on separate, incompatible wavelengths. A reasoned approach only heightens the child's sense of isolation: If his parents can't see things as he does, then he really is at the mercy of whatever he thinks is "out there."

The most effective approach is to first acknowledge the fear: "I know the dark can be frightening when you are three years old." Then identify with the child: "When I was three, I was afraid of the dark too." Finally, reassure him of your ability to protect him: "I'll be downstairs in the living room and I will take care of you".

Stay close enough to make the child feel protected, but not so close that your presence validates the fear.

(Q) Believe it or not, my three-and-a-half-year-old son is afraid of newspapers. He says he doesn't like the way they smell and refuses to enter a room if one is there. He is also afraid of other paper products. He won't sit at the table if there is a napkin at his place, won't blow his nose in tissue paper, and wants me to clean him after he uses the bathroom. He has become quite insistent about all this and has a tantrum if we do not cooperate. What should we do?

(A) Newspaper is a new one to me, but it isn't anymore significant than garden-variety fears of the dark or frogs.

Young children do not see the line we draw between fact and fancy. Their playful innocence makes them vulnerable, for the same process that turns bathtubs into sailing ships can also bring shadows alive in the night. With a bit more exaggeration the child sees himself as a victim of sinister forces beyond his understanding or control.

By accommodating his demands and rearranging the world in order to protect him, you inadvertently become part of the drama, thereby giving validity to his fright. "Newspaper can hurt me. I know it can, because Mom and Dad protect me from it. Other kinds of paper can hurt me too." He can also use this issue to manipulate you and gain control of certain family situations. It is no surprise, for instance, that his fears have disrupted mealtimes and hooked you back into helping him use the bathroom. Power struggles between children and parents almost always involve conflict over bedtime, mealtime, or the toilet.

Your son is saying, "I will come to the table only on my terms. I will only go so far in using the bathroom by myself." However, he is not actually in control of himself or the situation. He is convinced his fear is real. The more you cooperate, the more his original insecurities increase, and the more fearful he becomes.

You must help him distinguish between what is real and what is not. It is essential that *you* define for him the way the family functions. While I see no harm in letting him choose for himself whether to enter a room in which there is a newspaper, you must not let his panic persuade you to remove it. About meals and the bathroom, make no concessions. Tell him, "You are one person in this family, and your place at the table will look like everyone else's." Insist that he sit with the family during meals and use his napkin appropriately. Firmly refuse to assist him in the bathroom.

Give the problem back to him. After all, *he* invented it.

Intellectual Growth

Three-year-olds gradually learn to deal with delay of gratification. A two-year-old will always choose the immediate reward—even if it is less attractive—over one she must wait for. A three-year-old can hold off for a short time provided she has something to occupy herself with in the interval. This ability to postpone gratification indicates a strengthened tolerance for frustration and increased self-control.

Three-year-olds demonstrate a remarkable memory for past events. When my children were three, they continually amazed me with their ability to describe, in precise detail, events that had happened months before—ones I had almost forgotten and could not recall with comparable clarity.

Threes are also able to retrieve information selectively for problem-solving. For these reasons, children of this age show more variety on their approaches to problem situations. If a two-year-old's first attempt to solve a problem doesn't work, she will often fly into a rage. She sees no other alternative. A three-year-old, having experienced the same initial failure, is more likely to try one or two other strategies before she gets overwhelmed with frustration.

A three-year-old learns from her mistakes and uses this feedback to modify her problem-solving techniques. The emergence of trial-and-error thinking is one of the two most significant intellectual events occurring at this age. The other is the flowering of creative, imaginative thought. Threes are suddenly interested in making things. They enjoy coloring, painting, working in clay, and building things out of whatever material is available. But more than anything else, three-year-olds *pretend* and, if left to their own devices, will spend a major portion of their day engaged in self-directed imaginative activity. This timely happening is a perfect complement to their growing independence and initiative. For the first time in her life, the child is capable of occupying and entertaining herself for relatively long periods.

The three-year-old uses her intellectual freedom to explore and come to grips with her initiation into the social side of life. Her almost constant imaginative play is a way of practicing and preparing for greater social responsibility. The three-year-old is literally playing at growing up. This ability to mentally represent entire social scenarios also allows the three-year-old to keep enough distance between herself and actual events to keep her anxiety level under control and protect her still-fragile self-image.

Imaginary Playmates

One day shortly after my son's third birthday, I sat downstairs listening while he and another child played upstairs in his room. After nearly two hours of animated conversation and much activity, Eric bounded down the stairs. Alone.

"Who were you playing with?" I asked.

"My friend," he said, a gleam in his eye.

"And what is your friend's name?"

"Jackson Jonesberry," he said with obvious pleasure.

I have no idea where he got the name and like to believe it came from the same place Jackson did.

When my daughter was three, she created not one, but a

whole group of imaginary friends, including "Soppie," "Honkus," and the inimitable "Shinyarinka Sinum."

The appearance of imaginary playmates is an unmistakable sign of the three-year-old's interest in peer relationships. With a Jackson Jonesberry or a Shinyarinka Sinum, a child can satisfy this strong need for peer affiliation while at the same time practicing her social skills in a safe and controlled context.

When Eric was three and four, we lived in a rural area where there were few opportunities for play with other children. For nearly two years, he played with Jackson and several other invisible friends. Invisible to Willie and me, that is, for to Eric they were very real. I am certain he could "see" them.

There is no need to worry about the amount of time children spend in this sort of play. Adults should not interrupt or intrude when a child plays in this manner. When it is necessary to interrupt for practical reasons, do so with utmost respect for his "guest." Adults should *never* question the existence of such an invention.

In light of the importance of imagination to social and intellectual growth, I strongly urge parents to keep children this age away from television. It can distract and eventually overwhelm the young child's imagination.

A child watching television learns to depend on something outside herself for creative stimulation. She does not learn to be creative. A child watching television is not preparing for a larger role in life. She learns how to be a spectator instead of a doer, a follower rather than a leader. A child watching television is not practicing independence or exercising any initiative. She learns how to be complacent, dependent, resourceless, and irresponsible.

This is true regardless of the program—"Sesame Street" included (see Television, page 283).

Kid Klutz: He Trips, He Spills, He Stutters, He Walks into Walls

During the fourth year of life, children may act as though they are becoming *less* instead of *more* coordinated. Typically, they trip and fall more often, their feet get tangled when they run ("He's got two left feet"), and they drop and spill things and generally play the role of Kid Klutz. They may also begin stuttering—repeating themselves, backing up, and holding on to certain sounds.

Paradoxically, this physical and verbal awkwardness arises because the three-year-old is trying to orchestrate thought, language, and movement. Up until this time, the child focused on each of these developmental areas in relative isolation from the other two. Now, he is putting them together in a coordinated system.

Whereas before he concentrated separately on learning to walk and to talk, he now tries to walk and talk at the same time. This example, while oversimplified, expresses the essential character of this stage in the child's growth. It is a time of reorganization and integration, and at first the pieces don't work as well together as they did individually.

Unfortunately, parents often react as though the child has suddenly developed a problem. They become anxious, lose patience, and try to help the child overcome his "difficulties." All of this makes a problem where there was none. His parents' anxiety tells the child something is "wrong," and minor difficulties become traps. This is particularly true in the case of stuttering.

The general rule is, have patience and be supportive. If the child spills his milk for the thirteenth time in twelve days, instead of blasting his self-esteem ("What's the matter with you! Why can't you do something as simple as blah, blah, blah!"), say something like, "Oh, oh. Here, take this rag and help me clean up. I remember spilling my milk when I was three years old, too."

Stuttering can usually be prevented if parents take the time to listen and show interest in what the child is trying to say. If he starts stuttering, here is what *not* to do:

- *Don't* complete his sentences for him.
- *Don't* say things like "slow down" or "take a deep breath and start over."
- *Don't* discuss his stuttering when he can hear you.
- *Don't* interrupt him or tell him to come back when he is calm and can talk "better."

Talk slowly to a child who stutters. If he has trouble telling you something, ask him questions he can answer in three words or less. If he complains about his stuttering, let him know that sometimes even big people have tralking tubble.

Social Growth

By the age of three, the child's almost intolerable self-centeredness gives way to a more social view of herself in relation to others. She learns to take turns (which precedes true sharing) and to play *with* (instead of simply around) other children.

Three-year-olds occasionally act as though they can look at a situation from someone else's point of view. Expressions of empathy are rare, though, to anyone except their primary caretakers and children with whom they are familiar. Three-year-old playmates comfort each other and are sometimes even penitent when they bruise one another's feelings.

Three-year-olds can form transient play relationships with other children their age or slightly older. Proceed with caution, however, when mixing three-year-olds for the first time. They don't understand the value of social foreplay. Instead, they rush into intimate and risky interactions with one another. This causes as many disastrous first encounters as rewarding ones. And first impressions definitely count with three-year-olds. Children who hit it off well generally continue to do so, while children whose first encounter was filled with friction are likely to have subsequent difficulty getting along.

But close encounters of the worst kind can be prevented if adults are sensitive to the risks involved in putting children of this age together, and if they give the children adequate supervision, structure, and guidance until they are playing smoothly with one another.

This is a good age for introducing the young child to group day care. Be careful when selecting a preschool, because the value of the experience depends on the quality of the program. By and large, however, research indicates that developmentally-oriented group care produces (1) an increase in constructive, goal-oriented behavior, (2) an increase in cooperative play, (3) an increase in assertive behavior, (4) improvement in conflict-solving skills, and (5) improvement in the child's ability to adapt to new situations.

Three-year-olds carefully observe other children and imitate them. This "monkey see, monkey do" tendency, although exasperating at times, is important to the growth of social skills. On one level imitation is a game, an almost ritual exchange between children which forms positive, cooperative social bonds. On another, it is a way of acquiring problem-solving skills. Researchers have found that once a three-year-old watches another child cope with a stressful event, she can employ similar strategies to deal with the same situation. On yet another level, imitation is a low-risk way of experimenting with new forms of behavior. If they are nothing else, three-year-olds are experimental, and therefore somewhat unpredictable, little people.

It's a try-anything-once age. They go through this phase of their lives trying on any and every behavior imaginable, seeing if it fits or adds something interesting to either their own image of themselves or that image they see reflected in other people's reactions to them.

The first three years of a child's life are spent building a relatively enduring personality—a basic wardrobe. For the next two years or so, the youngster window-shops for "accessories"—bits and pieces of behavior to add variety and spice to her act.

She's likely to borrow these tidbits from anyone, but playmates and older children figure heavily in what she brings home. The three-year-old's love of mimicry is clearly a sign that she is beginning to identify with other children, and that they are exerting considerable influence as role models for one another.

Episodes of regression to behavior reminiscent of infancy are also common, and all the more so when there's a new sibling involved. These include increases in bowel and bladder accidents, asking for a bottle, using baby talk, and wanting to be carried and held more than usual.

Most of these harmless excursions back in time are best handled by looking the other way. However, if several repeat performances in a short period tip you off that a pattern is developing, then it's necessary to intervene authoritatively before the mortar sets.

(Q) My husband and I would appreciate your suggestions on a situation that has us puzzled. Our three-and-a-half-year-old son taught himself to use the toilet when he was just two. Since then, he has enjoyed playing with his diapers, training pants, and various articles of toddler clothing, which we let him do. Recently, after being at the home of a friend his age who is not toilet trained, he came home, put on several pair of training pants, and wet them, just slightly. He has done this twice since, and we aren't sure what it means. I've also noticed that, on occasion, his penis gets hard when he is playing with putting on diapers or training pants. Should we forbid him to wear them? I might add that we are expecting a new baby in four months. Could this have anything to do with it?

(A) I don't get a sense of anything unusual from your letter. Your son sounds like a typical three-year-old. Not that lots of threes dress "down" in diapers and old clothing, mind you, but typical in the sense that this age child is imaginative and experimental and enjoys role play.

There is no need to forbid him to play in his old clothes. I would suggest, however, that you convey clearly your rules and expectations about them.

It is probably unwise to let him play with the diapers. He may think he has permission to wet them, especially after the new baby arrives and he notices that his younger sibling enjoys this prerogative.

As for the arousal of his penis, keep in mind that a three-year-old's sexuality is diffuse and capable of responding to any form of pleasurable stimulation. In this case, putting on his diapers and training pants must arouse warm feelings associated with the many pleasurable experiences of infancy—being held, having diapers changed, wetting his pants, and so on. Similar physical responses are fairly common in boys and girls (although in a less obvious manner) who suck their thumbs or nuzzle favorite blankets.

Lies

A three-year-old's sense of fantasy is so much a part of her personality that the distinction between what is truth and what is not is hazy. The meaning of "truth" is not *really* clear until a child is nearly seven.

A young child doesn't completely understand the concept of responsibility either. To her, things simply happen, and the extent of her involvement is not always clear in her mind. Therefore, don't expect threes (or even fours, fives, or sixes) to be completely truthful. And don't regard it as a moral weakness when they aren't.

This age child is easily frightened into concealing the truth. If the threat of punishment is present, the child's natural defense is to try and avoid pain by saying, "Not me." If this works, the child will feel relief at having been spared from her parents' wrath.

There is also a certain rush of exhilaration at realizing that a concealment has "worked." This exhilaration can be habit forming. The greater the threat and the more risky the concealment, the greater the thrill of getting away with it. And so the child rolls the dice again the next time and keeps on rolling.

Occasionally, the concealment falls flat, and the parents "score" with a spanking. Some of the time, though, it works to at least confuse her parents, and so the child "scores." If the child tries five "hoodwinks," and only one is successful, chances are she will go on playing the odds.

(Q) Our little boy, who is three years old, will misbehave and then when we confront him, deny he did anything. We punish him anyway, but it makes us upset, because he acts so hurt. We wonder if he knows why he is being punished, or if he really believes he did nothing wrong. How should we handle these situations?
(A) Remember that "an ounce of prevention is worth a pound of cure." Don't give a child an opportunity to conceal something you already know he did. Instead of asking, "Did you tear all the leaves off my African violets?" make a firm, positive statement, such as, "You tore the leaves off my African violets. I am very angry. You must clean up the mess and then go to your room." Ask the child no questions, and he'll tell you no lies.

If you see a child misbehave, or if circumstantial evidence points to him as the culprit, don't open the door for argument by asking the obvious question. Extracting admissions of guilt or apologies is not necessary. Save time and trouble by making statements that tell the child you know what happened. Ignore his protests and alibis. You'll be doing him a favor.

When several children are playing together and something goes wrong, it's not worth the effort to play "Who-done-it." Besides, children are quick to make a scapegoat of one child in the group, usually the smallest, or one who has taken lots of blame in the past. They cannot be relied on as impartial witnesses. Where siblings are involved, say, "This happened while you were playing together, and you will both be punished for it." In cases where your child is one of a group, break up the action and direct the disciplinary lesson at your own.

Concealments are less likely if the threat of spanking is not an issue. Punish by taking away privileges—bicycle, outside play, having friends over and so on. It's true that spankings take less time, but in this case they seldom have a lasting effect. On the other hand, it's too easy to let "You can't go outside for three days" slide after the first day, so make the consequence short but meaningful.

Punish the act, and disregard the concealment. Don't promise a child that things will go easier if he tells the truth, or that he will be punished doubly if he lies. This sort of "plea-bargaining" is extremely confusing, and it tells the child you *expect* him to lie. Unless you want the seed to grow, this idea must not be planted in a child's mind. A child who misbehaves should be punished immediately. No deals or legal mumbo-jumbo should divert attention from what happened.

"Mine?"

Until recently, from the child's egocentric (self-centered) point of view, there was but one territory and one set of possessions—hers. Part of growing up is accepting the disappointing fact that everyone else owns a piece of the pie too. This requires that she civilize her view of the world by learning what is implied by the words we use to define "possession."

This is a difficult task, because the lines separating "mine" from "yours" are largely invisible. There is, for instance, nothing distinguishing about the "my" in "my firetruck."

The possessive pronouns—mine, yours, his, hers, theirs, ours—are abstractions referring to ownership. Three-and-a-half-year-old children find it difficult to comprehend abstractions, which are one step removed from the world of color and sound and touch and taste and smell.

To a three-and-a-half-year-old, "This firetruck is red" makes sense because red can be seen. It can be experienced *directly.*

"This firetruck is *mine,*" however, makes no sense. "Where and what is a 'mine'?" puzzles the child.

Attempting to understand abstractions, the youngster translates them into behavior. Oftentimes, this behavior runs counter to the intended message. For example, the word "don't" is also an abstraction, referring to the *absence* of some action. "Sit on the dog" makes sense to a three-and-a-half-year-old because the message is concrete, down-to-earth. On the other hand, "Don't sit on the dog" complicates matters considerably. The child is perplexed, and in an attempt to resolve his confusion, does the obvious, which is to plop down on the dog. Because we fail to see the child's behavior in its proper context, we say the child is "disobedient" and "knows better." Far from it.

(Q) During the past three months, on four separate occasions, our three-and-a-half-year-old daughter has shown me objects which she has concealed and taken from a playmate's house and the day-care center. After each incident, I have talked calmly and tried not to make a "big deal" out of it, but I'm not sure this is the right approach. Is this more serious than I'm willing to admit? Should I have punished her? How would you suggest I deal with it if it happens again?

(A) Not to worry. Nearly every child this age tries the "sticky fingers" routine. This is not to be confused with stealing. The motives are anything but similar. In fact, your daughter is, in the most literal sense of the term, *innocent.*

During the preschool years, "taking" is an experimental behavior—no harm intended. She is, first of all, testing your reaction: "What will Momma do if . . . ?" I applaud your daughter for inventing such a clever and ingenious way of defining the difference between "mine" and "yours." By taking what she has been told is someone else's, or what rests at someone else's house, your daughter is attempting to define the concepts of possession and ownership.

So whaddaya do now? Help her out. She's asking a question. Give her the answer. React calmly and directly. "Oh. You took a toy from Bobby's house. This toy belongs to Bobby. This toy is *his.* You and I are going to take the toy back to Bobby's house and give it to him."

It is extremely important that you return the item immediately, while the question is fresh in her mind. It is equally imperative that your daughter accompany you on this mission.

It is *not* important that she confess, apologize, or hand the item back herself. These requirements only serve to punish the question and muddle the answer. It is sufficient that she see you apologize and transfer the item to its owner. Keep the lesson simple and straightforward. No need to spice it with either guilt or grief.

"Play Wif Me!"

For the most part, three-year-olds have resolved the conflicts surrounding the issue of dependence versus independence. But not completely. There are still times when they are tempted to give up the ground they have gained and retreat to a lifestyle that guaranteed comfort and security. Independence involves risks and, remember, the three-year-old has no map to show him the way. Dependence, on the other hand, is secure and addictive. One way of expressing this internal tug-of-war is to pull on Mommy and say, in essence, "Be my playmate."

(Q) About how much time each day should I spend playing with my three-year-old? I don't work, so I've got just about all the time he needs.

(A) A very tricky question, for which there are no definite answers. At this age, there should still be plenty of time when the two of you sit down together just for the fun of it, but your responsibilities do *not* include being his playmate.

In fact, although he may want you to spend your day playing with him and be rather insistent about it, that is exactly what he does *not* need from you at this stage.

He does not require that much or that kind of attention from adults. He needs adults for protection, affection, and control. He needs adults to read to him, to organize and arrange his play space, to reinforce his initiative, to encourage his independence, and to give him ideas he can use to take off in new, self-sustaining directions.

Burton White, author of *The First Three Years of Life* and an authority on preschool children, has said that one of the most accurate indicators of developmental health in a three-year-old is an ability to occupy and entertain himself for significantly long periods of time.

That doesn't mean parents should stop playing with their children after their third birthdays. Three-year-olds need to know that their parents are still available to them. Keep in mind, however, that the more of a playmate a parent is, the more his authority and the child's autonomy are undermined.

Set limits on when you will play with him and when you won't. Don't be afraid to say "no" even if he screams. Find a morning preschool program and enroll him three days a week.

And while you're taking care of *his* independence, don't forget about your own.

Naps and Bedtime

(Q) My daughter is now three and a half. Even when given an hour's opportunity for an afternoon nap around two o'clock, she doesn't fall asleep. Then by 5:30, she falls apart. She cries and is touchy and can hardly sit up and eat her supper. If she goes to sleep around 3:30, I try to wake her after an hour or so, or she will be up until 9:30 or ten. Is this just another stage?

(A) It sounds as though your daughter may no longer need an afternoon nap. This transition from nap to no nap won't happen overnight though. For a while there will be days when she will obviously need a nap and days when she will not feel the need as strongly.

During this transition stage, she is likely to resist taking an afternoon slumber, for the simple reason that being awake is far more exciting than being asleep. Remember that children become upset when their routines are disrupted. This transition, then, because it involves shifting bedtimes back and forth, may be unsettling. You can count on her being cranky and out of sorts at times.

A routine would help her make this difficult adjustment. You must establish the routine, and you must enforce it in the face of occasional resistance. With this in mind, establish a bedtime. This decision should take into consideration such factors as work schedules, what time everyone needs to leave the house in the morning, where the child spends her days, and so on. In the end, however, parents should decide when *they* want the child in bed. Every child needs parents who spend private time together regularly. So let's say that you choose 8:30 as the time when you want your daughter tucked away.

To make this happen, begin at eight o'clock to prepare her for bed. Turn off the television, turn down everyone's activity level to idle, give her a warm bath, send her to the potty, offer a small (preferably sugar-free) snack, read a story (in bed), talk softly with her about pleasant things that happened during the day, kiss and cuddle her, turn out the lights, and leave the room. If she resists sleeping, make it clear that she must stay in her bed with the lights on. Enforce your decision calmly, but as firmly as necessary.

If her biological clock is turned to the norm, she will sleep until about eight o'clock the next morning. Depending on how active her day is, she may or may not want to nap. If she falls asleep of her own accord, allow her to sleep no more than one hour. In the evening, whether or not she takes a nap, begin again to wind things down at eight o'clock, aiming for that 8:30 bedtime. The most important thing to remember is that *you* establish the routine and *you* program her to fall into it through calm, consistent enforcement. The pattern will eventually become fixed, and she will make her own adjustments concerning naps according to her own needs.

Fours and Fives

The play of a three-year-old child is open-ended and improvisational. He is a self-starter and can occupy himself for relatively long periods of time, but he is playing solely in the present—the here and now. He has no objectives in mind; he plays simply for the sake of playing.

Four- and five-year-olds begin to establish goals and direct their activity toward accomplishing them. If you ask a three-year-old, "What are you doing?" you will usually get this answer: "Playing." A four- or five-year-old answers the same question more specifically, telling the purpose of his activity: "I'm building a boat."

This ability to conceptualize and work toward a predetermined goal is the next step in the child's drive to master the environment. It signals the emergence of achievement motivation—the focused desire to accomplish, to create, to do.

Fours and fives express their need to achieve in a variety of ways. They begin to form definite interests, and, more often than not, these interests are gender-related. Typically, boys identify with the role model their fathers present—showing an interest in similar things (sports, automobiles, gardening, and so on). They express more need for Daddy's approval and companionship and engage in activities associated with their fathers (playing with tools, cooking, and so on). At the same time, little girls are forming close ties with their mothers and exhibiting clear preferences for behavior and activities which are—relative to the standards in the home—feminine in nature.

This age child's gender identity also stabilizes. Four-year-olds realize that boys grow up to be men and girls grow up to be women. The emergence of precocious "sexual" behavior in this age children is their way of exploring and, thereby, understanding all that is implied by the mysterious difference between males and females.

As you might expect, the strategies they use to obtain answers to their questions are direct and unself-conscious. It's the age of "Let's play doctor" and "Show me" and it's bound to cause parents some consternation.

"You Show Me Yours, and . . ."

"I heard them all giggling and laughing upstairs in my daughter's room and went upstairs to see what was so funny. They all had their clothes off, every stitch! They were all hopping around the room, hitting each other with pillows. I just stood there. My mouth wouldn't work."

"Bobby had been in the bathroom for a long time, so I went to see if he needed any help, and there they were. I thought I had prepared myself for anything—but two boys?"

"Every time I look around, Julie has her hand inside her pants. She does it everywhere. I've tried everything I know to stop her, but it only gets worse. I'm embarrassed to take her any place."

It happens in the best of families. There you are, managing things smoothly, coping with the occasional, expected hassles, but at least there's *one* thing you don't have to deal with for another ten years—or so you think. Then one day you happen to look in on the little ones who have been playing so quietly together for a half hour, and . . .

Sometime between their fourth and sixth birthdays, most children discover that their bodies have pleasure places where touching feels almost as good as a chocolate ice-cream cone tastes. There's nothing perverted or wrong in a child's liking ice cream, and there's nothing unnatural about her wanting to know about her own—or someone else's—body once she discovers the mysteries within.

A child's curiosity does not readily obey the green and red lights that adults set up to define what is "right" and what is not. It never occurs to a child who indulges in immature sex play that she is doing something wrong, and the idea that this delightful discovery is forbidden can be confusing and destructive. After all, it's *her* body, and it feels good. When adults look sickened, shout, slap the offending hand, or say it's bad, the message is that making oneself feel good is wrong. She hears people saying there's something wrong with her body—that it mustn't be touched.

Eventually, what the child finds delightful and good about her body is scrubbed from her thinking and words like "disgusting" and "nasty" are written in. Embarrassment, shame, and guilt can easily become attached to her body-image and translated into ideas concerning herself. The final conclusion: "I'm *bad* to want to feel good."

There's a further danger in punishing or showing disapproval of such self-discovery. If a child's interest in her body is punished, if it becomes tinged with shame, then she will hide it from sight.

It is essential that our children feel free to talk with us about sex and related matters. If a young child's unashamed openness is punished, then later, as a teenager, it is unlikely that she will feel comfortable approaching her parents with questions, doubts, or problems concerning sexuality.

So, what to do? There are no easy prescriptions, but here are some general guidelines.

A child, like anyone else, has a need for, and a right to, privacy. Don't intrude on her world, at regular intervals or simply because she is being "too quiet." If you happen to find your child exploring her body in the privacy of her own room, let it be. She is doing no harm, physical or psychological, to herself and certainly no harm to anyone else.

Children who explore themselves in public places must learn that bodies are a private, personal matter. Tell them something like, "I know that feels good, but the living room is not the place to do it. If you like, you may go to your room where no one will bother you." This will help the child develop self-control without defining the act as "forbidden." In public, the straightforward approach is also best: "Please take your hands out of your pants while we are in the store. You may do that in your room when we get home." When there are two or more children together, simply divert their attention and briefly mention that what they are doing is not allowed: "You two are not allowed to play together like that. I want you to put your clothes on and come downstairs. I need your help with something."

Keep in mind that it is natural for young children to show an immature interest in sex in one way or another, and that there is no difference at this age between curiosity displayed toward one's own body and curiosity displayed toward other bodies of *either* sex. Be honest and simple when answering the questions that may come up. Keep a straight face even if you feel bewildered or shocked. Respect the child's right to privacy, but at the same time teach her that there are appropriate times and places for everything.

(Q) Our five-year-old daughter has recently started masturbating by rubbing herself between her legs. We have tried to ignore it, but several times have had to tell here to stop because we were in public. Her kindergarten teacher says she is also rubbing herself in class. In all other respects, she is a happy, well-adjusted child with no obvious insecurities. Can you help us understand why she started doing this and give some suggestions for handling it?

(A) In all likelihood, your daughter started masturbating because she accidentally discovered rubbing herself between her legs felt good.

In a well-adjusted child, who is active and enjoys good relationships with peers, there is no cause for concern. In fact, plenty of young children make this same discovery. You just don't hear parents talking about it for obvious reasons.

As you have learned, masturbation *cannot* be ignored. Nor *should* it be, since it is imperative the child learn that it isn't an acceptable thing to do when other people, even parents, can see.

So, you are obligated to say something about it. I recommend something along these lines: "We've noticed you seem to enjoy rubbing yourself between your legs. That's all right, but it is one of those things that shouldn't be done where other people can see you. We've decided you can rub yourself if you want to, but you must go to your room first. We also think there are better things to do with your time, like reading or playing outside. If you have trouble finding other things to do, let us know and we'll help."

Short, noncritical, and to the point. At school, her teacher should have a similar conversation with her and assign her a place to go if she feels an overwhelming urge. Chances are, she'll never have to use this special place.

She will probably continue to masturbate occasionally at

home for several months. Eventually, she'll tire of it and use her time more wisely.

If, however, you notice her spending increasing amounts of time in her room, then ask your pediatrician for a consultation.

(Q) Just the other day, I caught my five-year-old daughter and the boy next door, also five, playing at being a little more grown-up than I felt was appropriate, if you know what I mean. They had been playing in her room for quite some time when I went back to check and ask if they were interested in a snack. There they were, laughing and giggling with nothing but their underpants on. When I opened the door, their reaction told me they knew what they were doing wasn't proper. I'd rather not tell you how I handled it, because I don't want the whole world knowing if I blew it. But please tell me—and other parents who may someday find themselves in similar situations—how things like this ought to be handled.

(A) To begin with, what your daughter and her friend did is not unusual at all for four-, five-, and six-year-olds. Children this age have lots of questions and very few inhibitions, which can make for some exciting moments, as you've already discovered.

The naturally curious five-year-old is fascinated by the beginnings of life. She wants to know where babies come from, what pregnancy and birth are all about, what newborns are like, and so on. Sooner or later, she begins asking questions that deal with the sexual aspect of this whole mystery. And we answer her questions, with an emphasis on the general and simplistic, because that's all her little mind can grasp.

Our five-year-old is a concrete thinker, which is to say that she needs more than words to understand transcendental things like sex and death and fly-fishing. She needs pictures and demonstrations and other audio-visual aids. But when words are all adults will provide, and vague ones at that, our young one is left to her own creative devices. Somehow, she must translate the words into something concrete to which she can relate. So, at the first possible opportunity, she grabs some other child, who probably has similar questions, and says, "Hey! Let's act this whole sex thing out! Then maybe we'll understand it better!" They shift their gears into full-pretend and away they go, to the chagrin of parents who catch them at these innocent sports.

Low-key is the secret of success in situations such as these. Simply say something like, "You may not play this game, or games like it, until you are much older. Please put your clothes back on, and Billy, I think it would be best if you and Laura-Ann didn't play together for the rest of the day, so I'm sending you home."

In most cases, a "cooling-off" period of a day or so is advisable, but it shouldn't be put to the children as a punishment. In fact, there's no reason to punish at all, unless one or both of the children have already been told that the game is forbidden. You should also let the other child's parents know what happened and how you dealt with it. Under normal circumstances, and most of these circumstances are normal, there's no need to give the children the third-degree, or rush off to the psychologist's office. However, if this kind of behavior begins happening with some regularity, I'd recommend a professional evaluation. Repetitive behavior of this sort may be a symptom of sexual abuse.

A funny story, related to me by a single mother: One day, she caught her six-year-old daughter and an equally young male playmate out behind the garage pretending to be "married." Obviously, the game had gotten a bit out of hand, so she brought her daughter inside for the rest of the day. In the ensuing discussion, the mother asked, "Did the two of you pull your pants down?" A look of panic froze the little girl's face, and she quickly answered, "No, Mommy, we were just thinking about it!"

Art Linkletter was right.

Moral Development

Four- and five-year-olds are forming an elementary sense of moral values. They aren't capable of abstract thought, however, so they define "good" and "bad" in terms that are closely related to their need for approval. "Good" is doing what their parents approve of, and "bad" is what they disapprove of.

They are not yet able to apply moral concepts to a wide range of situations. For example, a four-year-old may be able to tell you that it would be wrong for him to take something from his friend's house (the concept of possession being fairly well established by this time), but he would not be able to apply the general principle that "stealing is wrong." If asked the question, "Why shouldn't you take a toy from Bobby's house?" he would probably answer, "'Cause it's Bobby's toy."

Furthermore, he doesn't understand why certain behavior is acceptable in some situations and not acceptable in others. He relies almost exclusively on signals from his parents and other adults to make these subtle distinctions and adjust his behavior accordingly.

For these reasons, it is essential that parents establish rules and guidelines solely in terms of what will and won't be allowed under each specific set of circumstances. The more talking and explaining parents do, the more the essential message—the rule—gets lost in the torrent of words.

Talk, Talk, Talk

Mikey is four years old. He's a smart little fella, full of mischief and stubborn as a mule. His parents are very conscious of the way they are raising him. They don't want to make *any* mistakes.

They believe the best way to teach Mikey the difference between right and wrong is to reason with him, thereby helping him to understand all the complicated "whys" and "why nots" of the world. Let's look in on the Mikey household to see if we can find an example. Ah, yes, his father is "reasoning" with him now:

"How many times do I have to tell you, Mikey, it's not nice to hit someone who is a guest in our home and then call him a 'pooh-pooh.' Reverend Diggs is our minister and he deserves to be treated with respect when he comes to visit. Hitting people and calling them names is bad manners. It's not polite, and you know better, don't you?"

Mikey nods.

"I thought so. When you hit someone who is a guest in our house and call them a name, they feel bad because they think you don't like them, and Mommy and I become angry when you do things like that because we've talked with you about hitting and name-calling before and blah, blah, blah. . . ."

Poor Mikey. He hasn't the vaguest notion of what his father means, but he knows enough to stand there and pretend to take it all in. He knows he's in trouble, but what's this about someone's name being called?

The truth is, Mikey isn't old enough to understand most of what his father is saying. In fact, the more his father talks, the *less* Mikey understands.

His father is well-meaning enough, and he certainly has a point—Mikey must learn to express his affection in some other way. But Mikey didn't know. He got carried away in his excitement. Unfortunately, at the end of his father's monologue, Mikey won't have learned much. In fact, the monologue is so confusing to a four-year-old that by the time it's over, Mikey will probably have forgotten how it all started in the first place.

The process of learning to talk involves more than learning to make certain sounds. It's like building a house, except this "house" takes at least twelve years to build and another six or eight years to put on the finishing touches. Talking involves learning thousands of associations between patterns of sound (words) and the things (nouns) or actions (verbs) they represent. Then the child must learn how and when to use all the qualifiers (adjectives and adverbs) that assign values to the nouns and verbs. Then he learns how to classify and organize words into larger units of meaning. Finally the child develops an appreciation for words which refer to ideas rather than objects. And through this entire process, the child is also learning a complex set of grammatical rules without which none of this makes any sense. Complicated, isn't it?

Mikey's "house" has a foundation. The walls for the first floor are slowly being put together. His father is throwing roofing shingles at him.

At four years, the Mikeys of the world can understand only words referring to things and actions—stuff they can see or feel with their senses.

Words like "respect" and "polite" evaporate in Mikey's brain. The key to understanding is *not* practice, it's *maturity.* Mikey's parents could drill him for a week on the meaning of "respect," and he still wouldn't know what it meant. He won't be able to understand "respect" next year or the year after that. In fact, an understanding of words like "respect" won't begin to emerge until Mikey is about seven or eight years old.

Let's go back to Mikey and his dad for a moment.

"Do you understand what I'm saying, Mikey?"

Mikey nods.

"Good. Now I don't want you being disrespectful to our guest and that includes name-calling. Do you understand?"

Mikey nods.

"Good. Now I want you to go tell Reverend Diggs you're sorry."

Mikey is a clever little munchkin. He has learned to escape the firing squad by nodding his head at just the right moment. He can tell when to nod by the changes in his father's tone of voice and facial expression.

Mikey will even apologize to the reverend, but he won't know why he's saying, "I'm sorry." He doesn't know what "sorry" means either. So, the next time there is a visitor, Mikey is just as likely to get excited and hit and say "pooh-pooh," and then everything will start all over again. Mikey's father will talk a mile a minute, and Mikey still won't know what he is talking about.

If you *must* reason with a young child, remember that you are helping him build a house. Make sure it's a solid structure. Don't try nailing on the roof before the walls are up. Observe three rules of thumb:

First, speak with the child immediately, before the memory fades away.

Second, use simple words that refer directly to *what* was done, *who* did it, and *who* or *what* was done to. Don't use words that refer to morals or ethics (such as "deserve," "respect," and "polite").

Third, do your reasoning in fifty words or less. Say your piece, and (if you feel it is necessary) assign some form of punishment. "Mikey, you hit Reverend Diggs and called him a 'pooh-pooh.' We don't hit or call people 'pooh-poohs.' Go to your room. Your timer is set for five minutes. You may come out when the bell rings."

Enough said. Mikey understands.

Ask Them No Questions, and . . .

Most lies young children tell are told because adults ask questions when they already know the answers.

For instance, four-year-old Minnie McSweeney is playing alone in her living room while her mother fixes their lunch. Suddenly, Mrs. McSweeney hears a loud crash from the living room and rushes in to find a vase in pieces on the floor and Minnie looking sheepish. In a demanding tone, Mrs. McSweeney asks, "Minnie McSweeney, did you knock this vase over?"

The question presents Minnie with a choice. She can admit to knocking the vase over, but Mom sounds angry, and that could mean a spanking. Or, Minnie can plead innocent and hope for the best. Either way, her odds aren't good, but Minnie decides in favor of deception. "No, Mommy," she replies, "I didn't knock it down. I was just playing and it fell. Honest."

Now Mrs. McSweeney has a dilemma on her hands. What's more important—the broken vase or the lie? If she responds only to the broken vase and ignores the lie, does she miss an opportunity to nip lying in the bud? Perhaps she should punish Minnie for lying, making it clear that had Minnie told the truth, she wouldn't have been punished at all. That, however, may give Minnie the impression she can avoid the consequences of her misdeeds by simply "'fessing up."

Suddenly, a minor incident has become thoroughly complicated. Every possible solution generates another problem. Furthermore, the problems aren't likely to end with the broken vase and Minnie's denial.

Because Mrs. McSweeney is sensitized to the possibility that Minnie will lie when confronted with a misdeed, she is likely to set up more "tests" of Minnie's truthfulness. The more questions she asks, the more lies she gets, and the bigger the issue of Minnie's moral depravity becomes.

A child caught up in situations like this learns parents expect her to lie, and so she does. To prevent this problem from taking root, remember the golden road to honesty and truth is by way of the old maxim, "Ask me no questions, and I'll tell you no fibs."

For instance Mrs. McSweeney could have said, "Minnie McSweeney, you broke my vase and now you must help me clean it up."

I'm reminded of an incident involving my daughter, Amy, who was five, and my son, Eric, then eight. Eric had begun saving his weekly allowance in a coffee can decorated with colored paper and crayon. One day, he and Amy were in his room and I was one bedroom over, relaxing. It registered that Eric came out of his room and went downstairs. Soon after, Amy emerged from Eric's room, walked into her bedroom, and shut the door. A minute or so later, Eric returned to his room. Amy then opened her door and went downstairs. Several minutes after all this, Eric was standing next to me, looking upset.

"Dad," he said, "I need your help. While Amy was in my room, I took my money out and counted it. Then I put it away and went downstairs for a drink of water. Now my money's gone and Amy's the only person who could have taken it. But if I ask her for it, she'll say she doesn't have it and we'll get into a fight. So, will you tell her to give it back to me?"

After thinking it over, I said, "Yeah, you're right. This is one situation involving the two of you that I'd best handle. You just go into your room and I'll take care of things." Walking to the top of the stairs, I called for Amy.

She peeked around the corner. "Yes, Daddy?"

"Come up here. I want to talk to you." When she reached the top step, I knelt down eye-level with her, extended my hand palm up, and said, "Go get the money you took from Eric's room and give it to me."

Immediately, her eyes grew wide, her chin dropped, and from behind this mask of utter incredulity she said, "What money?"

"Eric's money," I replied. "The money you took from his room."

Again the mask and the innocent voice. "I didn't take any money from Eric, Daddy. I don't know what you're talking about."

"Yes you do, Amy. When Eric left his room, you took the money from his can and put it either in your room or downstairs. Now go get it and put it in my hand and we'll all forget this ever happened. I'm not waiting any longer."

Slowly, the mask dissolved, only to be replaced with a look consisting of equal parts disgust and wonderment. Her eyes narrowed. "How did you know?" she asked.

I lied. "I know everything."

"Do You Believe In . . . ?"

(Q) I have a five-year-old daughter with whom I feel I have an open and trusting relationship. The problem that I am at a loss to deal with involves my religious views. Through family members, kindergarten, and friends my daughter is exposed to a belief system that I do not share. I am not necessarily opposed to this, but I feel reluctant to share my religious views with her for fear that if she repeats my thoughts and ideas, she will be ostracized at a time in her life when she is not able to deal with it. And yet, she is beginning to ask me questions about my beliefs. In the past I have responded to her questions with, "Yes, lots of people believe that." Now, she asks "Do *you* believe that?" How do I maintain the openness we have without endangering the relationships she has with others?

(A) More important than the need to protect your daughter from having differences of opinion with other children is her need to know exactly where you stand on these issues.

At this time in her life, her need to identify with you takes precedence over peer affiliations and peer approval. You are her primary role model and she is consciously striving to pattern herself after you—your behavior, your interests, your ideas. She looks to you to set the standards and wants only to follow your example. And yes, she *will* identify with your beliefs and claim them as her own.

You are also her primary source of security and will continue to be for the next seven years (or thereabouts) as she goes about finding a comfortable place for herself within her own generation. Before she ventures into new social territory, however, she must have a blueprint for behavior, and the directions must be clear. She depends on you to show her the way, but in this instance, it sounds as though she's having some difficulty "reading" you.

If you make it difficult for her to pin you down (remember, she doesn't know that you are trying to protect her), she will become "hung up" on the question, "What does Mommy believe?" The vague, evasive quality of your answers will frustrate her and stimulate feelings of insecurity. In an effort to reduce her anxiety, she will fixate on the religious issue until you clarify matters for her.

Furthermore, she may interpret your discomfort as a sign that you are ill-at-ease with your own beliefs—that perhaps *you* feel something is wrong with them. Otherwise, why the game of hide-and-seek?

I also think you may be overestimating the significance of her religious beliefs to her acceptance among her peers. A child's religious views, or the religious persuasion of her parents, is relatively insignificant to the social process at this age. Young school-age children don't ostracize one another because of differences in race, religion, politics, or what-have-you unless their parents encourage them to. The exception would be the child who wore her differences "on her sleeve."

Answer her questions. I would suggest, however, that instead of telling her what you *don't* believe, you answer her primarily in terms of what you *do* believe. Keep in mind that five-year-old children cannot understand philosophical abstractions. Explain your beliefs clearly, concisely, and concretely.

For the sake of trust.

"I Hate You!"

(Q) Whenever I make my five-year-old angry, she tells me she hates me. This happens when I make her do something she doesn't want to do or refuse to give her something she wants. Nearly every time I have to discipline. If I try to explain myself to her, she just gets more upset and more belligerent. What am I doing wrong?

(A) The only thing you're doing wrong is taking her seriously. Children your daughter's age think in absolutes. In other words, things are either black or white; there are no in-betweens. So, when you frustrate her by making her do something odious, like setting the table, or refusing to give in to a demand, she "hates" you. If, on the other hand, you let her do just as she pleases, she "loves" you.

You're attributing too much significance to your daughter's use of the word "hate." When an adult says he hates someone or something, it indicates a deep loathing, a repulsion that often carries with it feelings of ill will. When a five-year-old says "I hate you!" it means you've done something to make her mad. Since five-year-olds are still fairly self-centered, it doesn't take much to make them mad. It's part of a parent's job to set limits on what children can and can't do. Limits are frustrating. So, if a five-year-old is going to hate anybody, it's going to be her parents.

When you react to "I hate you!" as if it's something to be

taken seriously, you make matters worse. Acting as if she really understands the implications of what she's saying gives it credence. She sees it gets to you, so she starts saying it more often. The more she says it, the more seriously you take it, and the more credence you give it and . . . get the point?

At the very least, the more she says it, the more it's likely to become habit. A further danger lies in the fact that young children don't question their parents' beliefs. If the parent believes a certain way, the child "believes" it, too. It follows that if you act as if you believe your daughter truly hates you, she's liable to begin believing it as well.

For all these reasons, you must not tolerate your daughter saying things of this sort. On the other hand, you mustn't respond to it in an emotionally charged way. Letting her see that it makes you mad or upset will only make matters worse. You have to stop taking the words themselves seriously, while at the same time making it clear that talk of this sort is not allowed.

First, strike while the iron is cold by sitting down with her and telling her that, while you understand you sometimes make her mad, saying "I hate you!" isn't an appropriate way of handling her anger. Tell her you're going to send her to her room for fifteen minutes whenever she lets it slip.

This preliminary conversation puts you in position to strike while the iron is hot. The next time she loses control and says she hates you, don't threaten, warn, or admonish. Just send her to her room for fifteen minutes. If she quickly apologizes, say, "I know you're sorry, and I accept your apology, but you still have to go to your room." Use a timer to let her know when the fifteen minutes is up. That prevents having to deal with fifteen minutes of "Can I come out now?"

"I Need You"

(Q) My four-year-old is driving me up a wall. She can't seem to get enough of my attention. To begin with, she follows me from room to room all day long. If I tell her to leave me alone for a while, she looks hurt, so I find myself letting my frustration build until I can't take it anymore, at which point I explode. Then she cries and I feel guilty and things start all over again. In addition to following me, she asks me to do things for her that she is capable of doing for herself—help with her bath, dress her, zip her coat, carry her in stores, and so on and so on and so on. "Manipulation" is the term my pediatrician used. But labels won't solve the problem. Meanwhile, I feel like I'm going down for the third time. Help!

(A) Oh, all right! I'll help! Anything to get you to stop pestering me!

I'll bet that sounds familiar. Kind of stings a little bit too, doesn't it?

"But John," you might say, "I really need help, whereas she doesn't truly need me for all those things."

Maybe so, but keep in mind that she is as convinced of her needs as you are of yours. In other words, she is not, as your pediatrician says, manipulating you. She is as much a victim of the vicious cycle as you. Furthermore, she is not *in* control, she is *out* of control.

As things stand, your feelings of helplessness are a direct reflection of hers. You feel helpless to stop her and she feels helpless to stop herself. Furthermore, her independence is simply an extension of yours. Her only salvation (and yours) is your ability to control her, however misplaced it might be.

The least painful, fastest-acting method of reestablishing control in a situation such as yours involves three steps.

• Make a list of the things she asks you to do for her that she can either do for herself or that you want her to learn to do independently. Then assign a value of either 1 (things she can do quite easily), 2 (things which might frustrate her slightly, but which she is still capable of doing), or 3 (things which she doesn't know how to do, but can learn) to each item on the list.

• Draw an elongated rectangle on a sheet of paper, divide it into five boxes, and number the boxes left to right from five to one. Make thirty copies of this chart.

• This is the crucial step. I call it "The Conversation," and it must be done with *authority.*

Sit your daughter down at some relatively peaceful time and clearly spell out a new set of rules for the relationship. It could go something like this: "I'm going to talk to you about following me around and asking me to do things for you.

"First, following me around: I've decided that you can follow me five times a day and no more. I'm going to keep track of how many times you follow me by putting this chart up every morning and marking out a number, beginning with five, each time you follow me. When all the boxes are gone, you can't follow me anymore. If you do, I will put you in your room for ten minutes. Every morning I put up a new chart and we start all over again.

"Next, asking me to do things for you that you can do for yourself: Here is a list of all the things you want me to do for you that you could be doing for yourself (go over it). Now, here is a second list of the things I will still do for you (all the twos and threes from the master list). If you want me to do something for you and it's not on the list, I won't do it. If it's something new, I'll decide whether you need my help or not.

"If you scream or cry because I won't do something, you'll go to your room until you get control of yourself. In weeks to come, this list is going to get shorter and shorter and shorter until there is no list and you're doing everything you don't need me for on your own (cross out the twos over several weeks time, then start on the threes). We're going to call it 'Marnie's Growing Up List' because growing up means you learn to do things without Mommy's help."

The only thing left is to be firm and follow through. When she follows you, simply say, "You are following me, so I have to take a number off your chart." (Important! Don't threaten, just remove the number.) If she asks for help with something that isn't on the list, just point that out to her and go on with what you were doing—"Sorry, Marnie, but that's been taken off your list."

The first several weeks might be tough, as Marnie tests your resolve and adjusts to a radically new concept of what Mommy is for.

Then again, she might welcome the structure and the control and things might go smoothly from the start. In either case, just keep one thing squarely in mind.

You're doing this for her.

(Q) Our four-and-a-half-year-old daughter constantly asks for reassurance that we're not just going to take her someplace, like preschool or a baby-sitter's or church nursery, and never come back to get her. She separates from us easily enough, but never without asking, "Are you coming back for me?" and "When?" This happens regardless of how familiar the place and people we're leaving her with. Likewise, we always tell her that of course we're coming back and we'd never leave you and so on, but the next time we take her someplace, we get the same questions. We don't know how she became so insecure, because we've always been reliable and she's never had a bad experience away from us. Do you have explanations and/or suggestions?

(A) I'll bet you do the same thing with one another your daughter is doing with you. Proof: When one of you leaves the house to drive to some relatively distant place, your mate gives you a hug and a kiss and says, "Promise me you'll drive carefully." And you say, "I promise" as automatically as you say "fine" when someone asks how you feel.

In a sense, asking someone for a promise of safe driving is the same as asking, "You will come back, won't you?" Call it insecurity if you will, we all have it to one degree or another, and separation from a loved one is perhaps the likeliest trigger.

The problem with the separation issue is, it never goes away. It's with us from the day we're born till the day we die, and so is the anxiety. Most of us develop fairly effective ways of dealing with the insecurity of it all by the time we're three or four years old. One of the most common coping mechanisms is termed a "separation ritual."

A separation ritual, as the name implies, is an essentially meaningless exchange between two people about to separate from one another. The person who initiates the ritual is usually asking for reassurance that the separation isn't permanent. The other person, usually the one leaving, is obliged to reassure. Obviously, there's a certain amount of absurdity involved in all this, because no one can ever predict for certain that any given separation *won't* be permanent.

So, mothers tell their children to "be careful" when riding their bikes around the neighborhood, and wives make their husbands promise to drive safely when they're about to embark on a business trip, and your daughter asks if you're coming back when you drop her off at preschool.

Parents easily lose perspective on things like this when their own children are involved. I suppose it's because we're so afraid of warping them that we're supersensitive to any indication that we already have. But fear not! The fact is, your daughter's no more insecure about separating from you than the average four-year-old. And, relatively speaking, she's no more insecure about separating from you than you are about separating from one another.

The most truthful answer to "Are you coming back for me?" is "I don't know." But the point of ritual is that no one wants to face the truth, just like no one really wants to know how you are today, and you don't really want to tell them. The proper thing to do, therefore, is simply provide the reassurance your daughter's asking for: "Yes, we're coming back for you, because we love you."

(Q) At least ten times a day, every day, my four-year-old daughter asks me if I love her. Several months ago, when this first started, I thought it was a phase that would pass quickly, but instead of tapering off, it has gotten steadily worse. Whenever she asks, I tell her that, yes, I love her very much and always will. It's gotten to the point where I don't know what more she could possibly want to hear. The look of desperation on her face when she asks is disturbing to me, because I can't understand why she would need so much reassurance or what has caused her to become so insecure. What would you advise?

(A) I would advise that you help your daughter stop asking the question so much.

In the first place, asking "Do you love me?" ten times a day doesn't mean your daughter is insecure. It means she's four years old and doesn't know what "love" means or how long it lasts. Repetition is one way children answer questions of this nature for themselves.

Until a child is eight or ten months old, for instance, she does not know that objects are permanent. If you capture a six-month-old's interest by moving a brightly colored object through her field of vision and then hide it behind your back while she's still looking, she won't come in search of it because, in her mind, the object no longer exists. Several months later, she will respond to the same tease by crawling around behind you to find it. By this age, the infant is well on her way to establishing that objects do not cease to exist when they are out of sight.

I have watched a ten-month-old amuse himself by placing a block inside one of his mother's kitchen pots, putting the lid on the pot, and then immediately taking it off to rediscover the "lost" block. Just like a good scientist should, he repeated this simple experiment over and over again until he had proven to himself that the block was forever.

In like manner, your daughter is trying to establish the identity and permanence of an intangible concept—an invisible idea—by taking the lid off the question "Do you love me?" time and time again.

The problem, if there is one, is that adults are generally insecure about their ability to raise children and tend, therefore, to look for and seize upon every possible indication that something is terribly wrong. In our zeal to prove ourselves incompetent, we strive to blow the significance of things completely out of proportion.

At some point, your daughter probably began to sense that the question made you feel somewhat uncomfortable. Needing to understand why Mommy got so flustered, she began asking the question more frequently, in every possible situation she could think of. The more she asked, the more flustered you became, the more she asked and so on.

Both of you are riding the same merry-go-round. You don't know how to stop getting flustered and she doesn't know how to stop asking the question. So, as I said to begin with, help her.

Find a peaceful, relaxed time for the two of you to sit down together. Tell her that "I love you" is like a piece of candy people surprise one another with and that you want to begin surprising her with it, too. Make sure she knows that you can't surprise her as long as she continues to ask. In the future, when and if she asks, say something like, "Oh-oh, now it's not a surprise."

Meanwhile, make it a point to call her over to you several times a day to play "Guess What?"

"Guess what?"

"What?"

"I love you."

Personally, I can't think of a nicer surprise.

Six to Eleven: Middle Childhood

The psychology of the young school-aged child can be summarized in two words: acceptance and achievement. Her self-esteem hinges on her success at creating a secure place for herself in the social matrix of her peer group and at establishing and attaining specific goals of excellence.

A child must now learn to apply herself to a variety of challenging, and often demanding, tasks. In doing so, she draws on the trust, autonomy, initiative, and imaginative playfulness she acquired during her preschool years.

Children whose preschool years were a success are prepared to meet the social, intellectual, and emotional challenges of middle childhood. They are able to take reasonable risks with confidence; they are increasingly self-rewarding and self-motivated; they accept, and even seek, increased responsibility, and they continue to experiment with new expressions of independence and autonomy.

On the other hand, the child who arrives at this crossroads with a burden of "unfinished business" may have difficulty in the new roles expected of her by her parents, teachers, and peers.

Going to school introduces a child to new social, emotional, and intellectual pressures. For the first time she must adapt to a new set of intellectual and behavioral expectations. Being a "student" requires greater independence of thought and behavior, places greater distance between the child and her parents, introduces her to new authority figures, and brings her into closer proximity with her peers.

As a child broadens her social base and expands her range of interests and activities, she establishes significant and relatively enduring precedents for herself within her peer group. Her social personality is negotiated through interaction with other children her age and defined in large measure by the roles she is assigned or acquires within the tribe.

Most children, by the time they are six years old, have internalized the behavioral limits taught them by their parents. From this time on, a child's attention shifts toward learning the implicit and explicit rules that mediate behavior within the peer group. Her moral judgment is further elaborated through participation in rule-governed activities—competitive games, structured play, and so on—and the relatively formal atmosphere of the classroom.

Although she is capable of applying moral and ethical principles across a fairly wide range of situations, a school-age child's moral judgments tend to be dogmatic, rigid, and egocentric. Typical peer conflicts at this age involve arguments over whose point of view is "right," who behaved correctly, who broke a rule, and so on. Young school-aged children compare themselves to each other in every conceivable way. Everything is a contest, from the absurd to the trivial.

(Q) I have an eight-year-old who is supersensitive. He believes everything other children tell him. Recently, he proudly told one of his friends that he had sold twenty tickets to the school fair. The other child said that *he* had sold one hundred tickets (which wasn't true). My son believed him and felt terrible because he hadn't sold as many. I've explained how and why children sometimes stretch the truth, but my son continues to believe everything he is told. What can I do to help him understand?

(A) In any competitive situation, there is a risk that someone may experience emotional pain. Learning how to compete involves learning to accept and deal with losing in such a way that it doesn't threaten self-esteem.

In this respect, the "supersensitive" child is at a disadvantage. Supersensitive, however, is a label *you,* his parents, have selected and attached to him. It actually says more about *you* than your son. Because you think of him as "fragile," you are inclined to react protectively when the competition puts him down.

It is understandable for parents to feel protective when their children hurt, but reacting protectively is not *always* in children's best interest. Supersensitive becomes a self-fulfilling prophecy when parents' reactions prevent children from confronting situations on their own and learning from them.

In other words, you may be doing too much *taking care of,* when what your son needs is enough space to learn how to take better care of himself. An overdose of sympathy can be addicting.

I suggest that you simply reflect the content of these situations back to him in a fairly objective way, while acknowledging his feelings and helping him explore more successful ways of handling these problems. For instance, "Mark wants to be better at selling tickets than you, and you want to be better than Mark. When Mark told you he sold one hundred tickets, how did you feel? . . . Do you think Mark really sold one hundred tickets? . . . Why did he tell you that? . . . Let's talk about what you can do next time something like this happens, so you don't end up feeling so awful. . . . Have *you* got any ideas?"

Take the emphasis off self-pity and focus his energy on solving the problem. His self-confidence rests on being able to do that for himself, and he needs to hear you saying, "I know it's hard, but you can do it."

You may have to settle for a "sensitive" child, but he can still be "super!"

(Q) We recently moved into a neighborhood where there are many children about the same age as our eight-year-old daughter. The other children gang up and pick on her almost constantly. I have watched them take things away from her, tease her until she cries, make fun of her, exclude her from their games, and call her names. She comes home crying several times a day. I have talked and talked with her about staying away from them, but as soon as we talk and she stops crying, she wants to go back for more. She gets along fine with each of the children individually, but as a group they are mean to her. Should I handle it by not letting her play with them for a while or letting her play with them only if I supervise? Or should I talk with the children or their parents?

(A) Don't do any of the above. The correct answer is, stay out of it.

Something needs to be done, but the doing needs to be done with your daughter. There is more going on than meets the eye.

The treatment she is getting comes with being the new kid in town. Her arrival threatens to rearrange the fragile structure of the group as well as to break up some of the tenuous alliances the "old-timers" have with one another. So the group reacts protectively. You said it yourself: individually, the children have nothing against her—collectively, she is regarded as an untouchable. She is being slowly initiated into the group's pecking order.

The more serious problem is a paradox: You must act to prevent your daughter from growing into a victim role, but you must not interfere in the victimization. The role of "victim" is a seductive one because it evokes a potent, yet destructive, reinforcer—sympathy.

Furthermore, by accepting the underdog's definition of herself, along with the notion that she needs you (and only you) to help her, you can become that person's "lifeguard." You get to feel competent and needed; a strong temptation to resist. And finally, the "villain," by virtue of the "victim's" helplessness, gets to feel powerful. Each role complements the other two. Villains need victims who need someone else to give them sympathy and a helping hand. This triangular drama is addicting and self-perpetuating because everybody gets something out of the arrangement. It's a soap opera, every bit as enticing and repetitious as any you can find on the tube.

Back off. A victim without a "lifeguard" must either sink or swim. When a victim starts swimming, she's no longer a victim. I'll bet your daughter can swim. Obviously, she is in no real danger and wants to be with these other children, so let the problem be hers.

If you don't have a kitchen timer, get one. Every time your daughter comes home crying after an encounter with her tormentors, tell her she needs a "rest" and that she must stay indoors for thirty minutes. Set the timer to signal when she can go back outside. During this time, you can listen and reflect her statements back to her, but don't discuss her anguish in sympathetic terms. Persistent crying should be done in her room, alone.

If she is playing outside, and you hear her crying, go out and bring her in, with the same instructions (these suggestions do not apply to cuts, bumps, bruises, and other injuries to the body.) She may want to know why you aren't doing something about the horrible way the kids treat her. You can say something like, "Those aren't *my* playmates. They are *your* friends, and *you* will have to learn how to get along with them. I can't do anything except talk to you about it. Do you want to talk?"

Perhaps the most difficult thing about being a parent is having to make certain decisions that force your children to stand on their own, even when they tell you they can't.

(Q) We have a son, seven, who has a tendency to be rude and bossy to his friends when they come over. Not always, but often enough to concern us, he will refuse to share toys with them, order them around, and become angry and verbally abusive toward them when they don't do what he wants. We've spoken to him many times about his responsibilities toward his guests, but his behavior doesn't change. He tells us that these other children treat him the same way when he is in their homes. Even if this is true, it makes no difference. We have thought about sending his friends home when he is rude to them, and we have considered ignoring it altogether and just letting them work it out. Which approach do you favor?

(A) For the most part, I'd just let the kids work it out, but if the situation really gets out of hand, send the other children home and confine yours to his room for a few hours. There is another way of handling it, but first, understand that your son's behavior is perfectly normal for this age child. Furthermore, his little friends no doubt treat him likewise when he is in their domain, not out of spite, but simply because this kind of social behavior is more the norm than the exception at this age.

The territorial instinct is as basic to human psychology as it is in the animal kingdom, the difference being that among us humans, efforts are made to cloak it in a mantle of politeness. When we say that a child "can't share" or "must be the boss" in a group, we are referring to the fact that that child's territorial instinct has not yet been completely socialized.

For reasons that probably have more to do with biology than upbringing, the territorial instinct is stronger in some children than others. In a group of two-year-olds, for instance, the more territorial tots will occupy and aggressively defend certain play areas, while the less territorial ones will shy away from conflict.

Our culture, for better or worse, rewards territorial people; they create high expectations for themselves, pursue goals aggressively, and, consequently, get things done. They're the "go-getters" of the world and probably, as a rule, more intelligent. In thirty years, our highly territorial two-year-olds will probably be executives giving directions while more passive tots will be taking them.

So, your son is territorial. Slowly but surely, he's learning to socialize his inner yearning to always run the show when he plays with other children, particularly equally territorial ones, whom he is likely to choose as friends (birds of a feather, you know). As a three-year-old, he reluctantly learned to take turns. Later, he learned to give and take. At this stage, he can share, but if the sharing must take place on his turf, then it must also take place on his terms. When he's on a friend's turf, the roles reverse.

When my daughter was your son's age and equally territorial with her equally territorial friends, my wife and I would occasionally employ the "humiliation method." Most of the time, we just left the children to their uncivilized selves, but if Amy really started lording it over on the other children, one of us would step in and say something like, "Amy, I can't believe what I'm hearing from you. You're being very rude to your little friend, and that is certainly not the way we treat guests in our home. I'm sure that your selfishness is hurting your friend's feelings. It's also hurting mine to hear you treating her this way. If you don't stop right now, I'll have no choice but to send your friend home and keep you in your room the rest of the day."

We never had to follow through with our promise, because Amy would straighten up after one of these "talks." They took place every now and then for a couple of years until there was no longer any need for them. Eventually, if she was with a friend and wound up "running the show," she did so politely. I couldn't ask for more than that.

(Q) Our nine-year-old son seems uninterested in making friends. Both at school and in the neighborhood, he seems content to play by himself, even when other kids are available. He's been like this since he was very young, and we always thought he'd grow out of it, but the older he gets, the more concerned we have become. We've tried pairing him with more assertive children, but with little success. We'd like to help him improve his self-esteem to where he'd feel socially comfortable. Do you have any suggestions?

(A) Whoa! Slow down! What makes you think this is a self-esteem problem? The fact is, some children are socially outgoing, while others, like your son, are more introverted. The child who prefers solitary pursuits over social interaction doesn't necessarily have a problem. Introversion is simply a personality characteristic, and recent studies have determined that an individual's social style is strongly influenced by genetic factors. The fact that your son has never shown great interest in other children suggests this feature of his personality may have roots in his genetic makeup.

Don't confuse his social reticence with shyness, either. A shy person feels genuinely uncomfortable in social situations and avoids them for that reason. A person who is a "loner" by choice doesn't necessarily feel self-conscious or anxious when alone. The loner simply "wants to be alone."

Trying to stimulate extroversion by matching your son up with outgoing children isn't going to work and may even backfire. Children of similar social styles tend to get along better than children of opposite social styles. In other words, two outgoing children or two relatively passive children will play more successfully with one another than one outgoing child and one introverted child. Matching your son with an extrovert may cause him to become intimidated and make him that much more inclined to avoid social interaction.

As I said, this isn't a self-esteem issue, but it could become one, especially if your son begins to sense that you think something's wrong with his social performance. If he begins to feel that he's not living up to your expectations, he could conceivably develop feelings of self-doubt and experience a lowering of self-esteem.

I suggest you leave this issue alone. Don't worry about it. Like they say, "It takes all kinds." Let him find his own social comfort level and, for the most part, make his own social choices. When opportunities present themselves, you might match him with other children who are similarly inclined, but I wouldn't suggest that you go out of your way to manufacture these opportunities or push them in his direction.

Now, the fact that we're talking about the possibility of genetic influence doesn't mean this part of your son's personality is written in stone. This isn't like having either blue eyes or brown. Genes *influence* personality, they don't make final determinations. During his teen or early adult years, his social style may change in response to the peer group. Then again, it may not.

Either way, he'll work it out. Trust him.

(Q) Our seven-year-old is in the second grade in a public school. However, all of the other children her age in our neighborhood attend the local private school. We decided to "buck the system" and put her in public school because we believe in the concept of public education and want to support it.

We also feel that public school children receive a more well-rounded educational experience and, because they go to school with children from all walks of life, make a better adjustment as adults.

Our problem is this: Because she doesn't go to school with the children in the neighborhood, she finds herself left out of things like neighborhood birthday parties and spend-the-nights.

Likewise, she doesn't have classmates to play with after school and they don't invite her to parties and such either. We've invited some of her classmates over to play, but importing children to play with just isn't the same as having kids to play with in the neighborhood.

Our daughter has started to complain of having no one to play with, and we're beginning to worry that perhaps our decision to put her in public school is becoming a real handicap for her. What advice do you have for us?

(A) Like you, I also believe in the concept of public education. Both of our children have always attended public schools and will probably attend public universities.

However, I am also a realist who believes that there are times when practical considerations must outweigh philosophical ones. Your daughter is at an age when her social experience is of extreme importance. Increasingly, her social success will bear significantly upon her security and self-esteem.

In fact, the social and extra-curricular aspects of school are as important to a child's overall growth and development as the academic aspect. A frustrating social experience is likely to result in diminished self-esteem, which, in turn, can impair motivation and school performance. In other words, if the "social domino" falls, it's going to topple others as well.

In my practice, I've seen children who were seriously depressed and doing poorly in school because they felt they had no friends. When the social problems were corrected, these children usually began making better grades.

If you think you've given the present situation your best shot and it doesn't seem to be improving, and you're confident that your daughter would be happier with her friends in the private school, then make the move. All things considered, it sounds like the wise thing to do.

Your concerns that private school might adversely affect your daughter's ability to make a successful adjustment to a more pluralistic adult society is one shared by many; however, there really is no basis for believing that private-school children have any more adjustment problems in adult life than children who grow up attending public schools.

Nor is there evidence that private-school children are more narrow-minded, prejudiced, or suffer from any of the other personality quirks that some narrow-minded critics would attribute to them.

Junior Jekyll and Master Hyde

(Q) My son is six years old and in first grade. At home he is a real problem—disobedient, boisterous, and generally hard to handle. I went for my first conference with his teachers braced for the worst. Instead, they told me he is one of the best-behaved children and one of the best readers in the room. I had no idea. Since then, I've tried to get him to read to me at home, but he refuses (as usual). I don't get it. What am I doing wrong? Or, what are *they* doing right?

(A) Children are far more likely to engage in conflicts with their parents than their teachers. This is number thirty-nine of the time-honored Fifty Ways to Grieve Your Mother: Be the teacher's perfect precious and bite Mommy on the leg—or her ego (whichever is more vulnerable).

There are at least five reasons why number thirty-nine has become a tradition with children:

First reason: A teacher's role is more clearly defined than a mother's. Teachers are for teaching, which they do from eight A.M. until three P.M., Monday through Friday, nine months a year.

Mothers are for . . . everything, which they are expected to do . . . always. There's vast territory for a child to explore in his relationship with his mother, because the limits of that relationship are vague. So, anything goes—or can at least be tried.

"Teacher" is an occupation. Her status as an authority figure is clear and has institutional support. But, if it makes you feel better, consider that plenty of teachers who have no problem managing thirty children in a classroom can't get a handle on the one they have at home. A teacher's a teacher and a mother's a mother, and never the twain shall overlap.

Second reason: Mothers tend to take out one heck of an emotional mortgage on each of their children, with lifetime payments and no insurance. This investment makes objectivity almost impossible. A mother's self-esteem, sense of competence, and well-being are all too often tied up in her children and their behavior. There can be a problem of separating who is who.

Teachers are paid to be objective. Aren't they lucky?

Third reason: Rules are more clearly defined at school than they are at home. Parents often expect "good" behavior without defining exactly what "good" means. Furthermore, parents are more likely to make exceptions, overlook things (hoping they will go away) and fight with one another over how to enforce rules. Parents often act confused, which is not lost on children.

A teacher's rules are usually few and clear. She enforces quickly, makes few exceptions, and her spouse is not in the classroom. She is clearly "The Boss."

Fourth reason: In school, a child can observe the behavior of other children and follow their example. This *can,* and does, work both for good and ill, but the group usually pressures its members to behave in ways that enhance its image. Classmates expect every child to contribute to the collective identity and shun children who detract from that image.

Fifth reason: At home, within the family, the entire course of a child's upbringing is charged with the issue of autonomy and independence. The basic question of how much independence is possible, and by what means it is obtained, is central to a child's participation in the family. By its very nature, this issue *demands* that children be somewhat rebellious. Some conflict between parents and children is not only inevitable, but healthy. It is the parents' responsibility *to the child* to contain that rebellion within safe, reasonably appropriate limits.

At school, on the other hand, the central issue is achievement, which often requires cooperation. Because rebellion is incompatible with the expectations of the classroom, the likelihood of conflict between teacher and student is considerably lessened. Children who rebel in school are those for whom the challenge is too great or not great enough, those who have not been able to rebel effectively at home and those who have difficulty fitting in the social configuration of the group.

Your little James Dean is a rebel *with* a cause at home because he has developed a consuming sense of autonomy and an appreciation for his own individuality. He cooperates with the teacher because he has developed a sense of initiative and a will to achieve.

Congratulations on a job well done.

Organized Sports

(Q) What do you think about organized, competitive sports for children? Our son is eight years old, and the current craze among the neighborhood children his age is Pee-Wee Football. Actually, the adults appear at least as excited about it as the kids. The way the parents behave at the games makes me wonder whether they haven't got big money riding on the outcome. The same mania sweeps through the neighborhood in the spring, during Little League season. We are caught between wanting our son to feel that he's part of the group and not wanting him to learn, at this age, that winning a game is the most important thing in life.

(A) Organized activities of this nature are inappropriate during middle childhood (ages six to ten). Though organized sports might seem ideal for children at this competitive age, it's not so.

To begin with, adults are overly involved in these activities, both in terms of their presence and their emotional investment. Adults organize, raise the money, draw up the playing schedule, pick the teams, coach, referee, give out awards, and make up the biggest share of the audience.

But it doesn't stop there. Not only do big people play too

prominent a role in planning and organizing these events; they can also be found defining and mediating social issues, encouraging rivalries, conferring status as they see fit, and resolving conflicts.

Adults have no business being that entangled in the play of children. Their involvement is a complicating factor that prevents the children from learning to resolve certain critical issues on their own. Instead of being activities for children, Pee-Wee Football and Little League Baseball become theaters where youngsters are manipulated for the ego gratification of adults.

That these sports are competitive is not, in itself, disturbing. This age child needs and, left to his own devices, will seek out appropriate competitive experiences. What *is* disturbing is that children who are caught up in these sports don't play simply for the sake of the game—for the fun of it, that is—but play to obtain adult approval. In fact, they don't really *play* at all. They *work*, performing for the crowd.

The difference between competitive play and competitive work can be measured in terms of emotional outcome. When children band together to play a sandlot game, one group wins and one group loses, but everyone usually leaves the field feeling O.K. When adults direct an organized sports event, the children on the losing team often end up feeling angry, dejected, frustrated, ashamed, and depressed. This isn't play. This is serious business, and the stakes are high—too high. Under pressure from adults to perform, the child athlete's sense of achievement and self-esteem becomes defined in terms of winning and losing. Process and participation take a backseat to outcome, which isn't what being a child is about. Everyone suffers, including the children who don't get to play because they aren't "good" enough.

The basic problem—and one that isn't limited to this issue—is adults' tendency to act as though children will botch the job of growing up unless we engineer the process for them. The opposite is true. When we place ourselves *between* the child and the challenge of growing up, we are no longer in a helpful position. Instead, we are interfering and, to that extent, the child is ultimately less capable of dealing with life.

Guidance, support, encouragement, supervision—these are things children need from us. Carry them too far, however, and they become pure meddling.

Allowances

No one has more right to complain about inflation than this country's children. Recent trends have conclusively proven what old-timers in Maine have been saying all along—"As the economy goes, so goes the allowance."

Since the first of the year, this key economic indicator has plunged a record twelve points. In the wake of management's refusal to negotiate the level of this peculiar dole, episodes of panic bubble-gum buying have been reported in several junior high schools.

Concern over the effects this allotment can have on the economy is reflected in the increasing number of questions I've been receiving on the subject, including the following:

(Q) At what age should a child be started on an allowance?
(A) As a rule of thumb, it makes sense to start a child on a small allowance at the same time her teacher begins instruction in the mathematics of money. Preschool children are generally unable to grasp that the amount of money they have places an upper limit on *what* and *how much* they can purchase. In the child's eyes, there is no correspondence between the size or desirability of an item and its cost. Until a child is old enough to understand the idea of exchange and deal with the complexities involved, I recommend that parents limit her experience with money to certain exercises in *paying* for things.

(Q) Should a child be required to earn his allowance by doing chores around the house?
(A) Absolutely not. The question of how much the child is expected to contribute to household maintenance is *completely* unrelated to the allowance issue.

The child's allowance should be for the sole purpose of giving him opportunities to practice efficient money management. It should *not* be manipulated to persuade the child to carry out his assigned duties, nor should it be suddenly withdrawn to punish him for inappropriate behavior.

Chores are for developing responsibility, self-discipline, and other essentials, but it takes the better part of childhood for this lesson to take hold. Given a choice between developing some responsibility and riding a bicycle, most children will choose the latter. Therefore, parents must make the choice, and once made, enforce it.

It boils down to a simple matter of obedience, for which there is but one effective incentive—parental authority. In the end, children do chores because they are *told* to do them.

Parents who exchange money in return for chores are unwittingly undermining themselves. When money is used to mediate this aspect of the parent-child relationship, people lose sight of the basic issues of authority and obedience.

Every child needs to learn the value of chores, and every child needs to learn the value of the dollar, and parents need to make sure the lessons don't get mixed up.

(Q) Is it all right for parents to give a child a chance to earn extra money by doing special work beyond what's expected of her?
(A) Certainly. Chores are those jobs which are part of the household routine—taking out the garbage, feeding the pet iguana, and so on. It's perfectly acceptable for parents to contract with their children for work other than regular chores, though deals of this nature should be the exception rather than the rule. No one should forget that, within the family, work is *not* done for money, but simply because it needs to be done.

(Q) What should children be required to spend their own money for?
(A) That's an interesting question. In the first place, the child's allowance is *not her money.* It is the *parents' money,* which is shared with the child to teach her how to use it.

Parents should keep tabs on how the child intends to use the money and retain the right of refusing to let the child spend it irresponsibly or in ways which are incompatible with the values of the family. Parents need to teach their children how to be intelligent consumers—how to recognize quality, how to compare, how to shop for value, and so on.

It goes without saying that a child should *not* be required to spend her allowance on essential food, clothing, books, or school supplies. The allowance is not meant to *establish* the child's standard of living, but to *supplement* it.

(Q) How much should a child receive each week?
(A) Something between too little and too much. If the amount is either insufficient or excessive, the child may not learn to set responsible limits on his own spending.

Determine the actual figure by taking into consideration the socio-economic level of the family and peer group, the child's age, how involved he is with activities outside the family, where the family lives and, last but not least, the current rate of inflation.

Real Boys Don't Eat Quiche

(Q) My nine-and-a-half-year-old son prefers to play with his five-year-old sister's dolls and toys. When I tell him he cannot, that it isn't right for a boy his age, he pleads, begs, whines, and cries until I can't stand it any longer. If begging doesn't work, he becomes angry and verbally abusive, saying things like, "I hate you! . . . You're mean! . . . You hate me! . . . I hate my toys! They're no fun!" Eventually, I always give in. I don't think he's doing this to get more attention from his father and me, because even before his sister was born, he would play with the neighbor girls' toys before he'd play with his own. He has no really close friends (male or female), which also concerns me. I've tried speaking to him logically and quietly. I've tried yelling. I've tried ignoring it. I've even tried to embarrass him, telling him that other boys and girls will think he's strange. Nothing I have done will convince him to change. Do I have a reason to be worried? What can I do?
(A) Your son's preference for dolls and "girl" toys is unusual, but *not* necessarily abnormal. There is no law which says that boys must play with trucks and trains and sports equipment, or that girls must play with dolls and wear pink.

Unfortunately, we tend to be far more rigid in our attitudes concerning what is and is not appropriate sex-role behavior for boys than girls. For instance, we accept the little girl who likes to climb trees and play baseball, but criticize the little boy who wants a Barbie doll for Christmas.

The problem does not lie with your son's preference for his sister's things. The problem is that you have made his choice of toys into a major issue, at the crux of which is the question of his autonomy. As long as you fight with him over whether he has a right to like dolls, he has no choice but to fight back. In the process of defending his "turf," he builds walls around it which not only keep you out ("Eventually, I always give in") but keep him in. He won't have the freedom to expand his range of interests until you put an end to the battle.

I'm not suggesting that you ignore him. I'm suggesting that you give him complete permission to play with whatever he wants to play with, whenever he wants to play with it. Not just permission, but encouragement.

He needs to hear it from you, so tell him: "I've been making a big mistake. I wanted you to be like other little boys, so I tried to make you play with things like trucks and trains instead of dolls. Now I realize that what you play with isn't important. What's important is that you're happy. So, if playing with dolls makes you happy, then it's all right with me if you play with dolls. If you want some dolls of your own, we'll go out and buy some."

I can't guarantee that he will ever express more interest in "boy" toys than he does now. But I can guarantee that he will never feel comfortable with them until he is absolutely certain that you accept him, regardless.

The fact that your husband received only passing mention in your letter makes me wonder whether he is sufficiently involved with his son. If Dad isn't there enough to make a difference, he needs to realize that he should be, and can. Studies have shown that the quality of the father-son relationship has a direct bearing on a boy's success in social relationships. This seems to be more important when the father is in the home than when he is absent.

It sounds like your family has needs of the kind that are best, and more quickly, realized with the help of a competent, experienced family therapist. Ask your pediatrician or family doctor to find one for you.

(Q) I am a teacher and this concerns one of my students, a ten-year-old fifth-grade boy with pronounced effeminate mannerisms. He prefers to play with girls and is fascinated by makeup, women's clothing, hair styles, and other female things. He is not only an object of ridicule here at school, but according to his mother, catches a lot of flak from his father as well. Apparently, the dad is most disappointed at the way his only son is turning out. The boy talks to me a lot about the rejection he feels from both his classmates and his father, but I really don't feel qualified to counsel him. All I can do is lend a friendly ear.

My questions: (1) What is the likelihood of the boy developing into a homosexual? (2) If it is strong, is there a possibility that therapy can help him "turn around," or is it too late?

(A) Based on your description, I'd say that chances are considerably better than average that the boy will eventually become homosexual. Keep in mind, however, that personality and behavioral characteristics during childhood are unreliable predictors of an individual's later sexual orientation. Contrary to the prevailing stereotype, "effeminate" and homosexual don't necessarily go hand-in-hand. The boy's fascination with makeup and women's clothing is actually the more significant warning sign.

Under the circumstances, individual therapy probably couldn't do much more for the boy than help him cope with the ridicule and rejection with which he's faced. In other words, a therapist wouldn't be able to do significantly more than what you're doing, and since he already trusts you and feels comfortable with you, I see no reason to transfer that relationship to someone else. Don't underestimate your ability to give this youngster sound advice. As long as you don't take it upon yourself to "cure" him of his effeminate ways, you're as qualified as anyone else to talk with him. A "friendly ear" is exactly what he needs.

It's the parents who could truly benefit from counseling. It sounds like a predictable situation has developed in the family. The father is verbally aggressive toward the boy, partly out of disappointment, but in actuality his anger is a defense mechanism that masks deep-seated feelings of guilt and responsibility. I'd venture to guess that the father further projects his feeling of failure by blaming his wife for the boy's behavior.

The more rejecting and verbally aggressive the father is toward his son, the more the mother acts protective. This not only serves to strengthen the boy's identification with his mother, but further alienates him from his father as well. The closer the boy gets to his mother, the angrier the father gets and the more he blames his wife for the problem. The end result of all this mess is that the feminine side of the boy's nature comes to increasingly dominate.

What the boy needs more than anything else is an open, accepting relationship with his father. Therein lies whatever possibility still exists of helping the boy develop better self-esteem and a more appropriate sexual orientation.

The father needs to realize that his fears are self-fulfilling. The more angry and rejecting he is, the less effective he is as a role model. The mother, too, needs to understand that her protection is as much a part of the family problem as her husband's anger. Finally, the guilt both parents feel needs to be confronted. All these issues are much too explosive to be handled outside of therapy.

If you have any influence whatsoever with these parents, encourage them to talk with a qualified, professional counselor, and fast!

These, Too, Will Pass

(Q) We have a boy, six, and a girl, eleven months. Several years ago, our son went through a period of extreme defiance. We became firm with him, and although he remained headstrong, he settled down considerably.

Three months ago we began having the same problems with him again. Getting him to obey has become a constant battle. We generally prevail, but not before much arguing, crying, and gnashing of teeth. Robbie recently told us that we give more attention to his sister. Although he is loving and gentle toward her, he pouts when we spend time with her.

We've tried to explain she needs more of our time and attention right now, but he's not impressed. We don't know whether this is a normal reaction to a second child or whether we're doing something wrong.

(A) You're not doing anything wrong and Robbie's behavior is, for him, a normal reaction to a second child.

Dr. Burton White, noted researcher and author of *The First Three Years of Life* (Avon), has found that, generally speaking, three-and-a-half years is the ideal interval between siblings. Contrary to what many parents think, the chance of problems with the older child increases not only as the interval between siblings shortens from White's magic figure, but also as it lengthens. In other words, you are just as likely to have adjustment problems with a spacing of five-and-a-half years as you are with a spacing of one-and-a-half.

The problem with early spacing is that the first child has yet to resolve the conflict of dependence/independence that virtually defines most of the second and third years of life. By three and a half, most children have achieved a satisfactory degree of autonomy and are not threatened by the arrival of another child.

The problem with late spacing, particularly in the case of a firstborn, is that the older child has settled comfortably into the role of "only." That is his territory, so to speak, within the family, and he is not prepared to share it with anyone else.

For the first eight months of the second-born child's life, her relative passivity and helplessness pose few problems for the older child. But, as she begins to move about independently and make active demands on the parents, the older child's perception of her begins to change.

Where once she was cute and cuddly and where her helplessness made him feel big and responsible, now he sees her as an intruder.

The older child's response to this perceived threat varies according to his temperament and history. He may become somewhat aggressive toward the baby, or he may regress in one or more ways (baby talk, wetting his pants) to get attention.

Robbie has engaged in two predictable strategies. First, he is demanding more attention from you, even when you are obviously occupied with the baby and cannot give it. Then he puts on a display of pouting.

Second, he is engaging in behaviors which once brought him a great deal of attention—defiance, tantrums and so on.

As his role in the family changes, Robbie struggles to keep things as they were, using tactics that worked before.

The answer? Be firm. You must not cooperate with Robbie's perception of this situation. He is getting enough attention for his age, although less than before. You can help Robbie make the necessary adjustment by telling him the truth:

"Yes, Robbie, you are right. You *are* getting less attention than before because now there are two children who need attention instead of one.

"Your sister is a baby, and babies need more attention than six-year-olds. You are getting plenty of attention from us as it is. When you want attention and we can't give you any right then, you must find something to do on your own. We are also going to stop arguing with you about doing what we say. If you don't obey us when we tell you to do something, we will send you to your room until you decide to do it. That's the way it's going to be. Any questions?"

Robbie's security has been temporarily disrupted. Parental authority is the cornerstone of a child's sense of security. If you want to restore Robbie's security, therefore, you must exercise your authority.

(Q) Our eight-year-old occasionally asks me to hold him on my lap and cuddle him like a much younger child. Do you feel this is inappropriate for a child his age? Could it be an indication of insecurity? Should I let him or not? There are times when I'm simply not in the mood for an eight-year-old in my lap, but I don't know how to say "No" without making him think I'm rejecting him. Do you have any suggestions?
(A) To your first question—is it inappropriate for an eight-year-old to sit on his parent's lap?—the answer is: No, unless the child never wants to sit anywhere else.

During years six to ten, sometimes called "middle childhood," children are gradually transferring dependency needs from parents to peers. That is to say, they are becoming less involved with their parents and more involved with other children their age.

Up until now, everything the child did or wanted to do was measured against the parents' value system—consisting of a fairly constant set of do's and don'ts. During middle childhood, the peer group introduces a new set of expectations, which are not always compatible with the values the child learned at home. The almost inevitable discrepancy between what the child's parents have taught him and what the kids on the block want him to do in order to be part of the gang is one source of conflict for this age child.

Children seek to ease the tension generated by this conflict in a number of ways, always seeking to reconcile the often irreconcilable differences between the generations. They lie about their parents to their peers and lie about their peers to their parents. They deny that any conflict exists between the inclinations of the group and the values their parents hold dear ("I didn't think you'd mind."). They suffer mild, periodic spells of selective amnesia ("I forgot."). They scapegoat somebody ("Bobby did it! We told him not to!").

A second source of stress and conflict is the challenge of growth itself. Growing up is like conducting a guerrilla war, where the ultimate objective is to conquer some uncharted territory—in this case, adulthood. The child spends five years or so establishing a base of operations from which to develop and test his strategies. His subsequent forays, tentative at first, become increasingly bold and far-reaching as he becomes more familiar with the terrain. But always in the back of his mind is the knowledge that whenever things get too rough, he can always beat a hasty retreat to home base.

At this early stage of the game, the safest strategy is to take two steps forward and one step back . . . into Mom's lap (for instance).

Your son is simply seeking to maintain as close a relationship with you as possible during these trying times. He needs the reassurance of knowing that you will still be there whenever he needs you. There is no harm in his asking and no harm in your saying "sure."

Now, whether you say "sure" in any given situation should be solely a matter of whether you feel, at that moment, like having a relatively large child in your lap. If you don't feel like it, then say "No."

I suggest you talk with him about sitting in your lap. Begin by reassuring him that it's not only all right but something you enjoy doing for him as well . . . sometimes. Let him know that there will be times when it won't be convenient for him to sit in your lap and times when you will want to just sit by yourself. Prepare him to hear you say, "Not right now."

Then the next time he asks and you don't feel like having him sit on your lap, say, "Remember our talk? This is one of those not-so-good times."

When it comes right down to it, telling our children our true feelings is simpler and less painful than trying to conceal them.

(Q) Our eight-year-old son will not go up to his room alone after dark because he's certain there's "something" up there that's going to get him. We've tried leaving all the lights on upstairs after dark, we've talked ourselves blue in the face, we've even searched every upstairs nook and cranny with him to prove there's nothing for him to be afraid of.

Once he's under the covers he's fine as long as the hall light is on and his door is open. Are fears of this sort normal for a child his age? How would you suggest we deal with this?

(A) Yes, fears of the dark and carnivorous beasties lurking therein are quite typical of children your son's age. The cause is developmental, not psychological. This age child is highly imaginative and, recent studies tell us, extremely suggestible. It doesn't take much for even the most secure child of so-called "middle years" to talk himself into believing that the one-eyed flying purple people-eater lives in his closet waiting for that one unguarded moment.

As you've already discovered, no amount of talk, however logical, will dispel the child's irrational notions. Also, I hate to tell you this, but your method of proving that no monsters live in your upstairs was as counterproductive as it was thorough.

Looked at from the perspective of an eight-year-old, going from room to room on a monster hunt only confirmed his belief that one might be there. It's too bad that most adults can't remember how to think like children. We could save ourselves a lot of time and exasperation if we did.

The best approach involves a combination of understanding and nonchalance. You must also retain your sense of humor, even if the child has lost his. Above all else, the child must be given responsibility for the problem. You must be careful not to enter into the drama, which you do by taking the child's fears seriously. Handled properly, this situation can become a valuable lesson for the child in the power of positive thinking.

To illustrate, when our daughter, Amy, was around your son's age she, too, began expressing fears of the dark along with a reluctance to put herself to bed.

I told her, "When I was your age I thought there was a monster under my bed, too. He was so real I could almost see him. He had horns like a bull, scraggly yellow hair, one red eye, and green scales all over his face, like a fish. He was very, very ugly, and I knew that if I got too close to my bed after dark that he would reach out from under it, grab me and eat me!"

Amy laughed at the thought that her daddy could be so silly.

"Even though I was afraid of the monster, I knew I was just pretending. So, I pretended a way of beating the monster at his own game. Every night when it was time for bed, I would run down the hall that led to my bedroom, slap the light switch off as I came through the door, and dive into my bed. That way, I never got close enough to my bed for the monster to get me. And here I am! I lived to tell the tale! I suppose he got tired of trying to catch me and left.

"Now, your mother and I know that you're smart enough to figure out a way of beating your monster and getting rid of it. The reason you have to figure it out all by yourself is because anything we think up for you won't work. Also, once you figure it out, don't tell us, because it will stop working. That's just the way these pretend monsters are."

Over the next few days, I asked her several times if she had figured out a way to beat her nighttime monster, quickly reminding her that she wasn't to give me any of the details. Less than a week passed when, in answer to my question, Amy gave me a sly smile and said simply, "Yes."

And that's all there was to it.

Eleven to Fourteen: The "Tweenager"

"Whenever I ask him to do something, he just sits there, as though I don't exist. He's unpredictably temperamental, too—swings back and forth between joy and misery as if he's riding an emotional seesaw. And when he's in misery, watch out! Nothing I know of or have tried will satisfy him. But the worst thing to deal with is this idea that he can do whatever he pleases, without regard for anybody else. And stubborn? Hah! If I say go, he wants to stay. If I want to stay, he wants to go. Loving one minute, 'don't touch me!' the next. To tell the truth, I've about had it. There are times when I feel this urge to throttle the little monster, but I always snap back to reality moments before my hands wrap around his throat. Sometimes I think it's either him or me."

Another two-year-old, right? Wrong. The monster this parent is complaining about hasn't worn a diaper for ten years.

Introducing the large, uneconomically-sized version of the "Terrible Two": He pouts, he stomps his size-seven feet, he bellows at the top of his lungs. . . . Ladies and gentlemen! A big Bronx cheer for that second-most terrible of all terribles—The Tweenager!

(Author's note: the insertion of a "w" between the "t" and "e" in "teenager" is *not* a misprint. The term "tweenager" refers to an eleven-, twelve-, or thirteen-year-old person. I coined the phrase to distinguish this three-year period in a youngster's life, which is completely unlike the years immediately before and after. Most eleven-, twelve-, and thirteen-year-olds are no longer children, but they are not quite adolescents. They are betwixt and be*tween* definition; therefore, the term "tweenager.")

The tweenage years can be a miserable time for both "tweens" and anyone else who has to deal with them day in and day out—parents and teachers in particular. There are many outward similarities between the "Terrible Twos" and the equally "Terrible Tweens." So much so that many writers now refer to the second eighteen months of life as the "*first* adolescence."

Like the two-year-old, the tweenager is a rebel in search of a cause. His defiance of parental (and most other) authority is blindly reflexive. However, the tremendous growth of language during the intervening decade has replaced the monosyllabic *"no!"* with a peculiar form of self-centered ranting which makes no sense to anyone but the speaker.

And, like his predecessor, the tween is an emotional basket-case, careening wildly from one passionate extreme to another—a bull in the china shop of feelings.

It's another two years of almost certain temper tantrums, which burst forth any time the tweenager's inevitably unreasonable wants are not catered to. The more unreasonable they are, the greater the force of explosion.

This volatile character was portrayed brilliantly by young Michael Landon in *I Was a Tweenage Werewolf,* Hollywood's in-depth study of preadolescence. (Regrettably, the "w" was left on the cutting room floor by a junior editor who read it as a misspelling.)

The two-year-old is also father to the tween in his maddening self-centeredness. The tweenager is willing to inconvenience anyone to get what he wants. And excuuuuuuse *you* for leaving your foot where his royal tween-ness would step on it. Any empathic weaknesses which might interfere with this "me-first" obsession are suspended for the duration.

Again like the two-year-old, the tween cannot seem to make up his mind whether he prefers to be dependent or independent. But whichever role he chooses—Freddy the Freeloader or James Dean—it's darn sure going to be on *his* terms and no one else's. He will, for instance, curse his parents for having the gall to restrict his freedom, insisting that he's capable of taking care of himself, come what may; then he will ask them for money, a ride somewhere, or (more likely) both.

But there is method to this madness. Just like the two-year-old, whose behavior is the echo of a consciousness which is rapidly expanding and propelling him from explorer to experimenter and observer to doer, the tween is making a similar leap in his ability to flush out the mysteries of the universe. His mind, after ten years of grappling with the logic of concrete, measurable relationships, is beginning to grasp the abstract, the hypothetical, the stuff of no-stuff-at-all. No surprisingly, the tween is as hopelessly drunk on this process and its attendant revelations as the two was in his time.

Add an overdose of hormones, put the mixture under ever-increasing peer pressure, and you've got a guaranteed two or three years of Katy-bar-the-door-and-jump-back-Jack.

Ah, but amid this mayhem are two reasons to rejoice—most tweens are potty trained and very few of them bite.

The tweenage years are a time of transition—a symphony, or more aptly, a *cacophony* of change involving the whole child and dramatically altering his definition of himself and his world.

Changes in the structure and chemistry of the child's body and corresponding upheavals in his emotional nature bring him fact to face with his emergent sexuality.

About this time, a child's brain begins to process and organize information in a radically different manner, adding new dimensions to his perception of the world and further complicating his view of himself.

Preadolescents tend to be introspective; that is, they think a lot about themselves, sometimes to the point of obsessiveness. They reflect upon and evaluate their own behavior, feelings, and even their own thoughts. This ability to look within brings into clearer focus not just the person-that-is, but also the person-that-could-be—the *ideal self.* Comparisons between the real (present) and ideal self generate either aspiration or anxiety, depending on factors which include how much discrepancy there is between the two and whether the preadolescent has basically positive or negative self-regard.

Because they scrutinize themselves so carefully and speculate on the thoughts of other people as well, preadolescents often believe that they are constantly watched, usually by peers. Therefore, and quite understandably, they are given to "performing" for their imagined (but not necessarily imaginary) audience. This explains why tweens are so generally self-conscious about their personal appearance, spending hours (at least it seems like hours when *you're* waiting to use the bathroom) primping before every "public appearance," however routine.

During this critical period the child transfers most of his security needs from parents to peers. The peer group bridges childhood (when the child relied on his parents) and adulthood (when the healthy individual is primarily self-reliant); it is a social laboratory where rules and roles can be practiced, evaluated, and incorporated. Gradually, the clique becomes a thing of the past as the preadolescent turns his attention toward forming stable friendships and participating in large group activities.

Early adolescence is a time of great psychological vulnerability. The young person's self-concept is ambiguous, and therefore fragile. From a developmental standpoint, the child's task is to establish identity—an enduring sense of who he is and is becoming. This is not so easy for someone caught, for the moment at least, between the comfort and security of childhood and the uncertainty of adolescence.

(Q) Do you have any suggestions for parents on how to successfully endure the early teenage years?
(A) There are four keys to parental success during early adolescence.

The first is understanding. Parents must realize that the needs of a child are changing radically during the early teenage years. Socially, the peer group is becoming more important, both as a source of approval and as a source of values. For better or worse, the young teen begins pulling away from family and identifying more with his own generation.

The child's intellectual processes are maturing, unleashing the capacity for abstract, critical thought. The "tween" tests his newly expanded mind on none other than his parents, arguing and criticizing at every possible opportunity.

The young teen's physiology, both internal and external, is changing at a pace more rapid than his self-image can maintain. In defense, he projects his dissatisfaction with himself onto the outside world. Complaint, thy name is tweenager.

The second key combines tolerance and accommodation. Tolerance because early adolescence is rarely permanent. Accommodation because the radical changes taking place during this critical developmental period necessitate equally radical changes in how parents respond to their children. Oftentimes, the child's accelerating need for freedom catches parents off guard, and they react by hanging vainly onto a "style" of child rearing that no longer works.

True, most tweens want more freedom than they can handle. On the other side of this coin, however, are parents who fail to let the young teen experiment with a sufficient amount of freedom. The child, faced with parents who want to keep things the same, rebels. It is important that parents learn when to restrain and when not to, so that this time in the child's life is not defined primarily in terms of a struggle with us. Parents who hope to weather the "onslaught" of early adolescence by digging themselves in are fighting a losing battle.

The third is communication. Parents must be willing to listen to this age child, even when they make no sense. To listen to their fears, their expressions of insecurity, their hopes, their ideas and opinions. To listen to their many complaints—about friends who don't do right, clothes that don't look right, hair that won't lay right, and parents who are never right—and to reflect the majority of their moanings and groanings back to them in an accepting, nonjudgmental way.

There are still plenty of occasions, however, when young teenagers need to hear what their parents think about a certain subject or issue. Parents should not ever be reluctant to say, "We understand how *you* feel; now we want you to listen to how *we* feel." Note the subtle difference: Parents need to understand their children but require only that their children listen. During childhood, understanding is almost always a delayed reaction.

The fourth is involvement. There is no better antidote to the potential pitfalls of peer pressure than parents who are interested and involved. Take the time to ask questions, to listen, to participate. It's one of the best investments you can make in your child's future.

I Was a Tweenage Misanthrope

When I was twelve years old, I hated everything. There was so much to hate I couldn't remember it all. To keep it straight, I wrote it all down. In keeping with this stark, no-frills view of the world, I entitled it my "Hate List."

My Hate List filled several pieces of lined notebook paper, both sides. It was in my possession at all times so I could refer or add to it at a moment's notice. Nothing and no one was immune. Naturally, my parents were at the top of the list—in CAPITAL LETTERS, surrounded by exclamation points. I hated every one of my teachers, even the ones who were tolerant of my abrasiveness. I hated them if they gave me a C, and I hated them if they gave me an A. I couldn't be bought.

I hated my brother. I hated my sister. I hated my neighbors. I even hated my friends. Each one took a turn on my list. I hated books, homework, the guy who ran the neighborhood store, the barber who cut my hair too short every time, grass because it had to be mowed, leaves because they had to be raked, cars because they had to be washed, my room, girls, white socks, white Levis, police, and all food except for hamburgers, french fries, and Cokes. I hated my mother's hamburgers. She made them awful just to punish me for spending my meager allowance at the Burger Palace. I hated having an allowance. It was demeaning. I hated having no money.

I hated acne medications, my clothes, my shoes, my jacket, the stupid hat my mother bought me, and the galoshes my father made me wear when it snowed. But most of all, I hated me. I couldn't stand the sight of myself in the mirror.

"Yuk! Look at that face. No wonder Linda avoids me. I'm ugly! I hate Linda. I'm short, I'm skinny, my face breaks out, I've got freckles, my biceps are concave, my ribs show, I have dandruff, my hair is red, I can't suntan, there's no hair on my face . . . Oh Lord, please don't make me put on shorts for gym anymore—my legs are too skinny and my knees are too knobby. Why do I have to wear glasses? Why do I have to wear braces? My arms are too long, my nose turns up, my ears stick out, my chin is too pointy, I can't play football, I can't fight, nothing good ever happens to me! I'm a reptile! I'm a worm! I'm a bug! I deserve to be squashed!!!"

What a dirty trick it is to be twelve. You ain't nothin'. You aren't a child. You aren't a teenager. You aren't an adult. You need your parents, and you wish they'd leave you alone. You want friends, but you don't know how to be friendly. You want to be one of the crowd. You want to be different. You're always on guard, protecting a fragile sense of who you are or wish you were.

Confusion. Resentment. The victim of a cosmic joke. Twelve is the pits. But there is one way out.

Thirteen.

Keep Both Hands on the Wheel

Preadolescence can be emotionally tumultuous and confusing for all concerned. Unfortunately, in many families it is a time when limit-setting begins to break down. It is easy for parents to let themselves be intimidated by the child's emotional upheavals and begin allowing her more responsibility than she can handle in order to avoid confrontations.

Exactly the opposite is called for. This is a time for reaffirming your authority rather than allowing the child to dismantle it. Although she will surely reject the notion, it's also a time when the child needs to know that hands other than her own are ready to take the wheel.

(Q) Six months ago, we moved from the East Coast and settled in a nice community in the Midwest. The adjustment has been somewhat difficult for all of us, but it seems to have particularly affected our twelve-year-old son. This once outgoing and popular child has formed no close relationships since the move. In fact, he seems to avoid children his own age and has taken to associating with children several years younger. We have spoken to him about making more of an effort to find a friend, but he stays put, spending most of his free time in his room, watching television. He has also become more dependent and attached to his father and me. How can we help him?

(A) I suggest that you start by talking with your son about how generally upsetting the move has been to everyone in the family, how difficult it was to leave old friends and find new ones, and so on.

The disruption of a move often causes the preadolescent to regress to earlier forms of behavior. He may seek out younger children because they are more accepting, and because his status among them is virtually guaranteed. He is also likely to act more dependent on his parents.

Be understanding and supportive. Encourage and help him expand his activity away from home. A gentle assist from you in the form of arranging for his involvement in activities sponsored by the church, Y.M.C.A., and so on may be helpful.

Finally, I can't urge you strongly enough to remove the television from his room and limit his access to the family set to a maximum of one hour in the evening. His absorption in the television is a way of retreating from the challenge of carving out a niche for himself in his new surroundings. Every hour spent staring at the tube further dampens his initiative and increases his inertia.

(Q) Our thirteen-year-old has recently started threatening to run away from home. He is the second of three children and is almost exactly three years younger and three years older than his brothers. He complains about everything—we expect too much of him, he never has anything to do, we are "easier" on his younger brother, his older brother gets to do more than he does, and so on. It seems as though he's miserable nearly all the time. He can be loving and cooperative—but has not been for at least three months. Should we be concerned about his threats? We hear them two or three times a week. What should we do?

(A) I don't think there's much possibility that he actually will leave for good—not anytime soon, that is. The ones who run with the intention of staying gone don't talk about it much beforehand. They just *go,* and the pressures which push them to that extreme are far more serious than the typical "Tweenage Blues" you're describing. In a similar vein, people who repeatedly threaten suicide are seldom the ones who (except through miscalculation) end up in the morgue. In both instances, the threat is a dramatic way of calling attention to oneself: "Hey! You better look at me, 'cause it might be your last chance!"

There are victims and there are "victims." Included in the former are real-life runaways and real-death suicides. A "victim," on the other hand, is nothing more than a caricature of tragedy—too involved in wearing this particular mask to even consider playing a lesser role. Included in the latter are, quite often, middle children and "tweenagers." Congratulations! You've got two for the price of one!

In one sense, the middle child is a "tweenager" throughout his childhood. Born both too late and too early, he rails against the injustice of having an older sibling who enjoys more freedom and a younger one who seems to get more attention ("You let him get away with murder!").

The middle child wants the best of both worlds, without having to pay the price. He wants to be gloriously independent and securely taken care of at the same time. The lure of becoming a victim is almost impossible to resist in this irreconcilable dilemma. "I'm gonna run away!" is a frustrated, exaggerated expression of this conflict. It is both a battle cry for freedom and a plea for more attention.

As the middle child moves into his "tweenage" years, his middle-ness is compounded. Woe is him! Insult upon injury! The straw that broke . . . and all the rest.

I would be less concerned about his threats than the feelings behind them. Understand that this is a particularly stressful transition in his life and an equally important time in the life of your family.

Keep communication open, but beware of allowing the child too powerful a voice in defining crucial issues. The questions (or challenges) children of this age raise are often superficial or irrelevant, only distracting from, and preventing resolution of, more important problems facing the family.

For instance, concern over threats of running away can mask the more salient issue of, "What does being a member of this family mean when you are thirteen years old?"

(Q) Several times in the past six months, we have found panty hose, usually several pairs at a time, in our twelve-year-old son's room (he will be thirteen soon). He says he took most of them from his aunt's house (he sometimes baby-sits for her children). He denies ever wearing them, but can't (or won't) explain why he is so interested in them. We don't understand what his problem is, since he seems like such a typical, well-rounded boy in every other way—he is active in sports, makes good grades, and has lots of friends. Who do you think is going on, and how should we handle it?

(A) You're right. What you have is a typical, well-rounded twelve-year-old boy expressing his emerging sexuality in a rather unusual, but no means abnormal, way.

And *he's* right, too. He probably *doesn't* know why he's attracted to panty hose; he just knows he is. Let's face it—part of the mystery and magic of sex at any age is that words are inadequate to express why it feels so darn good. It just does, and that's enough. For instance, if I try to explain why I'm sexually attracted to my wife, I end up describing *her.* Fine, but why am I attracted to that particular combination of characteristics? I dunno. Just am.

The only problem with the panty hose is that most adults are narrow-minded about expressions of sexuality by a child. We tend to have definite ideas about what is and is not appropriate. So when a twelve-year-old elopes with a pair of panty hose, we freak out because it doesn't fit our preconceived notions of what is O.K. Another facet of the problem is that we think of the differences between children and adults in purely quantitative terms. A twelve-year-old possesses less "adultness" than a thirty-year-old—he is smaller, less practical, and so on.

But childhood is not just the lower eighteen rungs of life's ladder; it is a different ladder altogether. Children play at a different game, particularly when it comes to things like sex. In fact, the basic difference between children and adults is that children learn about such things *by playing,* while adults think of learning as a very serious undertaking.

At around the age of twelve, your son became increasingly, irresistibly, attracted to the female body. He could hardly contain his curiosity! But he had to. The average twelve-year-old has enough presence of mind to know that the female body is off limits for another few years. But it just so happens that there are these things called panty hose that women wear over a very intriguing area of their anatomy. So . . .

He's only playing. Just learning, in a safe and harmless way. In this case, panty hose are "transitional objects"—items the youngster uses to help him come to grips with the changes taking place in his body, in his mind, and in his emotions. He is interested in them because the "real thing," besides being off limits, is too threatening for the moment.

If your son were not "typical"—if his behavior were extremely unusual in other respects or if he isolated himself from other children his age or seemed depressed—then more concern would be appropriate. But even in that context, panty hose would be the *least* relevant detail.

Take this ideal opportunity to let him know that you understand how panty hose could be so intriguing (but *don't* analyze his interest for him). Tell him that as his body matures and his feelings about women change, you are there to help answer his questions and discuss his concerns. If the door is open, he will walk through it, and when he discovers that you're willing to listen without judging or criticizing him, he will seek your counsel more often.

(Q) A communication problem has recently developed between us and our eleven-year-old son. We used to be very close and affectionate toward one another. He's always been a child who would tell us what was going on in his life and talk to us if he had a problem. That all changed shortly after he started school (sixth grade) this year. He's more distant, seems uncomfortable when we show affection toward him, and is no longer open with us about what he's doing in school or with his friends. If we try to engage him in conversation, he gives us one-word replies to anything we say or ask him. According to his teachers, he's well liked by his classmates, but his grades are starting to slip. What would you suggest?

(A) I'd suggest that what's going on may be nothing more complicated than preadolescence, and that you would do well to stay pretty much out of the picture, at least for the time being.

Preadolescence, or the tweenage years, as I call them, begins around age eleven and lasts through age thirteen. Before this important transitional stage, the child's security is invested primarily in his relationship with his parents, self-esteem is primarily a function of parental approval, and the quality of sense of identity (self-concept) is tied predominantly to his or her role within the family.

The "task" of preadolescence is to find a secure niche within the peer group. This requires the youngster to put some distance between himself and his parents. And so, around age eleven, the child begins withdrawing security from the family and investing it in the peer relationships. Increasingly, self-esteem becomes a function of peer approval and self-concept a measure of how successful the youngster is at finding a relatively stable role within the peer group.

As you can imagine—and probably remember—this metamorphosis generates its share of anxiety and insecurity, which explains why this age child often looks worried and troubled.

But to whom can he talk? Not to his friends, because to do so would be a tacit admission of weakness. Not to his parents, either, because that would be an admission of continued dependence. The tweenager is having to make a lot of adjustments and—outside being understanding, patient, and supportive—there's probably little that parents can do that will significantly ease the process.

Although he may at times act like he wants nothing to do with you, your son is actually trying to figure out how he can develop a place for himself among his peers and still keep you "on his team." Without realizing it, you're doing half his job for him. Every expression of concern on your part affirms the security of his relationship with you. And so, he seizes the opportunity to turn the tables on you a bit. You pursue, and he plays hard to get.

I'd suggest you back off a bit and let him begin assuming a greater share of responsibility for the relationship. You might issue an open invitation of the "if you want to talk, you know where to find us" sort. As far as his grades are concerned, a slight slip is no cause for alarm, but if they continue to deteriorate, you might consider reading my previous book, *Ending the Homework Hassle* (Andrews and McMeel, 1990).

Childhood's End

(Q) Our eleven-year-old daughter recently told me she has been having "scary thoughts" lately, including thoughts of dying, us being killed, and other vague feelings that something terrible is about to happen. The thoughts not only frighten her, but also cause her to feel guilty, particularly the ones about us getting killed. We have a good relationship and she's been open with us about this. We recently read an article about a psychological disorder that involves obsessive thoughts of this sort. Could something serious be going on here? How should we handle it?

(A) The psychological disorder you read about is called obsessive-compulsive disorder (OCD). It often begins during adolescence and is characterized by obsessive thoughts and/or compulsions—ritual behaviors which the individual feels compelled to perform. Recent research suggests that OCD results from a chemical imbalance within the brain and is best treated using a combination of medication and psychotherapy.

I am in no position, of course, to make a diagnosis. Chances are, however, your daughter's problem isn't serious. Persistent disturbing thoughts of one sort or another are fairly common to preteens and teens. Often, they are a byproduct of the transition from childhood to adolescence.

Along with physical changes that are taking place during this time, profound changes are taking place in how a child organizes and processes information. Specifically, the child becomes capable of thinking in far more complex and abstract terms—in other words, like an adult. Comparing the child's brain to a computer, it's as if the child's "thinking program" is suddenly and significantly upgraded. This new capacity is exciting, but some aspects also may be initially confusing, even frightening.

When my daughter, Amy, was about twelve, she began having fears of dying. They usually began after bedtime, preventing her from falling asleep. When she shared her anxieties with me, I explained them in terms of "mental growing pains."

"At this point in your life, Amy," I told her, "You're beginning to change from a child into an adult. You can see the changes happening in your body. What you can't see are the changes happening in your brain that affect the way you think about things. As you go through this transition from thinking like a child to thinking like an adult, it may sometimes feel that you're not in control of what's going on in your mind. Sometimes, a frightening thought may just pop into your head, or the same thought may occur over and over again. No matter how powerful these thoughts may feel, however, they don't have the power to cause things to happen that wouldn't have happened anyway.

"The important thing," I went on to say, "is that you talk about these things with either Mom or Dad. The worst thing you can do is bottle them up inside because then they have nowhere to go and they just start bouncing around in there and make you feel more and more confused. The best way to get them out of your head is to talk about them, and that's one reason why we're here."

Amy and I continued to have occasional talks about this over a period of about six months. Each time, I provided the same reassurance and basically the same explanation. To my knowledge, the thoughts didn't go away that quickly, but Amy became less and less fearful of them and, therefore, better able to control them without talking.

The fact that your daughter shared the problem with you indicates you have a healthy relationship in which there is good communication and lots of trust on her part. With you there to provide the foundation of support and security, there is little chance that this will develop into something major. If, however, the problem persists longer than a few months without any improvement, it would be prudent of you to seek professional help.

"Hello? Is Anyone at Home in There?"

The phone rang and Eric (thirteen years old at the time) jumped to answer it.

"Hello? . . . Huh? . . . No . . . Uhhhh . . . Yeah."

He emitted a series of unintelligible sounds and hung up. The "conversation" lasted less than thirty seconds.

"Wrong number?" I asked.

"My girlfriend."

"Your girlfriend!? You've got to be kidding, Eric. You actually talk that way to someone you know? It sounded as if you have a speech problem—sort of semi-human, you know?"

"That's the way we talk to each other all the time."

"No it's not."

"Whadayamean?"

"I mean it may be the way some of you talk to each other, but it's not the way you are going to talk to anyone, not on our family phone, you're not."

Soon thereafter, my wife and I put both children through a crash course in making and receiving telephone calls, including "Hello?" "May I take a message?" and "Thanks for calling."

Good phone manners, we pointed out, are as important as manners in any other area, perhaps even more so, since your voice is all you have with which to make your impression on the other person.

From that point on we never cringed when one of the children picked up the phone, because they projected a friendly, positive attitude.

As time went on, however, I discovered in at least one respect, Eric was right—they do all talk to each other that way. Many of them do, at least, "them" being young people in their early teens.

I think it has something to do with their self-consciousness, which has something to do with wanting to appear aloof, which has something to do with wanting to make one's self less vulnerable. In any case, their phone manners are generally abominable.

I was brooding on this problem one afternoon shortly after Eric had drawn my attention to it, when the phone rang. I picked it up.

"Hello?"

"LemmespeakaEric."

"Chip (not his real name)? Is that you, Chip?"

Chip was one of Eric's friends. I would kid around with Chip a lot.

"Yeah."

"Listen, Chip, that was just atrocious. I mean it was just awful, and I'm just going to pretend you never called and hang up. You call back and let's try it again from the top, O.K.?" and I hung up.

Fifteen seconds later, it rang again.

"Hello?"

"Uhhh, I wannatalkaEric."

"Better, Chip, better, but not quite right, if you know what I mean, so let's try it one more time, from the top again," and I hung up.

It rang again.

"Hello?"

"Uhhhh, ha, ha, ha, Uhhh . . ."

"What do you mean, 'Uhhhh, Uhhhh,' Chip? I mean, do I have to spell it out for you? Look, try it one more time, but this time when I pick up the phone, I'll say, 'Hello,' and you say, 'Hello, Mr. Rosemond, this is Chip and I'd like to speak with Eric if he's home.' Got it? Oh, and Chip, a British accent would really snap it up." And I hung up again.

It rang again.

"Hello?"

"Hello, Mr. Rosemond, uhhhh, this is Chip and I'd, ha, ha, ha, like to (phony British accent) speak with Eric, ha, ha, ha."

"Gosh, Chip, I'm sorry, but Eric's not at home. Can I take a message?"

He hung up.

The "Talk"

(Q) Our oldest, a son, just turned twelve. He's in the sixth grade and beginning to show some interest in girls—talking on the telephone, mostly. When and how should we begin his sexual education? Neither of our parents ever sat down to talk with us about such things, so we don't know how to go about it.

(A) As a young teen, one of the things I dreaded, and hoped to forever avoid, was "The Conversation." That's when your father walks casually over to you and says, with this real serious, I mean *terminal* look on his face, "Son, I think you and I need to have a conversation." And you act stupid at first, like you don't have any idea what he's talking about, all the while calculating how you're going to handle this uncool situation. But before you can say anything, he's already started his spiel, and all you want to do is get out of there, but you can't because it's your father. So you pretend to listen.

Or you do what I did, which was to lie: "Hey, listen, Dad, before you go any further, I think I can save you some time. This guy came and talked to our health class last year about, you know, and, well, he was pretty good and, well, I don't think it's really necessary for me to hear it all over again, but I appreciate your concern and I'll be sure and come to you if I have any questions, O.K.?"

Boy, did *he* ever look relieved.

As my son approached adolescence, I looked back on that truncated conversation with a mixture of humor and perplexity. I wasn't comfortable with the format my father chose, and neither was he. But what was the alternative? In the process of pondering this dilemma, I realized that my feelings of unease as an adolescent were due in part to the fact that sex was, at the time, a threatening subject for me, and so it is for many adolescent males. One way of keeping the anxiety it arouses at bay is for the young teen to deny that he needs to know anything about it.

But a second reason for my discomfort was that I had no choice in the matter. Dad had decided it was time for my education and that was that. In other words, *his* needs dictated the moment. I'm sure he felt obliged to "do his duty" toward me and approached the subject the only way he knew, but I felt backed into a corner and so took the quickest way out.

I came to the conclusion that what my son needed from me was not a rundown of "the facts," but the freedom to ask questions. If his sexual education was going to be meaningful, he would have to feel in control of it.

So, I took the initiative to issue an open-ended invitation. I think we were going somewhere together in the car when, for whatever reason, the time felt "right" for me to say what I had to say.

"Son, as you get older, you're going to become more and more interested in girls and you're going to have questions and . . ."

He interrupted. "Uh, look, Dad, before you go any further, this guy came and talked to our health class last year and . . ."

"Yeah, I know, he was pretty good and answered your questions, right?"

"Right. How'd you know?"

"Same guy came to my health class when I was your age. But I'm not finished. All I want to say is that when you have questions or anything at all you want to discuss concerning women and men and sex, I'd like you to ask me. I'd rather you asked me instead of one of your friends, because their answers and opinions might not be correct. And remember: There's no such thing as a dumb question."

Boy, was *he* ever relieved. But he *has* come to me with questions on more than a few occasions, and I've taken those opportunities to not only answer his questions, but add a few editorial comments as well. In addition, he occasionally says or does things that allow me to make further adjustments in his attitude.

With our daughter, the only modification my wife and I made in this basic approach was to prepare her for her first period.

Basically, we tried to get across to both of them that the

secret to a successful sexual relationship with someone has less to do with techniques and biology than with attitude and values—specifically, how well you respect yourself and how well you respect the other person. You can't package that attitude in one fact-filled conversation. It's something you model for them every day in what you say and what you do. In that sense, a child's sex education begins the day he or she is born.

Fourteen to Nineteen: The Teen Years

The Mall. If you have teenage children, it becomes an issue. So do parties and "riding around" and dating and curfew and concerts and going to the beach and . . . need I go on? All these things became issues in our home when our children entered their teens.

Not since the children were two were my wife and I confronted with such a push for independence. Even though we knew it was coming and did our best to prepare, adolescence still occasionally managed to sneak up behind us and yell "BOO!"

Thankfully, those times were few and far between, but then we've been blessed with two children who take pride in doing the "right thing." I think about parents who haven't been so fortunate, for whom life with a teenager or teenagers has been like dominoes falling, and I wonder how things can go so right for some and so wrong for others.

After twenty years of working with families, no one can tell me that luck—for lack of a better term—doesn't have something to do with it. I've heard enough horror stories from caring, conscientious parents to convince me that caring isn't all it's sometimes cracked up to be.

Please don't misunderstand me. If you don't care, then you will most certainly reap the harvest of your neglect. But caring and doing all the things caring parents are supposed to do still doesn't guarantee everything's going to be all right. And that's what's so scary, isn't it?

The question I am most often asked by parents of teenagers is "How much freedom should we give?" I must admit to not having a specific answer to that one. I only know that teens are generally guilty of wanting more freedom than they can handle. But then parents are likewise generally guilty of giving less freedom than teens can handle. Somewhere between the urge to fly the nest and the urge to keep them from flying so far, so fast, there is a happy medium. Finding it is the trick.

Then comes "What should teenagers be doing in their free time?" and again I have no formula. "A variety of things" is perhaps the closest I can come to an answer. I smell trouble when a teenager seems obsessed with doing only one thing, or only a few, whether the thing(s) be listening to rock music, hanging out at the mall, or doing homework.

For my wife and me, things like going to the mall and riding around were not issues as long as they were but two of many things our children wanted to do. Nor were there magical ages at which we allowed our children to go to concerts or wear makeup or date. The better our children took care of the privileges they had, the more we gave them.

That last question is followed closely by "How can parents tell if their teenage children are doing things they shouldn't be doing?" The answer: If you care to know, then you will know. You'll know because they'll act like they're keeping secrets.

If you want to minimize the possibility that your teenage children might, among other harmful things, become sexually active and/or experiment with drugs (including alcohol and tobacco), the best insurance policy involves open lines of communication.

I find that humor is perhaps the best medicine for opening those lines of communication and keeping them open. Likewise, nothing clogs those lines quicker than a parent who takes things too seriously.

I once heard a parent jokingly remark that the teenage years were, for parents, "the best of times, the worst of times." That may be so, but let's not forget that the teenage years are possibly the best and worst of times for our children, as well. The fact that we've already walked in their moccasins means we can understand them better than they understand us. And a little understanding can go a long way.

(Q) We are worried about our fourteen-year-old daughter. She's become extremely rude and disrespectful, and the more of an audience she has, the ruder she is. She constantly calls attention to herself by acting silly and/or obnoxious and seems determined to provoke us, one way or another. We're also concerned that she seems to have little or no interest in either school or spending time with friends. Up until a year or so ago, she was a sweet, affectionate child. What could be the matter and how should we handle it?

(A) Prior to adolescence, a child's self-concept is closely tied to parental approval. As adolescence approaches, the source of self-esteem shifts from parents to peers. The task facing the young teen is one of finding a viable niche in the culture of the peer group, one that draws positive attention.

This important transition involves a certain amount of insecurity. To gain approval from peers, the youngster must conform to prevailing peer group standards. In the process, parents come down off the pedestal they previously occupied and are replaced by friends as a major source of influence.

As the parents and the child adjust to new roles and expectations of one another, some friction is inevitable.

An abnormally high degree of conflict/rebellion, however, usually spells trouble. It means that either the child's friends are exerting a decidedly negative effect on her values, or the child is having social problems and, outward appearances aside, is depressed. Depression can wear a number of masks, but self-directed anger is almost always a feature.

Your daughter's lack of involvement with peers may mean she has yet to find her niche. Feeling rejected and self-conscious, the draws attention to herself by acting silly and obnoxious. This has the unintended effect of driving peers farther away. Inwardly, she blames herself for her social problems, but deals with her anger by projecting it outward, toward you. You become her whipping post.

First, confront her in a way that opens the door for communication and support. Say, "We think your recent behavior is a way of hiding some unhappiness that you need to talk out. If you don't feel you can talk with us about what's bothering you, let's find a counselor you can talk to."

During this conversation, it's important that you not criticize her or imply that her behavior has hurt you in some way. This kind of approach will put a quick damper on communication.

Second, encourage involvement with peers. Urge her to do things like invite a friend over to spend the night or go to the movies. Depending on how much social paralysis has set in, you might even need to insist. Consider getting her involved with a church-sponsored youth program. If you don't attend a church, you can still find a program that would welcome her participation.

Third, keep your cool when she lashes out at you. Don't take it personally, because it really isn't. Let her know, however, in straightforward, nonemotional terms, how her behavior appears to others. Be honest and straightforward with your feedback, as in, "That was rude. It's not necessary for you to behave that way to get our attention. What is it that you're really wanting from us right now?"

In a sense, her verbal barbs are a test of your strength. She wants to know, "Are you strong enough to see me through this uncertain time of my life?"

If things don't get better quickly, call your family doctor or area mental health association and ask for a referral to a therapist who specializes in adolescent issues.

(Q) Our fourteen-year-old daughter recently told an adult friend that she didn't get along with us. This came as quite a surprise because although we have occasional conflicts over the usual things—what she can do, when she has to be in, and so on—we didn't feel we had any major problems.

We don't want to betray the confidence she has in the adult friend by confronting her with what she told him, but we feel we need to do something. How would you handle this situation?

(A) Unless you have reason to feel that there is something amiss in your relationship with your daughter, I wouldn't advise that you do anything. The fact that she told someone that she doesn't get along with you is more of a comment on her age than it is on the status of your relationship with her.

In the first place, it isn't cool to get along with your parents when you're fourteen. Even if you do, you're reluctant to admit it. This age child is seeking to establish autonomy and identity separate and distinct from who her parents think she is or want her to be.

This struggle to become your own person, to define yourself, is, in fact, the central theme of early adolescence and the reason for most of the tension that exists between parents and children during this stage of development.

So, if someone asks a fourteen-year-old, "Do you get along

with your parents?", the likelihood is great that the answer will be "no." But that "no" doesn't mean that there is more than a normal amount of tension in the relationship. "No" may simply be an expression of the young teen's need to feel autonomous.

Consider also that your daughter may have unburdened to her adult friend shortly after a conflict with you. Teens are given to dramatic exaggeration. If they've just had an argument with their parents, they'll say they never get along with them even if they generally do.

In short, I wouldn't worry about it, and I certainly wouldn't confront her with what you've heard. Bringing her feelings out in the open will give them more attention than they probably deserve, and attention can make a mountain out of a molehill.

(Q) Our fourteen-year-old daughter's room is a pigsty. Her clothes are heaped on the floor where she takes them off, her closet looks like the aftermath of Armageddon. Papers, books, and records are strewn everywhere. Gaudy rock posters are all over the walls and her bed is never made (except on the day I change the sheets). Millie and I have had a running battle over the state of her room for as long as I can remember. Her position is that she lives there and so should be able to decorate and maintain it according to her standards, rather than mine. I don't see how she can stand to live in such a mess, much less find anything she wants in there. She says it's none of my business whether she knows where things are or not. What do you say?
(A) I say your daughter's argument is far better than yours. She's perfectly right—whether she can stand the mess or knows where to locate her possessions is none of your business.

Here's your argument: Millie should keep her room orderly and clean because she'll be happier if she does.

Question: How do you know? Answer: You don't. Millie has told you she's perfectly happy with her room as it is. It's really quite presumptuous of you to tell her she'll be happier if she does things your way.

I say it's time you told Millie the truth. The first part of the truth is that the reason you want her to keep her room clean is because you'll be happier if she does. The second part of the truth is that you pay the mortgage, so your standards should prevail.

Now get in there and insist that your daughter keep her room clean and orderly. Sure, her tastes are different than yours, and you can respect that, can't you? Millie can have her rock posters and her Michael Jackson bedspread and her record collection, as long as they're tacked neatly to her walls, spread neatly on her made bed, and put neatly away in their sleeves.

The issue is not what constitutes good taste; it's what constitutes "clean," and whether children should obey their parents.

Apply the Godfather principle and make her an offer she can't refuse. On school days, her room must be neat and clean before she leaves for school or she can't socialize with her friends or talk on the phone after school. On other days, freedom and privilege are earned by first accomplishing the same chore. If she wants to trash her room while she's in there, fine. But it must be untrashed before she can do what she wants to do. Define "neat" and "clean" as (1) clothes picked up and put away properly, (2) floor cleared of obstructions, (3) closet organized, (4) top surfaces of furniture kept likewise, and (5) bed made. (In the future, have her change her own sheets).

She's bound to want to fight you about this. Don't! Just enforce the rules, without concern for whether she likes them.

(Q) Do parents ever have a right to search a teen's room and/or read a diary? My fourteen-year-old daughter and I are having a dispute over this issue. Although I've never searched her room or looked in her diary, I maintain that, as her parent, I have the right to do so at any time, especially if I think she's up to no good. My daughter says her room is her "private domain" and that I do not have the right to even step foot in there without permission, much less conduct a search. Who's right?

(A) That's a tough question. Both points of view have merit, but neither can claim to be the final word.

For instance, I agree with your daughter that parents should respect a teen's privacy. With that privilege comes certain responsibilities, however. Your daughter's concept of "private domain" implies that she is responsible to no one but herself where her room is concerned. That is simply not so.

She earns and maintains her privacy by, first, keeping her room clean and orderly, in keeping with the standard that prevails in the rest of the home. Second, she is not entitled to do as she pleases in her room. The rules of the household extend beyond her doorway, and she should be expected to abide by them. For instance, she should keep the volume on her stereo low enough that it doesn't interfere with someone else's peace of mind.

Nor does your daughter have the right to shut herself in her room for long periods of time, only coming out to eat and perform other vital functions. With the benefits of membership in the family goes the requirement of participation. For some teens, however, the only question is "What can my family do for me?" They have little appreciation for the flip side of the coin, which is "What can I do for my family?"

In other words, you should expect of your daughter exactly what society expects of us. We are entitled to privacy, but we are not allowed to do as we please with the privilege. Our homes are our castles only as long as we abide by certain rules and regulations.

In most communities, for example, there are restrictions that prevent using a private residence as a commercial business. Nor are homeowners allowed to accumulate garbage in their front yards or disturb the peace of the neighborhood with loud noises. If your daughter wants to be treated as an adult where the privacy of her room is concerned, she must be willing to act like one.

For the most part, you are wrong in saying that parents have the right to search a teen's room at any time. A search motivated by mere curiosity will do nothing but undermine trust and communication. If the teen's conduct is above suspicion, then the parents have no right to violate a young person's privacy. On the other hand, if parents have significant reason to believe that the teen is, indeed, "up to no good," they have more than a right to search for evidence, they have a responsibility to their child to do so.

If the teen has been lying about her whereabouts and activities, if she has been violating curfew and other rules with regularity, if she frequently comes in looking and acting unusual, if she has been skipping classes in school, if her grades have taken a sudden turn for the worse, if she tries to keep you from finding out who her friends are—then trust has already been broken and parents do have sufficient cause to conduct a search.

If, however, a search reveals that the parents were wrong to suspect wrongdoing, then the child deserves a "confession," along with an explanation and an apology. Trust is, after all, a two-way street.

(Q) I've heard that the more organized activities—church youth groups, athletics, scouting, school organizations and so on—teenagers are involved in, the less likely it is they'll get messed up in drugs and sex. Do you agree, and if so, how much should parents dictate to a teenager concerning extracurricular activities?

(A) I agree that there is nothing so deadly as boredom during the teenage years, and believe that parents should promote involvement in the types of events and activities you mentioned.

The recipe for "Teen in Trouble," whether the trouble be alcohol, drugs, or sex, is equal parts negative peer pressure, parental underinvolvement, and boredom. Let a teenager just wander in search of something to do, and he'll eventually wander into a crowd of kids who are themselves wandering. Sooner or later, they'll stumble onto the opportunity to experience something forbidden. Lacking anything better to do, they will accept, and keep on accepting, the invitation.

Several years ago, I did an informal study of well-adjusted teens. These were young people ages thirteen through seventeen who, according to their parents' reports, made good grades, got along well with their parents, enjoyed an active social life, and seemed happy with themselves. Without exception, these youngsters were active in at least one extracurricular activity through their school, church, or community. In addition, every one of them had a hobby. To their parents' knowledge, none of them was using drugs or alcohol, nor were they sexually active.

I know what some of you are saying: "C'mon John, don't be so naive! Just because their parents don't know something is going on doesn't mean it isn't."

I disagree. Parents who are interested and involved in what their children are doing with their spare time will usually know when something is wrong. They may not know the specifics, but they will *know,* nonetheless. The test for trouble is simple: Ask yourself, "How often do I have a feeling of general discomfort concerning who my child is with, where he is, and what he's doing?" If your answer is once a month or more, then you better take a closer look. Parents often ignore the signs. Then when the beast finally rears its ugly head, they claim ignorance.

Remember also that most teens will sooner or later drink a beer or two, take a drag off a joint and tread dangerously close to "too far" sexually. There's a difference between trying and using. The difference is made by parents who care.

Concerning how far parents should dictate to a teenager how he uses his spare time: I don't see anything wrong with parents mandating that a teen get involved in a certain activity as long as that mandate is the exception rather than the rule. Part of our job, after all, is to help create and maintain "well-roundedness" in our children's lives. If we see a gap, we have every right to fill it—if our children won't take the initiative to do so. Oftentimes, their reluctance to get involved in something is based on inadequate information, misperception, or the unfounded fear that they won't "fit in."

There have been a few occasions when my wife and I told our teenage son what he was going to do with his time. Although he might have initially complained about our decision, he always ended up appreciating it.

Sometimes it pays to remind ourselves that we really *do* know best.

(Q) About two months ago, our fourteen-year-old son got mad at us and ran away from home. We finally found him two days later at the home of a friend, whose parents didn't know we were looking for him. He left because we put him on a week's restriction for not coming home on time. He was a perfectly delightful kid until about a year ago, when he began acting like a complete jerk—talking back, giving us grief every time we asked him to do something, becoming belligerent when he didn't get his way, and so on. We're at our wits' end with him. To make matters worse, he's using this running away thing to get what he wants from us. If things don't suit him, he starts talking about leaving. He obviously knows how upset it makes us. To hear his teachers and friends' parents talk about him, you'd think he was a saint. What should we do?

(A) For starters, you should stop living in fear of his running away. Based on what you told me in your letter, it's not a likely possibility.

I make a distinction between running away and running off. Lots of kids run off. They get mad at their parents and escape to what is usually a fairly safe haven—a friend's house, a neighbor's barn—for a few days. It's an impulsive, dramatic way of handling frustrations. Kids who run off have every intention of coming home, and often make it very easy for their parents to find them.

Running away, however, is a horse of quite a different color. This is serious stuff, not soap opera, and these kids don't want to be found. They're almost always from very unstable families, where conflict is the norm. Frequently, these kids have been the victims of physical and/or sexual abuse. To escape the dead-end street, they hit the road.

Your son didn't really run away; he merely ran off. And there's nothing in your letter to suggest he's likely to decide suddenly to leave on a cross-country hike.

Yes, living with a young adolescent can certainly be the pits at times. It's important to distinguish between normal adolescent behavior and real problem behavior. Here's my "Test for Truly Troubled Teens":

- Was he/she a behavior problem long before the onset of adolescence?
- Do other adults (teachers, neighbors, other kids' parents) also have difficulty with him/her?
- Is he/she using drugs or alcohol?
- Is he/she sexually active?

If the answer to all four questions is no, then there's every reason to believe this, too, will pass. If the answer to even one of them is yes, then I would advise that you get some professional help, and fast.

Your letter suggests a "no" to all four. Therefore, I don't think you have anything to fear, save fear itself. In that regard, you mustn't allow your son to intimidate you with threats of running away. The next time he lets one slip, shrug it off by saying, "Help yourself, but when you decide to come home, remember that you're going to be grounded a week for every day, or part of one, you are gone." That will give him something to think about.

The more you soften your approach in order to prevent another incident, the worse his behavior will become and the more likely it is he'll pull this kind of stunt again. When he needs discipline, discipline him. In fact, it sounds like a major crackdown may be in order.

I won't wish you good luck, because luck has nothing to do with it. Instead, I'll wish you "good hanging in there!" You're certainly going to need to.

Curfew

When Eric and Amy were in their early teens, my wife and I made an astonishing announcement to each of them. We said, in effect, "We don't want to be your parents anymore."

By that we meant we no longer wanted to reprimand, scold, restrict, or exercise the power of "office" in any punitive manner. We went on to say, "You are well aware of the rules, and well aware of the consequences of violating those rules. You're also intelligent and responsible. So, we're counting on you to keep us from having to be parents.

"Here's the deal: If you obey the rules, you'll find that not only will we stay off your back, but your freedoms will steadily grow, and grow, and grow."

Having secured their undivided attention, we popped the Big Q: "How would you like to have more freedom than just about anyone you know?"

"That would be cool," they said, feigning nonchalance.

"Then all you have to do is obey the rules. We want you to have lots of freedom, but with freedom comes responsibility. You prove to us that you're responsible by respecting the limits we set on your freedom. You respect those limits and the freedoms expand. It's as simple as that."

Take Eric's curfew, for example. When he was fourteen, his curfew was ten o'clock on nonschool nights. The rules were simple. We had to know and approve of where he was and what he was doing, and he had to be home before ten.

"But some of my friends can stay out later," he complained.

"So, if you obey the rules for six months, your curfew will become 10:30. You break the rules and we start counting another six months from there. If, after earning a 10:30 curfew, you obey the rules for six months, your curfew will become eleven, and so on. Sound good?"

"It's a deal!" he said.

Two months later, he came in 15 minutes late. He gave us some song-and-dance about not knowing what time it was, and he forgot to wear his watch, and his friend's pet iguana got sick and they had to take it over to the vet, and we just smiled and shook our heads and said, "See, now we have to be your parents." His six-month waiting period started over from there.

He figured things out quickly. Six months later, his curfew became 10:30. Six months later, it became eleven o'clock. By the time he was seventeen, we trusted him enough to let him spend spring break at the beach with a couple of his buddies.

The principle is a simple one. A child will take responsibility not for things that are handed to him on a silver platter, but for things he must earn. The things he earns, he takes care of. We all take care of the things we invest in, don't we?

I never cease to be amazed at parents who give their children nearly everything they want and then wonder why their children (a) don't take care of what they have, (b) take their parents' benevolence for granted, (c) behave irresponsibly and even dangerously, or (d) all of the above.

Willie and I have not dedicated ourselves to making Eric and Amy happy. Instead, we've tried to instill in them the qualities and skills they'll need to create their own happiness. The payoff was twofold. First, the children obtained nearly all the freedom they could want. Second, so did we.

You know, it's kinda fun not being a parent.

T-shirts

This is the story of Eric and the T-shirt. Eric was fifteen at the time these events transpired. The story finally can be told because I bought the rights to it from him for an undisclosed sum. Fifteen-year-olds, I found, drive hard bargains.

The story begins at a Van Halen concert Eric attended. Before he went, he had asked us permission to buy a tour T-shirt. We granted it with the stipulation that the T-shirt not be black, sleeveless, or bear any reference to drugs, alcohol, or sex.

"Why can't it be black?" he asked, in that indignant, I-demand-an-explanation-for-this-injustice tone that is universally characteristic of fifteen-year-olds.

"Because we don't like black T-shirts," we replied.

After several exchanges, the issue was put to rest by offering to rescind permission to buy any T-shirt at all if agreement on color could not be reached. Eric agreed to our terms.

He returned from the concern with a white, long-sleeve jersey emblazoned with the Van Halen logo and the words "World Tour '84." On Monday morning of the following week he came downstairs ready for school wearing you-guessed-it.

"Sorry, Eric, but we aren't going to let you wear your T-shirt to school," I said.

"Why not?"

"Eric, would you like to donate your new T-shirt to Goodwill?"

"I won't wear it to school."

It's truly amazing how quickly he sees the light.

Eric didn't wear it to school but he wore it everywhere else. It seemed like weeks went by when he wore nothing but the T-shirt. I was beginning to think maybe the band had bought advertising space on his chest.

Meanwhile, Eric spurned the other clothes we had bought him—clothes he had picked out himself, clothes that were supposedly "in," clothes that were not getting any bigger, but he was. No only this, but there was a certain, let us say, "attitude" that Eric projected when he wore his Van Halen T-shirt. It wasn't quite defiant. It wasn't quite macho. It wasn't quite anything else we could put our fingers on, but it was definitely an "attitude." The final straw was when he wore it to school on the final day of his junior high school career. Upon discovering this, his mother confiscated the T-shirt.

Several weeks later, as Eric, his godfather Rob, and I were driving to the beach to play golf, the subject of the T-shirt came up. Eric began complaining that he couldn't understand why Mom had taken it away, and he didn't see anything wrong with wearing it to school anyway, and it just wasn't fair.

I agreed that it didn't seem exactly fair.

He got excited, "Will you talk to Mom about giving it back to me, then?" he asked.

"No," I said, "I won't."

Again: "Why not?"

"Because I plan on living with your mother for at least another forty years and with you another three years. I think you can figure that one out."

All I heard from the back seat was a disgusted sigh.

Rob and I spent a good hour talking to him about the importance of proper dress and the impression one's clothes make on other people. At the end of this eloquence, all Eric could say was, "I want my T-shirt back."

"Eric," said Rob, "if you were smart instead of mad, I'll bet you could get it back."

"How? Steal it?"

"I'm not going to tell you how, because you should figure this one out for yourself, but I'll give you a hint: It's called 'diplomacy.' "

For several moments, the car fell quiet. Then, all Eric said was, "I'm never going to get my T-shirt back, I just know it."

"Diplomacy, Eric," said Rob, "diplomacy."

About a week later, Eric came down to the dinner table wearing the T-shirt. I asked my wife how Eric had managed to get the shirt back. "He asked me for it politely and promised not to wear it away from the house," she answered.

Good going, Eric. I'm proud of you.

Wheels

"Dad! I've decided what kind of car I want to get when I'm sixteen. Look at this!"

"Eric," I said, brushing away the copy of *Car Trader* he'd stuck in my face, "I've told you a hundred times, I'm not buying you a car when you turn sixteen. Look here! Read my lips! I'm . . . not . . . buying . . . you . . . a . . . car . . . when . . . you . . . turn . . . sixteen."

"Why not?!"

"I've told you why not."

"Yeah, but why not?"

"Because I've told you why not."

"But, can we talk about it?"

"We've talked about it before."

"But, Dad, can we talk about it today?"

"No."

"Why not?!"

He wouldn't give up. He started in on me when he was fourteen and kept it up relentlessly for two and a half years. I mean every day. And every day I told him he wasn't getting a car.

"Why not?!"

"Because you won't need a car of your own, Eric. We have two cars. You'll be able to use one."

"Right! The station wagon! Forget it! I won't drive a station wagon!"

"Nerd-mobile, eh?"

"Right!"

"Well, Eric, nerd sort of runs in the family. I was a nerd, you know. It's probably inevitable—genetic, even—you'll be a nerd, too, sooner or later. If driving a station wagon doesn't do it, wearing glasses will."

"I don't wear glasses."

"Then you have to drive a station wagon. It's either one or the other. We nerds don't have a lot of options."

"Dad?"

"Yes, son."

"Will you buy me a car when I'm sixteen?"

"No."

"Why not?!"

Relentless.

My reasons for why not were philosophical (giving a sixteen-year-old a car served only to reinforce, one more time, to a kid already firmly convinced it was so, that something could be had for nothing), ideological (parents who bought cars for their kids were indulging their children's capitalist/materialist/bourgeois obsessions), and psychological (buying a teen a car was a way of compensating for never having spent time with the kid when the time really mattered).

And finally, I had practical objections, firmly rooted in reality. (I didn't think I could afford it.)

Then, sixteen came and so did the driver's license and Eric started driving my car. (He was true to his word—he *wouldn't* drive the station wagon.) And it was inconvenient and it was irritating to get in my car after he'd driven it to find the seat pulled up under the steering wheel and the rearview mirror aimed at the floor and the gas gauge on empty. And he couldn't get a job because he didn't have reliable transportation, which meant I had to pay for his gas and insurance. And so, tossing my self-righteous, pompous principles out the window, I broke down and bought him a car—a completely restored 1966 Mustang. It was the car I wanted when I was sixteen.

I surprised him with it during our summer vacation at the beach. You should have seen the look on his face. It was worth every penny of it.

And, I've since concluded, it was one of the best moves I've ever made.

I put the title in his name, you see, and I said, "This car is yours, lock, stock, and barrel. I bought it, but you have to pay for the insurance, the gas, and all repairs. Welcome to responsibility!"

Eric got a job soon thereafter. He was never late with an insurance payment, never late to work, and never was his car anything but clean. He grew up two years in the first nine months of ownership.

And, man, was I happy! Not to mention proud.

Wheels, Part Two

(Q) With the start of the school year upon us, and with a child about to turn sixteen, my wife and I were wondering what your feelings were about high school kids having jobs during the school year. Our daughter, who has always been a fairly good student, says she wants to get a job. We're not sure it's a good idea. Do you think we should let her, and if so, what kinds of rules should there be?

(A) I think you should let her. Your daughter's initiative and willingness to accept obligations outside of home and school, especially one that will allow her less time with her peers, should definitely be encouraged. At the very least, she'll find out that she really isn't ready for a job. Either way, it will be a tremendously valuable learning experience, one she shouldn't be denied.

Now, if she was not already a fairly good student, I would probably advise that you tell her she can get a job when her grades come up. She shows improvement in her grades, you allow her to work a certain number of hours per week. She shows further improvement, you let her increase her hours, and so on, and so forth. In that case, I would point out that her desire to work presents you with what I call a "strategic opportunity"—a chance to turn her motivation for doing one thing (getting a job) into motivation for something else (better grades). In the long run, seizing upon a strategic opportunity benefits the child more than the parent, although it may take the child a while to figure that out.

When our children turned sixteen (separately), we told them that if they wanted to drive, they had to pay the difference in the insurance premium. That meant they had to get jobs, the only stipulation being they could not work more than fifteen hours a week to start. We gave them a two-month "grace period," during which we picked up the insurance tab. After that, no work, no drive.

So, they each went out and got a job. Eric stocked shelves in a drugstore. Amy worked behind the counter in a yogurt shop. They started at minimum wage, which meant that after they paid us their share of the insurance, they had a little more than half their paychecks left to do with as they pretty well pleased. We should be so lucky!

We also informed them they couldn't keep their jobs unless they kept their grades up. "We'll give you one grading period to adjust to this," we told him/her. "If your grades go down, you'll be allowed to continue working, but you'll be on probation until the next report card comes out. If the grades haven't come back up by then, you'll have to quit your job, which means you won't be able to drive."

By linking grades, job, and driving privileges together, we created circumstances that began to approximate adult realities. This age child needs experiences of that sort, ones that prepare him or her for dealing with the complexities of independent living.

And that's what it's all about, remember? As I've said before, the purpose of being a parent is to help your children get out of your life and into successful lives of their own.

Letting Go—Part One

Raising my son, Eric, has been the most significant learning experience of my life. Through him, I discovered more about children than a hundred books could have taught. I also discovered a lot about myself, particularly during his teen years.

Not just living with a teenager, but living with a teenage son has opened a window on my own adolescence. More than a breath of fresh air, it's been a look backward in time.

Like most, if not all, teenagers, I never truly knew who I was or understood why I did the things I did. I only thought I understood myself and tried to get everyone else to go along with the deception. In order to cover my insecurities, to hide them from myself and the world, I cultivated an attitude of insensitive aloofness.

Nothing bothered me. I did not run through the rain. I did not wear a hat or earmuffs in below-zero weather. In other words, I was cool. This was the early sixties and cool was "in" for the teenage boys of my generation. We were masculine only to the extent that we were cool. There was only one alternative to cool and I was definitely not an alternative.

In this little charade, I was also in control. I was in total control of myself and my surroundings. No one ran my show but me. Not even my parents. You had to be cool to be in control, and since I was obviously in control, I was cool, right? Wrong!

I wasn't cool and I wasn't in control. I was kidding myself and the joke was on me. I was insecure and not a little frightened of suddenly losing my tenuous grip on reality according to Rosemond. But I would not admit this, even to myself.

Eric has helped me see all this, to put it in new perspective, to recapture those lost years of my life. As I watched him grow into and through adolescence, I saw him doing pretty much the same things, for the same reason. Holding the hounds of insecurity at bay. There's been déjà vu quality to the whole experience, as if I was at times watching myself, twenty years younger. Sometimes, I haven't been able to keep from laughing at the teenage me I've seen in Eric.

When he was in the seventh grade, for instance, I drove him to school nearly every morning. The junior high was on my way to work, so it was convenient and gave us some time together. When eighth grade rolled around, I continued to drive him.

One morning about a month into the new school year, I stopped at an intersection two blocks from the school. Without warning, Eric jumped out of the car, saying something like "I'm gettin' out here, Dad. See you later. Bye."

He continued to get out at the same intersection over the next two weeks. Unable to figure it out, I finally asked why, and he gave me some lame excuse about joining up with friends and walking the rest of the way. No, he wasn't telling me the real reason, which I became determined to figure out. There was something about what he was doing that looked vaguely familiar, but I couldn't get in touch with it.

Several weeks later, after having all but forgotten my mission, it came to me. Of course! I remembered being thirteen years old, and I remembered how hard I worked at that age to create and maintain the illusion within my peer group that I didn't have any parents. Come to think of it, none of my friends had parents, either. We were cool.

Thank you, Eric. Thank you for helping me be a kid again. In some ways, it's a lot more fun the second time around.

Letting Go—Part Two

He was gone.

Number One Son Eric, that is. Just like that.

One day he was home, the next he was off to his first year of college at N.C. State University.

We took him up on a Thursday, helped him move in, and were back home on Friday. Seemed like the fastest twenty-four hours of my life.

Try as I did, I just couldn't make it go any slower. Besides, it was obvious he was doing his best to get us back on the road as quickly as possible.

Once he was all settled into his dorm, we said our goodbyes and left, stopping downstairs for a soft drink. As we sat there, talking with two other parents, Eric walked by the window, headed in the direction of the women's dorm. The kid doesn't waste any time.

That's when it hit me, watching him walk away from us like that.

He looked so, well, *purposeful.* Like he knew where his life was going, and it sure as heck wasn't going back in the direction of home.

And right then and there I realized his childhood was over. He'd never be the same again, and neither would I.

There were many times during his last three months at home when I caught myself trying desperately to fix some minuscule flaw I thought I had detected in his behavior. I found at least one of these must-fix-its a day.

"Eric," I'd say, "You need to listen to me. It's high time you realize that . . ."

"You can get away with that kind of stuff when you're in high school, but college is a different ball game. . . ."

Most of the time, he'd sit politely through these exercises in last-minute parenting, indulging my need to hang on to the job I'd been doing the past eighteen years. Then he'd acknowledge I was right and promise to do better.

Other times, he'd just smile and cut me off, saying something like, "It's O.K., Dad. I know what you're going to say, and, well, I don't mean to be impolite or anything, but I really don't need to hear it. I'm going to be all right, really I am."

He knew I needed to talk more than he needed the lecture, and he was right.

I thought it would be easy.

At least, I tried hard to convince myself it would be. His mother was having a rough time of it because, said I to my smug self, mothers have more difficulty with separation.

Dads can handle this stuff. We encourage our kids' independence and look forward to them leaving home. We're tough.

Who was I fooling? Only me.

I wasn't handling this any better than his mother; I was just better at hiding my feelings, at kidding myself.

The truth is, I missed him terribly. The truth is, I worried about him.

The truth is, there were times after he left when I walked into his almost-empty room, expecting to find him there. And then there were times I walked into his room knowing he wasn't there and just sat and tried to come to grips with the whole thing; tried to convince myself this was the way it should be and that everything would work out and he'd be fine and so would I.

All I can say is, he'd better bring me some grandchildren one of these days. He's got to do something to make up for this.

Looking Back

On the afternoon of Friday, November 13, 1969, Willie and I, along with three other college friends, piled into a van lent us by her father and headed east out of Chicago. After driving all night, we arrived in Washington at daybreak, joined hands and spirits with nearly a million other intrepid travelers, and marched in protest of the Vietnam War.

Twenty years later, Woodstock gets all the hype, but the March on Washington, as it was called, was truly the most significant event of, by, and for our generation. Woodstock wasn't in the same league. In Washington, there was purpose and passion, commitment and risk. Woodstock was nothing but a party.

When it was over, when the last speech had been made, the last anthem sung, we ate and piled back into the van for the drive west. Arriving back in Chi-town at noon Sunday, we showered, slept a few merciful hours, and drove downtown to see the Rolling Stones—the "World's Greatest Rock 'n' Roll Band," as they had come to be known—in concert. It was a fitting climax to the most exhilarating weekend of my life.

Twenty years later, Willie and I, along with our two children, Eric—then in his third year of college—and Amy—a high school senior—and two of their young friends, made the trek from Charlotte to Carter-Finley Stadium in Raleigh to see the Stones hit the boards for their first tour in eight years.

I had looked forward to the concert for months and knew it was going to be good, but it exceeded my wildest expectations. Though I'd seen many rock 'n' roll shows, this one was *it.* From the stage (a futuristic industrial ruin that towered above the band) to the show (twenty-eight direct hits to the body), to the fireworks at the end of "Jumping Jack Flash," the night was perfection.

When Mick and the boys finally came on, there were dark storm clouds gathering to the west and the clean, electric smell of rain in the air. From the opening chords of "Start Me Up," the Stones charged through a set that included familiar favorites, a few only diehard Stones fans would know, and a few off their latest album. About a third of the way into the two-and-a-half-hour performance, the storm blew away and a full moon rose above the stadium as if to say, "You didn't think I'd miss this, now did you?"

It was the best, but it was more than rock 'n' roll to me. As the band played, I looked at Eric and Amy and could tell that they, too, were transported. Looking around, I saw many other parents our age with their kids, all bouncing up and down to the Stones' infectious beat.

Watching my kids singing along to all the songs, it occurred to me that ours is a generation perhaps unlike any ever before, certainly unlike our parents'. Somehow, we have managed to bridge the so-called generation gap. The span may not always be in good repair, but it's there, always capable of a crossing.

I remembered with regret that in 1969 when my father heard I was going to Washington, he ceased all contact with me for three years. He not only didn't understand, he couldn't. After all, he'd gone to war. He'd been willing to lay down his life for a noble cause. To him, my politics were a slap in the face.

As the Stones segued into "Two-thousand Light Years From Home," I thought of the distance that had separated many, if not most, of us from our parents and said a silent prayer of thanks that we have somehow found the means of communicating with our kids through thick and thin, of understanding their trials and tribulations, of having patience with their determination to head down blind alleys, of tolerating their naive idealism.

And at the center of this reconciliation, there was the music—by groups such as the Beatles and the Stones and Led Zeppelin and the Grateful Dead. A music for our time, but a music for all time. A music we could share with our children. A music we could dance to with our children and sing with our children. And not just a music, but a culture with a heart of hope and healing.

It's only rock 'n' roll? Not in my life.

PART THREE

So, What's Your Problem?

As I travel around the country, doing my talks and workshops, I collect questions from people. Most of these are the "What should I/we do when . . . ?" variety. As in . . .

"What should I do when my five-year-old refuses to eat what I put in front of her at suppertime?"

"What should we do when our eight-year-old misses his ride to school because he dawdled about getting up and getting ready?"

"What should we do when our children bicker with one another?"

"What should I do when my six-year-old says she hates me?"

Questions of this sort are answered in this section. My first aim is to help people understand that most child-rearing problems are, in fact, typical. I'm trying, therefore, to bring a lot of this stuff "out of the closet."

My second aim is to clarify that a behavior problem is not necessarily indicative of an emotional problem. All children, at one point in time or another, exhibit behavior problems. Very few children have full-blown emotional problems. Another way of looking at this is to say that all children, because they are human, and humans are gifted/cursed (depending on your point of view) with emotions, and learning to tame one's emotions always involves a struggle, have "emotional problems." But very few of these problems, or the behaviors that accompany them, are out of the ordinary. Most of them are just part of the struggle.

My third aim is to give answers that are practical, workable, down-to-earth, and which speak to people's common sense rather than to their intellects. Again, raising children is not an intellectual proposition. If it were, then the smartest people would be the best parents, and I haven't noticed that to be the case at all.

My fourth aim is to help people laugh at things they've been taking all too seriously, like kids pooping in their pants, or telling you they hate you, or threatening to run away, or throwing up at the dinner table because you've served broccoli, or letting the air out of your tires for an April Fools' joke. Ha, ha.

I hope I've succeeded.

Toilet Training

Readiness Signs

"My pediatrician says that parents shouldn't even *think* about starting to toilet train before a child is at least two and a half," a mother once told me.

Any doctor who makes such a statement should be sentenced to hard labor in a diaper laundry. There is no such truth. In fact, there are no general "shoulds" at all pertaining to the age when a child can learn to use the toilet. Some children are ready to develop this skill when they are fifteen months old. Others show no signs of readiness until nearly age three.

Both these examples are exceptional. Most children are ready sometime between the ages of eighteen months and two and a half years. In any case, there is no "normal" age for toilet training, and there can be no prescriptions for when this learning must take place or how long the process should take. The important variable is *not* age. It is the child and the signals she will send to let you know when she is ready to give potty sitting a try.

Don't hold your breath waiting for your child to say something akin to, "Mom, I believe it's time you told me about the legendary great white water chair." She might not say anything. Chances are, however, she will begin by dropping little hints that can be translated to mean essentially the same thing. These hints, or readiness signs, include (but are not limited to):

- waking up dry in the morning for several weeks,
- being dry after naptime fairly regularly,
- staying dry for more than two hours between diaper changes.

This tells you her bladder is holding more, and she is developing some ability to work the muscles that control urination.

To continue our list:

- telling you when she is about to release,

• taking her diaper off when it is wet or soiled,
• asking you to change her when she is wet or soiled,
• imitating you when you use the toilet,
• showing a definite interest in the toilet and some indication that she knows what it's for,
• asking to sit on the potty.

When these signs will emerge depends on both the child and her environment. One important question is, "Does Jennifer have the opportunity to express her readiness?" For instance, is the bathroom door left open? Is she allowed and even encouraged to watch the big people in the house use the toilet? Does she have a seat her own size to sit on and pretend?

Another important question follows closely on the heels of the first: "If Jennifer exhibits several of these signs, will someone pay attention?" Sometimes a mother isn't ready to listen, because she wants the closeness and affection that spin off the diapering ritual to last longer.

At some time during the second or third year of life, a child's toileting readiness peaks. This peak lasts for several weeks. Parents who initiate toilet training during this critical period will probably find that the child will master the process quite smoothly.

It is important, therefore, that parents be sensitive to the child's expressions of "I'm ready!" If the critical period is *not* responded to, the child's natural eagerness will wane. Later, it will be difficult for everyone to paddle back upstream.

On the other hand, if parents act too pushy and eager to get the whole business over with, the child will become negative and uncooperative. It's just her way of saying, "I'd rather do it my way!" You can lead a child to the water chair, but you can't make her sit.

Every child is unique, and every home is different. No two children will show the same signs at the same age, nor are there any methods which can guarantee success.

Give your child ample opportunity to discover why mommies and daddies and brothers and sisters sit on the water chair. Don't push the process, but be aware of the readiness signals and prepared to initiate toilet training when they appear. Remember that once the readiness signals occur, several weeks of hesitation may let the best opportunity slip away. Above all else, watch the child—not the calendar.

A Family Affair

(Q) A professional in the town we live in will come into your home and toilet train your child for about $300. He uses a method which he claims virtually guarantees complete success in one day. We have a twenty-six-month-old daughter who seems ready to use the potty, and we want to know what your thoughts are on having him perform this service for us.

(A) Frankly, the whole idea is profoundly disturbing to me. I do not believe it is within the legitimate province of a professional to offer such a service.

Learning to use the toilet is a normal part of every child's socialization. Given time, the child's readiness, and gentle encouragement from the parents, it will happen without undue stress or any great investment of effort. In this respect, it is no more significant a skill than learning how to drink from a cup, use a fork, or get dressed.

Toilet training does, however, involve more of a mess and a smell than buttoning a shirt, and after two or more years of changing diapers, parents are usually eager to get it over with. It is this eagerness that your friendly neighborhood professional is capitalizing on by offering his tidy service.

Any specialist in child development should be able to comment on the acquisition of this skill and identify, for instance, factors which facilitate the child's success. However, except in cases where either the child or the circumstances are exceptional, the firsthand, on-site services of a specialist are not necessary for the actual learning.

In fact, it is probably better for both parents and children that professionals keep a respectful distance from natural developmental processes of this nature.

There is more going on during toilet training than meets this professional's eye. Apparently, he has little appreciation for the transition which toilet training brings about in the parent-child relationship.

Not only is the child learning where to put his b.m.'s, but he is learning to be less dependent on his parents. This usually involves some ambivalence. Does he really want to give up the creature comforts that come with being an infant in exchange for dry pants? This ambivalence, and the anxiety that accompanies it, can be resolved successfully *only* with his parents.

For parents, toilet training means readjusting their manner of relating to the child and their perceptions of him. It is crucial that parents and their children work through this transition together, in their own way and their own time.

You want your child to use the potty? Here's how, in less than fifty-five words (see pages 203–4 for readiness signs).

Buy her a potty and some training pants, consign her diapers to the rag bag, and tell her where to put her business. Help at first with the details. Then, stand well out of the way so she can experience this as an exercise in independence.

Simple, yes? You don't need a Ph.D. to do that.

This professional probably has enough candy up his sleeve to persuade a toddler to use the potty, but most children are smart enough to go poop in the corner as soon as he leaves.

Better Late Than Never

(Q) My almost-four-year-old shows no interest in using the toilet. When he was two, I decided I would let things be until he showed me he was good and ready. Now it's almost two years later and all he shows me is wet, messy training pants. When he was about three, I became panicky and upset at his lack of progress, but then I felt bad about having made such an issue of it and backed off entirely. When he has an accident (five or six times a day), he is very good about cleaning himself up and putting his wet clothes in the right place. At night, he still wears diapers. He goes to a day-care program (which he lives for) five mornings a week, and while he's with other children, he controls himself. He has even used the toilet there on several occasions. But as soon as we get home, he floods. Don't tell me to withhold privileges, as there is nothing he cares enough about to make him cooperate. The nurse at our family doctor's told me that this is a sign of emotional problems and that we need to make an appointment with a psychologist. Do you agree?

(A) Nope. He doesn't have emotional problems—he's a four-year-old who has never been given a straight message about using the toilet. He has probably never heard you clearly say, "I want you to put your wee-wee and b.m.'s in the potty . . . and nowhere else, mind you."

There is a difference between making an *issue* of something and making a *statement* about it. Unfortunately, toilet training has become a major issue, full of myth, anxiety, and misinformation. Consequently, we have difficulty *thinking* effectively about it, much less making effective statements about it to our children.

Only in America, for instance, will you find entire books devoted to the subject. Several of the more recent ones come complete with stories to read to the child. One has drawings showing a fireman, policeman, and teacher, all sitting merrily on toilets. What a production!

Only in America would someone think to write, for a public hungry to buy, a book entitled *Toilet Training in Less Than a Day* (Azrin and Foxx, Simon and Schuster).

Only in America will you find professionals with impressive credentials offering, for a modest fee, to come to your home and, with the aid of a doll that wets, toilet train your child in one day while you sip coffee and watch "As the World Burns."

It's the Twentieth Century Medicine Show: "Amazin', just amazin'. Yesiree, folks, just step right up and watch as I demonstrate in front of your very eyes with a real live two-year-old just like the one you've got at home how you too can toilet train your child in one day. . . . That's right! One day! Not two, but one! You heard me . . . no more poopy pants, no more ammonia smell clogging up your nostrils, no more disposable diapers clogging up your septic tanks, and all accomplished in one amazingly short day."

Amid all the hocus-pocus, confusion reigns. We have made a mystery out of something that is simply a practical, unamazing exercise in self-sufficiency—like learning how to eat with a spoon. Think about it. First, the child sees you using a spoon, and he experiences what it's like to have you feed him with a spoon. When you see that he has developed enough manual dexterity to hold a spoon and guide it to his mouth, you give him his own little spoon. Initially, he slops his food everywhere—he has "accidents," which you patiently, and with words of encouragement, clean up. And lo and behold, in time he learns to eat with a spoon. Through this whole process of learning to eat with a spoon runs the message, "You can feed yourself." And so he does. I never yet have heard of a child who was psychologically traumatized by spoon training.

Two years ago you could have shown your child how to use a potty his own size and said, "You can use the potty just like everyone else does." And he would have done his business there and everywhere else for a while. And you could have been patiently encouraging. And he would have learned.

But he never got the message. Then, a year later, he sensed your anxiety, heard conflicting statements, and said to himself, "Well, if *they* don't know what they want me to do, then I don't know what I want me to do either."

So now? Now you gotta convince him. But first, convince yourself. Do you want him to use the potty like the rest of the world's four-year-olds, or do you want to continue acting confused and paralyzed by words like "emotional problems"?

Don't tell me there's "nothing he cares enough about," because you also said, "He lives for day care."

So here's a four-year-old who knows what to do but won't. Convince him! Say to him, with no uncertainty, "I want you to put your wee-wee and b.m.'s in the toilet . . . and nowhere else, mind you."

Give him an "allowance" of one accident a day for the first two weeks: "If you have two accidents, you don't go to school the next day." At the end of two weeks, take away the "allowance."

During this time, keep an accident scorecard posted in a prominent place (such as on the refrigerator). Put a check in the box-of-the-day for each accident.

Oh, and don't ever, ever, ask him, "Do you have to go to the bathroom!" Make *him* responsible. And he will be.

The most delightful story I ever heard about toilet training was of a mother who gave her two-year-old a set of training pants and a potty of his own and said, "Use it."

Well, the little fella just flat refused. "NO!" he said. "I wanna poo in my didee."

"Fine," his mother said, taking a diaper and laying it in the bottom of his potty. "Poo in your didee—right here."

It was all the convincing he needed.

Don't Ask, Tell

(Q) Our almost-three-year-old son absolutely refuses to use the toilet. He responds with a firm, amplified, "NO!" nearly every time I ask him if he would like to use the potty. If I try coaxing him, he wails. Actually, I have caught him "off guard" several times during the past six months, and he has shown me that he does know how to use it. Otherwise, he refuses to cooperate. I am looking forward to getting rid of the diaper pail. Help!

(A) Why should he cooperate? Obviously, you have yet to tell him, in definite terms, exactly what it is you expect of him. As long as you continue to ask, in whatever way, "Won't you *please* use the potty instead of using your diapers?" he has your permission to say, "No!"

Children spend nearly the first two years of their lives viewing the universe as though they sit at its center. Because of their obvious limitations, we wait on them hand and foot—we carry them, bathe them, powder them, comfort them, feed them, and dress them.

It should come as no surprise to any of us that almost every child emerges from this cocoon feeling as though he is the world's most significant person, rightfully in control of everything and everyone. This fantasy has obvious appeal, and most children are reluctant to give it up.

For parents to survive the "Terrible Twos" they must develop an uncanny ability to sense and avoid power struggles. Whenever we react to the two-year-old's natural inclination to oppose us (after all, from *his* point of view, *we* are the ones who are stepping out of line) by attempting to force cooperation, the game is lost. The struggle itself is our undoing. A person in control has no need to struggle.

So far, so good. You are definitely *not* in a power struggle with your son over the use of the toilet. You say, "Please?" he says, "No!" and you back down. Under the circumstances, he has no need to struggle. He is in control.

Ah, but *avoiding* power struggles is only part of the picture. The real trick is to learn to maneuver *around,* rather than retreat from, opposition. In other words, you don't fight, but you don't run away either. Up until now, you have not taken an assertive stance on the question of whether your son uses the potty or not.

Because of your indecision, your son has seized the opportunity to proclaim, "I'm more powerful than you are."

For seven days, make no mention of the potty. Change his diapers on schedule, without protest or impatience. If he tells you he *wants* to sit on the toilet, give him an assist and then excuse yourself. If he calls you to see his accomplishment, acknowledge what he has done in a positive, but matter-of-fact way: "That's very good. I'm going to put your diapers back on now."

During the week, purchase several pairs of heavy cotton training pants. On the morning of the eighth day, greet him with this announcement: "Today is a brand-new day! Today you begin to use the potty. You are not going to wear diapers anymore. You are going to wear these big-boy pants and learn how to keep them dry. Come with Mommy. I want to show you something."

Take him to the bathroom and show him an alarm clock you put there the night before (as an alternative, the timer on your stove will do).

"This clock has a bell that will tell you when you need to sit down and use the potty. It's called the potty bell. When you hear the potty bell, I *want you* to come in here and sit on the potty. The bell will ring four times today (set it to ring in the morning, after lunch, before dinner, and before bed), but you may use the potty any other time you need to. You aren't wearing diapers anymore. I *want you* to keep these big-boy pants dry."

Set the alarm to ring at the same times every day for the next few days. When it rings, tell your son, "It's time for you to use the potty. Call me if you need some help." Don't become overly involved. Prompt him when the bell rings and then keep your distance.

If he tells you he doesn't want to sit right then, don't push, but gently remind him that he needs to keep his pants dry.

Respond to his successes with encouragement, but without unnecessary razzmatazz. Deal with accidents (and there will be some) in a calm, direct manner: "You forgot to use the potty. That's all right. You will do better next time. I'll help you put dry pants on. Remember, I *want you* to keep these pants dry by using the potty."

By using an alarm to signal "potty-time," you are gently turning his resistance away from you. At the same time you are making clear, authoritative statements which convey what you expect of him.

Instead of giving him permission to say, "I won't," you can give him an opportunity to grow. It's an offer he can't refuse.

Just One of Those Things

The parents of a four-year-old boy recently asked my advice concerning a toilet-training problem. This little guy learned how to use the toilet when he was about thirty months old, which, for most children, is neither too soon nor too late.

For reasons unknown, however, he became anxious and resistant about using it for bowel movements. Whenever he felt a "Number Two" coming, he asked to be put in a diaper.

Wisely deciding not to press the issue, the parents cooperated with the minor fetish, thinking the problem would resolve itself in due time, which it didn't.

As the months became years, he became increasingly stubborn toward any suggestion that he use the toilet for bowel movements. The unsavory prospect of having to clean bottoms and buy disposal diapers for several more years brought the parents to my office.

Sometimes a problem of this nature is complicated by a pattern of "holding," which can, over time, result in medical problems. Fortunately, this youngster was regular, and a pediatrician had recently given him a clean bill of health.

My first question, then, became, "What's going on here?" An evaluation of the child and family failed to reveal anything that might implicate emotional disturbance, family dysfunction, or faulty toilet training. It would have been convenient to presume that the problem was a manipulation or a form of attention seeking, but that didn't seem to fit. I finally concluded that it was just one of those many unpredictable, inexplicable things that can develop in the course of raising a child.

However, whereas the problem wasn't psychological in nature, it could eventually have culminated in serious emotional and social problems. Therefore, given that this little fellow knew the mechanics of using the toilet and was both medically and psychologically healthy, I advocated a "cold turkey" approach.

His parents began by informing him, in no uncertain terms, that he was henceforth expected to use the toilet just like everyone else in the family. Under no circumstances would he ever again be allowed to wear a diaper. When he demanded to know why, they said, "Because we won't let you." Period. End quote. As in, "We are in charge here, and we know what's best for you. Trust us."

If, when a bowel movement was imminent, he became agitated and/or began throwing a tantrum, his parents were to put him in the bathroom and tell him not to come out until he was calm. They were not, however, to even suggest that he might want to try using the toilet while he was in there.

When and if he had a bowel movement, no matter how small, in his pants, he had to go to the bathroom, take a bath, and hand wash any and all soiled clothing. The parents stocked the bathroom with the necessary supplies and showed him how to accomplish this task. After cleaning up after himself, he had to get into his pajamas and go to his room, where he spent the remainder of the day.

During the day, the parents were not to make any mention of using the toilet. If he had an "accident," they were to respond patiently and with encouragement, but were to enforce the rules dispassionately. Furthermore, if he had success, they weren't to lavish praise. Be positive, I told them, but be matter-of-fact.

One week and one accident later, the boy was using the toilet regularly and without anxiety.

But be not deceived, it wasn't the technique that turned the trick, it was the clear, authoritative message from his parents that he was going to use the toilet appropriately, along with the proof of where they stood. Children like it when parents take control. Yes, they do.

Power Struggles

(Q) My four-year-old daughter holds her bowel movements. Her pediatrician assures us that there is nothing physically wrong with her. She lets out only a little at a time and therefore is still in diapers. I have been playing it cool and not forcing the issue, but she has a young brother who is an infant, and the thrill of changing diapers is wearing thin.

(A) I would not hesitate, with a four-year-old, to communicate some firm expectations about where to put b.m.'s. Young children are quite intuitive and can sense when their parents have a big investment in an issue. I suspect that your daughter has seized on this passive form of rebellion to keep attention focused on her, rather than on her younger brother. In this way, she continues to get her importance confirmed. What you need is a method which will get her to use the toilet and at the same time reassure her that she is important.

Tape a sheet of paper daily to the refrigerator door or some equally visible place. Tell her firmly that she is not going to wear diapers anymore and that she will use the toilet for b.m.'s. Inform her that when she has an accident, she will receive a large check on her scorecard.

Now consider what privileges she enjoys daily. Playing outside after supper? Riding her tricycle? Going to a friend's house? Make a list of three activities she values most. Tell her that you will eliminate one activity for every accident, starting with the activity that is most important to her.

Expect two to three weeks to pass before you see steady progress. Don't be discouraged by a relapse after a good start. Stay firm, but gentle, and always be encouraging. Your confidence in her, combined with a steady attitude of authority, will make more of a difference to her than anything else.

It's None of Your Business

(Q) Bobby, our four-year-old, is not bowel trained. He holds his b.m.'s and constipates himself for several days at a time, sometimes nearly a week. When he can't hold any longer, he usually releases in his pants. Sometimes he tell us when he is about to go, and one of us literally runs him to the bathroom, but once we get there he usually loses the urge. Later he will have his inevitable accident. We have tried laxatives, and they made him somewhat more regular, but no more cooperative. We have him clean himself with supervision after every mistake. He also needs help taking his pants down and getting up on the potty. We've tried everything.

(A) Wow! I'm exhausted! Frankly, your son is not putting his b.m.'s in the toilet because you are doing all the work. *He* may not be trained, but *you* certainly are. And by the way, he *is* cooperating—in the confusion.

You are investing a tremendous amount of energy in monitoring, supervising, and helping him with something he should be in charge of by the age of four. This long-term investment has created a climate of chaos and confusion concerning "Bobby's b.m.'s."

No one, including Bobby, knows exactly what to do when Bobby feels like having a b.m. The statement, "we've tried everything," probably means that over the years there has been an accumulation of inconsistent responses and messages in reaction to his gestures, requests, and mistakes.

Your son is confused. He is probably wondering, "Who's having the b.m., me or my parents? Is a b.m. something that should or shouldn't happen? Can I have one by myself? Who am I doing it for? Am I really four years old?" Because there are no clear definitions, the confusion has never been resolved.

It is essential that you back out of the picture. First, define the situation.

Teach him, if he *really* does not know, how to pull his pants down or off and position himself on the toilet seat. If he has difficulty, dress him in elastic-waisted shorts. A wooden stool will give him any additional boost he needs.

Most four-year-olds are capable of cleaning themselves *without supervision.* Some initial guidance for Bobby will help to define this as his responsibility. Take the time to teach him exactly what he should do when he soils himself. However, this lesson should take place *when he is clean.*

Organize the necessary equipment (washcloths, sponge, liquid soap, towels, clean underwear, and so on) in one specific, accessible area of the bathroom, and put him through the paces of cleaning himself. Practice the sequence several times, in an encouraging and positive manner.

When he tells you he feels the pressure of a b.m., tell him to go to the bathroom and sit on the potty, "just as everyone else does." If he wants you to take him (after all, he hasn't had to do the work up until now), tell him, "I will not help you have a b.m."

If he has an accident (count on it), send him to the bathroom to clean himself. If he comes out before either he or the room is clean, simply say, "You are not finished. Go back in and finish—then you may come out."

During the day, do *not* ask him if he needs to go or provide him with reminders. This age child no longer needs to be protected from the consequences of his own mistakes.

When he has success, keep your reactions low-key. After all, he's learning to accept this responsibility for *his* benefit, not yours. Furthermore, success is not a big deal—it's expected of him. "That's fine. No, I don't need to come see. You can do it all by yourself. You don't need Daddy to look."

Finally, give him plenty of time to adjust and expect some lapses along the way. If you can stay with the program, and roll with the initial ups and downs, he will eventually match the pace you set for him. Just as he has all along.

Bed-wetting

If your child wets the bed almost every night, then you undoubtedly know that none of the "home remedies" are much help. Punishment, restriction of liquids, getting her up at intervals—none of these works. Some of these methods may provide temporary relief, but all of them together won't stop a child from wetting the bed.

Somewhere along the line, most of us have been taught that wetting the bed is a symptom of laziness or insecurity, and that it's a child's way of saying that things aren't going right at home. While it is true that many children who wet the bed do feel ashamed and are under a great deal of stress because of it, there is no reason to believe that bed-wetting is an expression of a damaged emotional condition.

Actually, bed-wetting happens, in most cases, because the child is an unusually deep sleeper. This deep sleep prevents her from waking when the bladder sends an "I'm full" signal to the brain. The signal is too weak, or the brain is too deeply asleep to "hear" it. In either case, the bladder does the natural thing, which is to empty itself. It's easy to see why the home remedies described above will be no more useful than beating one's head against a brick wall.

However, there is a way to approach bed-wetting which re quires nothing more than your patience and understanding. First, give the problem back to your child. Stop trying frantically to solve it for her. It's *her* body and *her* problem, and she can solve it only if *she* has possession of it.

Stop making "Did you wet the bed last night?" the first question of every day. Her bed-wetting should not be a topic of family discussion.

Tell her that when she wets the bed she is to change her pajamas, lay a heavy towel across the wet spot, and go back to bed without waking the family. In the morning, she is to strip her own bed and place the wet linens and wet pajamas in a pile just inside her bedroom door. After you have done the wash, put the folded linen back on her bed. At bedtime, have her help you make the bed, patiently teaching her how and letting her take over more and more of the chore until she is able to do it by herself.

Give her as much liquid as she wants all day. It's probably good to remind young children to use the bathroom just before bed, but do it casually.

Help your child understand her problem by providing some basic education. Tell her that there is a muscle just below her bladder (you can call it the "doughnut" muscle) which is normally closed. When she goes to the bathroom, she relaxes this muscle and it opens (open and close your fist to demonstrate). Suggest to her that she might want to make this muscle stronger by practicing tightening and holding it for several seconds off and on during the day. And when she goes to the bathroom, she can further strengthen it by turning off and on her flow of urine. Most children will cooperate willingly in this exercise.

A number of pediatricians now advise parents of children who wet the bed to eliminate all refined sugar from the children's diet. Substitute fruits, nuts, raw vegetables, or peanut butter and crackers along with a glass of unsweetened juice for bedtime snacks instead of sugar-sweetened "goodies."

If, after doing these things for about six weeks, the bed-wetting has not stopped, then I recommend that you purchase a bed-wetting alarm. A typical system consists of a set of pads which are arranged under the sheet and an alarm connected to the pads which sounds immediately when the child begins to wet. Through repetition, this device eventually teaches the child to wake to the feeling of a full bladder. Then use of the alarm can be discontinued.

This alarm operates on low voltage batteries, is completely safe, and when used properly, it usually works. The wee-alarm is *not,* however, to be used with children younger than four, many of whom are still developing nighttime control. Nor is it to be used without the child's consent and a definite indication from her that she wants to stop wetting the bed.

Bed-wetting kids are not "bad" kids. However, you can bet that the more of an issue you make of the problem, the more overwhelmed the child will feel, and the longer it will be before she can solve it for herself.

(Q) Our five-year-old, who has always been a bed-wetter, has recently started wetting his pants during the day. He doesn't tell us about it, but waits until one of us points out that he's damp and suggests that he change his clothes. We haven't criticized or reprimanded him for these accidents, and the bed-wetting is not a topic for discussion either. Do you think he could be wetting himself for attention? Do you have any suggestions?

(A) My first suggestion is that you break your vow of silence. Bed-wetting can become an increasingly burdensome handicap for a child as he grows older, one which limits his social life and damages his self-concept.

Your decision not to discuss it, although motivated by good intentions, is actually preventing him from initiating any work toward a lasting solution. You seem to be giving tacit permission for the problem to linger indefinitely. This is not in anyone's best interest.

To begin with, I would wager that you *are* upset—about both the daytime accidents and the bed-wetting. Your frustration at having to change and wash smelly sheets, pajamas, and now clothes, nearly every day, needs to be acknowledged and accepted as legitimate. *How* you express that frustration, rather than *whether* you express it, is the central question.

You have probably succeeded admirably at suppressing your annoyance. But our children are more sensitive to us than we generally imagine. Although neither situation has been a topic for discussion, you probably cannot avoid sending subtle, nonverbal cues that tell of your displeasure—an expression, a gesture, an exchanged look. Your silence itself is perhaps the most blatant message.

The topic needs clarification, but because no one has permission to talk about it, your son can't ask, "Are you mad, or aren't you?" So, in an attempt to resolve this ambiguity, he begins wetting his parents during the day, when you can't fail to notice. Will you say anything *now?* How much will it take to bring you out of hiding?

It is probably wrong to say that he's doing this for attention. The fact that he waits for you to mention it strongly suggests he is trying to draw you out. It's time to show your hand.

Begin with a discussion of his bed-wetting. Define it as a problem for you. Tell him you don't enjoy changing and washing sheets and pajamas every day. Bring it out in the open, so you can begin helping him solve this difficulty.

Be careful, however, that you *don't* take responsibility for it. The responsibility must be *his.* He needs a clear, straightforward message from you regarding your feelings and a commitment of understanding and support.

"Junior, we want to talk with you about wetting the bed. You are wetting your bed almost every night, and we both think it's time you began staying dry at night. We want to know how you feel about this. Do you want to continue wetting the bed, or do you want to stop?"

Some indication from him that *he* wants to stop wetting the bed is essential, but you cannot force this point of view upon him. However, it will be much easier for him to make that statement once he knows where you stand.

He also needs to hear a clear message concerning the daytime accidents: "We also want you to stop wetting during the day."

Once you have squarely faced the issue and settled your ambivalence, he will no longer need to wet his pants. The chances are also good that he will stop wetting the bed. If he doesn't, and he begins to express some frustration at not having the success he wants, I would recommend that you purchase a bed-wetting alarm.

I have heard these alarms criticized as artificial, impersonal means of conditioning a child to stop bed-wetting. This is completely off the mark.

My son began wetting his bed shortly after we moved to North Carolina when he was four and a half. Nine months later, a friend and colleague told us about the bed-wetting alarm. We bought one and asked Eric if he would like to try it out. The first night, he wet the bed before he went to sleep just to hear the alarm go off.

Over the next three weeks, he *alone* triumphed over what all of us struggling together had managed to make worse. At the end of that three weeks, he proudly informed us that he did not need the unit anymore. I'm certain he had never felt so proud of himself. If that smacks of something impersonal, then I must have missed something.

The manufacturer does not guarantee success, and it would be foolish of me to imply that it's foolproof. However, your child's self-esteem is worth the relatively few dollars it will cost you to give it a try.

A Tantrum Place

Children usually begin having tantrums around the age of two. Tantrums happen for a variety of reasons. First of all, they are an inevitable by-product of even the most normal, healthy childhoods. Children become frustrated and angry just as we do, but they can't see that there is "more than one way to skin a cat." They also have difficulty expressing their frustrations and knowing what questions to ask. If at first they don't succeed, they just might have a tantrum.

A cardinal rule is don't respond to tantrums by taking over the problem for the child. If parents rescue a child often enough, she learns that tantrums solve problems. If a child has a "this-dumb-toy-won't-obey-me" tantrum, take the dumb toy and tell the out-of-control child that it will be returned when she is calm.

A second rule of thumb is don't give in to demands because of tantrums. It's true that giving in turns off the screams, but it also guarantees their eventual return.

Spankings don't cure the tantrum habit. In fact, they *increase* the likelihood that tantrums will occur. You can't fight fire with fire.

The occasional tantrum can be handled best by letting it run its course and then being there when it subsides to help the child cope with whatever is making her upset.

Frequent tantrums are often an indication that the parents are not enforcing rules consistently. One day, Miranda wants a cookie before supper and gets it because Mom is too tired to be firm. The next day, she is refused a cookie before supper because Mom took an afternoon nap. She throws a tantrum. Mom may (A) spank her, (B) give her a cookie, (C) put her in her room, (D) throw a tantrum, (E) all of the above. This kind of inconsistency places stress on a child. Stress provokes tension, fatigue, and tantrums.

Remember what Grandma did when you told her you were

running away from home? She probably said, "That's a wonderful idea. You should have left home to see the world long before now. After all, you're six years old and time's a-wastin'. So, I'll help you pack and fix you a sandwich. . . ." And there you were back at Grandma's door twenty minutes later, having seen quite enough for six years old.

Grandma had some fine ideas. She could tell the big people from the little people without a program, and she never needed a scorecard. So let's lift a page from Grandma's memoirs and see if tantrums can be handled with some homemade "reverse psychology."

Pick a calm time when everyone in the family is feeling relaxed. Sit down with your young one and say something like, "Miranda, we want to talk with you about tantrums. A tantrum is when you are very angry and scream and throw things and foam at the mouth.

"You make about ten tantrums every day, so we have decided to give you a special place to have tantrums in. We call it your Tantrum Place. Your Tantrum Place is the downstairs bathroom" (or any relatively private place in the house).

"From now on, when you want to make a tantrum, go (or we will take you) to your Tantrum Place, close the door, and make it. You may make all the tantrums you want in there. No one will bother you while you make tantrums."

Whichever place you choose, make it seem it's the best location in the whole house to make tantrums in. Nowhere else is quite good enough for the fine tantrums that Miranda makes.

"We decided to give you the bathroom, because it seems just right for making tantrums. It's small, so the tantrum will be louder. It has a toilet you can use if you have to go potty. There is a light switch for you to turn off and on to make tantrums bigger. You can lie down on the comfy rug and kick and scream. When the tantrum is done, you have tissues to dry your tears and water to wash your face. We hope you like it. In fact, it would be all right if you want to go in there *right now* and make a tantrum, just to see how well it works."

Chances are that she will make a few trial runs the first day, and then, finding that the thrill is gone, will begin having shorter tantrums less often. As she begins having fewer tantrums, point this out to her, and thank her for helping keep the house quiet.

Should she forget about her special place and begin making tantrums in the living room, say something like, "Oh-oh, remember the Tantrum Place. You had better get in there quickly before it's all gone." If necessary, take her there while she is screaming, firmly but without anger.

If she continues to have an occasional tantrum outside while you aren't around, or in her room by herself, let these run their course without notice.

Is it a trick? No. The parents are not one-upping the child with an elaborate practical joke. It's actually a game in which everyone learns something valuable about dealing with stressful situations.

I've seen this technique work with children between the ages of two and a half and five, the ages at which tantrums occur most frequently. Children older than five probably will not cooperate in the game so readily and may simply have to be told, "I do not like tantrums. From now on, when you have a tantrum, I am going to put you in the downstairs bathroom. When you go in there, the door will be closed. You are not to open it and come out until the tantrum is completely over. If you come out before it's over, I will put you back in again."

If Grandma's game doesn't appear to be working, then you may need to be more firm. If nothing you try appears to be having any positive effect, consider seeking professional help. Whatever you decide, if at first you don't succeed, don't throw a tantrum.

Head-banging

(Q) We have a three-year-old who is a head-banger. At six months, she began banging on the bars of her crib, hard enough to cause bruises. When she was nearly two, the banging shifted from bedtime to almost constant banging on the floor, a chair, and so on. There are two types of banging: one to soothe or put her to sleep; the other to express anger or frustration. She knows this gets to us, and we have been known to give in to her just to get her to stop. I know this is not a solution, but nothing else we do seems to have any effect. Our pediatrician insists she cannot hurt herself. He does, however, feel that she has a psychological problem. Friends and relatives are beginning to ask what's wrong with her. What can we do to stop her?

(A) To begin with, your pediatrician is correct: She is not likely to hurt herself. That certainly isn't her aim.

But head-banging isn't necessarily indicative of a psychological problem. While it *is* true that many emotionally disturbed and autistic children head-bang, it is also a fact that many normal children do the same thing.

Head-banging is fairly common among infants and toddlers. Generally speaking, it begins around the sixth month, shortly after the infant is first able to raise herself to a crawling position. At this stage, infants test their balance by rocking back and forth on their hands and knees, looking as though they're trying to build up enough momentum to take off. If a solid object, such as a wall or headboard, is immediately in front of them, they are likely to discover the untold pleasures of head-banging.

The monotonous combination of rhythm and self-stimulation is hypnotic, lulling the child into a blissful, self-absorbed trance. In this respect, head-banging is no different from thumb-sucking or nuzzling a favorite blanket. All of these behaviors are soothing, and the child who discovers their benefits has found an ingenious way of providing for herself some of the comfort she might otherwise be demanding of her parents. By sucking her thumb or banging her head, she is able to put herself to sleep, separate from her mother, occupy idle time, and even postpone the need to be held or fed. In one sense, then, it's a fortunate parent who has a head-banger.

But that's *not* the way most parents look at it. In the first place, good parents don't allow their children to hurt themselves. Furthermore, rocking and head-banging have been associated with severe emotional problems. The idea that we might be raising a child who is so disturbed that she actually enjoys pain is too much to deal with.

So, we try to stop her. First, we give her something else to do. The distraction works—temporarily. A short while later, we hear a thud-thud sound coming from the den. We rush in to find that she has crawled over to the wall and is steadily ramming her head into the baseboard. We pick her up, carry her into the kitchen, and offer her a cookie.

This goes on throughout the day, and eventually she puts things together—banging her head not only feels good, but is a form of communication. When you want Mommy, just bang your head on something—it's like Morse code.

The more she bangs her forehead, the greater her threshold for pain in that area becomes, and the harder she must bang to feel anything at all. Bruises become discolored bumps, and people begin eyeing us suspiciously, their imaginations in high gear.

But the harder we work at getting her to stop, the more she bangs. When she reaches her "Terrible Twos," the head-banging is absorbed into her tantrums, and, since she is already out of control, the banging becomes more violent. By this time, we will go to almost any length to stop her, and she learns that head-banging can get her just about anything she wants. What started as an irrelevant self-indulgence has become a focus of tension in the family. The entire family is obviously edging closer to the brink. You must gain control of this situation.

What should you do? Do very little. The more fuel you funnel into this issue, the higher the flames will leap.

Find a time when the house is calm and running in tune for both parents to talk with her about the head-banging: "We have decided that you need a place to bang your head. Banging your head is O.K. with us, but we don't want to watch or listen. If you want to bang, go to your room. You can bang on anything you want in there. Mommy and I will help you remember the rule."

Keep it short and to the point. Don't expect her to remember. Every time she bangs, whether it's to soothe or express rage, say, "You forgot the rule. You may bang your head in your room. I'll help you get there."

Whether she resists or not, take her there and leave her, saying, "When you finish banging, you may come out."

You may not see any results for several weeks. In fact, an upsurge may occur as she pits her will against yours. The more violent form should subside within six weeks, but she may continue to bang her head as a means of relaxing for several years to come.

After all, it still feels good.

Zeke and the Tar Baby

In one of Joel Chandler Harris's Uncle Remus stories, Brer Fox and Brer Bear make a tar baby, hoping to catch Brer Rabbit once and for all. Sure enough, pretty soon Brer Rabbit meets up with the tar baby and makes some remark about the weather, but the tar baby says nothing. After failing several more times to strike up a conversation, Brer Rabbit becomes angry and hits the tar baby smack in the piece of coal Fox and Bear had used for its nose. Naturally, Brer Rabbit's fist sticks in the tar baby's face, which makes him even madder. So he hits the tar baby again with his other hand, which also becomes stuck. Furious, Brer Rabbit begins kicking the tar baby. In no time, he is covered in tar and unable to move. Enter Fox and Bear.

Sometimes parents get bogged down in problems with their children the same way Brer Rabbit did with the tar baby. First, they make the mistake of attributing more significance to something than it deserves. Then, instead of learning from their mistakes, they become frustrated and begin flailing away at the problem. The more they flail, the more stuck they get. Eventually, the issue begins to infect nearly every aspect of their lives together, and as Brer Rabbit would surely testify, once the tar baby gots you, you ain't goin' no place.

Several years ago, a young couple asked my advice concerning their three-and-a-half-year-old son, whom I shall call Zeke. Zeke was not unlike many other three and a half year olds in that he refused to take "no" for an answer and was determined to run as much of the show as his parents would allow.

And how Zeke's parents had allowed! At three and a half, Zeke did pretty much as he pleased. His parents claimed to have run out of ways to control him. "Nothing works!" they chorused. Guess who was in control?

They had tried spanking him. Small spankings made him laugh, and big spankings made him furious and frenzied. To make matters worse, Zeke's parents spanked too late and always felt guilty afterward, which Zeke was sensitive to and made the most of.

Taking privileges away didn't work either. And no wonder. After all, what's a mere privilege to a child who is calling most of the shots as it is?

His parents had tried talking to Zeke. Oh, and how they talked to him. Like a lawyer in his closing argument they talked to him. When they were finished, Zeke would say, "I'll be good," and proceed to do whatever it was they had asked him not to do. With a smile on his face, no less!

Putting him in his room didn't work. Oh, Zeke would go in all right, but then he would go berserk, turning over bookcases, emptying drawers, and throwing toys and clothes everywhere, all the while giving forth a shrill, lunatic scream. If his parents told him to clean up his mess, he would get worse (if you can imagine that), continuing to scream and thrash about until one of them came in and picked up for him. Maid service in the booby hatch!

After describing all this, they asked me what I thought they should do when Zeke misbehaved.

"Putting him in his room sounds fine to me," I told them.

"Well," they countered, "what are we supposed to do when he goes on one of his rampages?"

"Is he capable of cleaning up afterward?" I asked.

"Oh, yes," they said. "The problem is not that he can't, it's that he won't."

"Well, then," I ventured, "since he's capable of cleaning up after himself, make him stay in his room until he does."

They thought that was funny. "He'd be in there for days," they chortled.

"So? What's a few days?" I replied.

After convincing them that I wasn't kidding, and that what I was suggesting wasn't too extreme (just a minor, and rather fitting, inconvenience), we made a list of Zeke's most frequent transgressions. Zeke would go to his room whenever he did any of the things on the list.

And a new rule was created: If Zeke went on a rampage, he had to remain there until he had completely cleaned up his damage, regardless of how long it took. Meanwhile, he could come out to go to the bathroom, attend his preschool program (three mornings a week), eat meals with the family (with no discussion of his room), and accompany his parents whenever they both left the house. Otherwise, it was full quarantine for Zeke.

Here's what happened:

Day 1, at 3:45 P.M.: Zeke hit his mother and was sent to his room where, just as expected, he went bananas. Refusing to undo any of the destruction, he spent the rest of the day in seclusion (except for supper), screaming insults at his parents (example: "Doo-doo heads!").

Day 2: Except for morning at the preschool and a brief trip to the store with his mother, Zeke stayed in his room.

Day 3: Zeke remained in his room, refusing to budge.

Day 4: Still in his room, Zeke showed signs of weakening. At one point, Zeke offered to clean up some of his room if his mother would do the rest. Wisely, she refused the deal. He called her a "doo-doo" (dropping the reference to her head was a definite sign of progress).

Day 5: That afternoon, a friend dropped by, bringing her son, who was also three and a half. In less than fifteen minutes, Zeke had his room in order.

Zeke tore up his room several times in the following weeks. Each time, he straightened it up before the end of the day. To my knowledge, he hasn't torn up his room since, and that's where his parents send him when he misbehaves. Because it works.

Another tar baby bites the dust.

Bedtime

A Very Hoppy Bedtime Story

A long, long time ago, in a bedroom far, far away, there lay a three-year-old boy named Grumph Nadly, who would not sleep.

Every night at 8:30 his mother would say, "Grumph Nadly, it's time for bed."

He would yell, "I don't want to!" and his mother would ask, "Why not?" Grumph would reply, "Cuz."

He would scream, "I'm scared!" and his father would inquire, "Of what?" Grumph would earnestly answer, "Things."

His mother would say, "Let's go Grumph, it's time for munchkins to be asleep," and Grumph would collapse in a heap on the floor. The heap that was Grumph Nadly would not move, but it would sob and moan piteously.

At last, Grumph's father would pick him up and carry him, shrieking, off to bed. Then, when Grumph was finally quiet and looking the other way, his parents would scurry off and hide. But it was no use. The sound would always find them.

It began softly. ". . . Mommy?"

But if the sound got no answer it grew louder and louder until it fairly shook the rafters: "MOMMEEEEE!"

Then the sound would get an answer. "Yes, Grumph, what is it?"

Sometimes Grumph would say he was hungry or had to go to the "bafoom" or wanted to tell somebody "sumpun." Whatever it was, he would make all the noise he could until the whatever was seen to properly.

Grumph usually went to sleep around midnight and woke up with the sun. His parents had dark circles under their eyes and shuffled when they walked.

One day, Grumph Nadly's mother set out from home and shuffled deep into the woods, seeking peace and quiet. She had shuffled for several hours and was passing a small pond alive with water lilies and butterflies, when she heard a small baritone voice ask, "Are you lost, or what?"

"Who's there?" she asked, startled and looking around.

"Me. Look down here, lady."

And sure enough, when she looked, there he was, a rather unremarkable frog. Unremarkable, that is, except for the fact that he talked, which is *quite* remarkable for frogs.

Before the startled woman could say anything, the frog spoke again, asking, "What brings you to my front yard?"

And Grumph's mother felt suddenly moved to tell the frog everything about how Grumph would not sleep and the heap and the sound and the rest until the frog, having heard quite enough, said, "Hold it! You wanna know how to get this Grumph-child into bed and off to sleep?" With hardly a pause, he went right on, "I'll tell you. But first you have to promise *not* to kiss me when I'm done."

"But why on earth should I want to kiss you in the first place?" asked Grumph's mother.

"Mark my words, you'll want to, and if you manage to grab me and do it, I'll turn into the most handsome and charming prince you ever saw, which is the worst thing that could *ever* happen to a frog who wants to just spend the rest of his life sitting on water lilies, eating bugs."

"All right, I won't kiss you," promised the woman, who had never kissed a frog anyway. "Tell! Tell!"

"Well," the frog began, "you make a book, see, called 'Grumph Nadly's Bedtime Book.' All you need is some sturdy paper, paste, a hole punch, and yarn.

"First, make a list of what's done to prepare the heap for bed.

"Then, gather up several magazines and find pictures to go with each of the things on your list. Make sure you find one of a kid sleeping—draw one if you have to.

"Paste each picture on a separate sheet of paper, put them in order, with the picture of the kid sleeping last. Punch holes in the left-hand side, and tie a loose loop of yarn through each hole.

"Then, write a story to go with the pictures, and every night, read the story to Grumph right before bed.

"For example, the book might begin, 'It's eight o'clock, and time for Grumph Nadly to begin getting ready for bed. The first thing he does is . . .' and you show him the picture of a child taking a bath. Together, you and the Grumph say, 'Take a bath.' The next page reads, 'After his bath, the Grumph dries himself and puts on his pajamas.' And Grumph sees a picture of a kid in pajamas. Keep going until the last page, which says something like, 'And when everything is done, Grumph's mommy and daddy tuck him in, kiss him good night, and Grumph Nadly goes to sleep like a good little tadpole."

When the frog finished his description, he looked at Grumph's mother, adding, "By the time you get to the end, the Grumph should be so involved in his story that he'll take the cue and go right off to sleep."

Grumph's mother thanked the frog profusely, being careful not to kiss him, and hurried home with nary a shuffle in her step. She did exactly as the frog had told her and, lo and behold, that night Grumph Nadly was asleep by 8:45.

Every night thereafter, Grumph and his mother would read the "Bedtime Book" together, and he would go quickly and quietly off to sleep—which is where our story should end, but it doesn't, because . . .

Several years later, Grumph's mother was skipping through the woods when she happened across the same pond.

"Well?" a familiar baritone voice intoned. "Did it work?"

Grumph's mother stopped short and, looking down, saw the very same frog, looking not a year older. "Yes! Oh, yes! It worked, just like you said!" she replied. Then, remembering what the frog had said about being a handsome prince, she grabbed him and planted a big kiss in the middle of his face. Nothing happened.

She kissed him again, longer this time (with her eyes closed). Still nothing happened.

"Hey! What's wrong?" complained Grumph's mother. "Turn into a prince, already."

The frog just laughed as he hopped back onto his lily pad.

"Sorry, lady, but I'm just a talking frog who likes to be kissed." And without even a goodbye, he jumped off his pad, landing in the center of the pond with a great splash, and was never seen again.

The moral, good reader, is simply this: Don't ever kiss a frog, no matter what he may have . . . toad you.

More Than Meets the Eye

(Q) Our first child is thirteen months old. For thirteen months, I have been rocking him to sleep at night and also for his naps. I don't mind doing this—I'd rather rock him than listen to him cry, which he does if I put him in his crib before he's completely asleep. Although I'd like for him to be in bed by 8:30 P.M., the actual time varies because there are nights when he just doesn't seem tired until nine or ten o'clock. But regardless of when I put him in bed, he always sleeps the night. Recently, my pediatrician told me to stop rocking him, put him in bed at the same time every night, and let him go off to sleep on his own, even if it means some crying. The doctor says Robbie is learning that if he cries at bedtime, I'll pick him up. Do you agree with this?

(A) Almost. I definitely agree with your pediatrician that you need to stop rocking young Robbie off to sleep, establish a definite bedtime (with allowances built in for occasional times when it isn't possible to keep him on schedule) and let him go to sleep on his own.

There's far more at stake here, however, than a relatively simple matter of learning to connect crying with being picked up. In fact, it's what Robbie *isn't* learning that warrants the lion's share of attention and concern.

For instance, Robbie *isn't* learning how to go to sleep by himself. Instead, he is becoming increasingly reliant on you. There's a strong possibility that he may eventually think that being next to you is essential to falling asleep. Having a thirteen-month-old cry for a while at bedtime is one thing; having a three-year-old *fight* you at bedtime is quite another.

Robbie *isn't* learning how to predict when bedtime is at hand. It is important that there be some certainty about this, because a child's feelings of security rest, in large measure, on being able to "read" the environment for cues that certain events are about to happen.

In a child's world, *time* needs to be as well organized as the furniture and other things. Confusion over where-things-are *or* when-things-happen encumbers a child's attempts to make sense of his surroundings.

Routines help a child develop a clear sense of cause and effect (logical thinking), and they contribute to his feelings of competence and confidence.

Robbie *isn't* learning that you control when things occur. Instead of deciding when Robbie's bedtime is, you seem to be looking to *him* for a signal, a vague sign of some sort that he is ready. This puts him in the driver's seat before he has even learned to be a good passenger.

But the biggest "isn't" of all is that Robbie *isn't* learning how to let go of you when the day is done. You aren't learning how to comfortably let go of him either.

The importance of bedtime has little to do with *when* children get tired or how much sleep they need. It has, on the other hand, *everything* to do with parents who need time together and, most of all, with teaching children that letting go is O.K. Bedtime is really nothing more than a ritual of separation.

Virtually every important issue that comes up between parent and child involves, to some degree, questions of attachment versus nonattachment. To the extent that these questions are successfully resolved, a child can be less dependent upon his parents. In other words, learning how to let go of parents (mother in particular) is learning how to grow up.

Bedtime problems often bring up this larger issue for the first time. How they are handled will set a precedent for dealing with future separations of many kinds: staying with baby-sitters, going to school, and so on.

It's up to you, as Robbie's parents, to take the lead and set a good precedent. If you are indecisive about letting go at bedtime, he may interpret your hesitation or reluctance as a signal that something is wrong with separating. And, believe me, few things are more stressful to a family than a clinging child.

If you want Robbie in bed at 8:30 P.M., first establish a routine that begins at eight o'clock and lets him know that bedtime is coming. Cap the routine with a tucking-in ceremony; then leave the room.

If he cries (as he almost surely will), you and your husband should take turns going back into his room every five or ten minutes to calm him and reassure him that you are still there, taking care of him. Don't pick him up, and don't hang around.

Bedtime Is for Parents

(Q) We have a three-year-old son who is afraid of the dark and will not go to bed unless one of us stays with him until he is asleep. This started about one year ago, but he was O.K. at bedtime as long as the hall light was on. Now that's not enough. When we put him to bed (at 8:30 every night), he screams about being afraid of the dark until one of us goes back in to stay with him. If we do that, he usually stays up until eleven and sometimes twelve o'clock; then he sleeps until 6:30 A.M. and is rarin' to go. I don't see how he could be getting enough sleep. We have tried spanking him and keeping him up later to make him sleepy, to no avail. My doctor said to let him scream, but the first night we tried that, he went on for three hours. We are all about to go crazy. Can you offer any suggestions or hope for the future?

(A) I'll take a stab at both.

To begin with, let's get this whole *reason for bedtime* business straightened out. Once we do that, I believe everything else will fall right into place.

It is my sworn professional obligation to inform you that bedtimes do *not* exist because children need to sleep. Yep, you've been hoodwinked.

Rumor has it that three-year-olds need ten to twelve hours of sleep each night. Hogwash. Except in the most unusual of circumstances, children get all the sleep they need, *regardless* of when they fall asleep or how long they stay that way.

Generally speaking, a child will let you know when he's tired, and if he needs twelve hours of sleep, he'll get it. On the other hand, there are some three-year-olds who need only eight hours of sleep (and some even less) a night.

In other words, every child's need for sleep is different. That makes sense, doesn't it? Why should we expect that two children who have different appetites, dispositions, and activity levels will both need ten hours of sleep each night?

You may not understand how he can get up at the crack of dawn all bright-eyed and bushy-tailed while you feel like leftovers, but that's the way it is. I assure you, he is getting all the sleep he needs.

But that has nothing to do with bedtime, because (I repeat) bedtimes are not necessary because of children's need for sleep. A bedtime is for the *parents'* benefit, *not* the children's.

Only after the children are in bed can parents renew their acquaintance with one another without being interrupted for "feed me's" or "hold me's" or whatever the latest "me's" may "be's."

What difference does it make if the children aren't asleep? Who cares if they want the lights on? Not I.

When Amy, my daughter, was three and a half, she absolutely refused to go quietly off to sleep at her appointed time (also 8:30 P.M.). She pulled the old cry-awhile-and-then-come-downstairs-for-one-last-look routine.

"Yes, Amy, what is it?"

"Uhhhhhh . . . I wanna as' you sump'in."

"Well, what is it?"

"Uhhhhhhhhhmmmmmmmmmmmm . . ."

"We're waiting."

"Come on, Amy, let's hear it!"

"When's my birfday?"

And so it went, night after night, until we realized that sleep wasn't what she needed and wasn't necessarily why we were putting her to bed in the first place. We put her to bed because of *lust!*

At that point, we simply told her she had to go to her room at 8:30 P.M. And stay there. But she didn't have to sleep if she didn't want to. She could, after we tucked her in and kissed her "night-night," turn on her light, close her door, and play to her heart's content while we relaxed our bodies and renewed our relationship.

By the time we were ready for bed, she was usually asleep on the floor, surrounded by her playthings.

Never Say Never

(Q) Our two-and-a-half-year-old usually goes to bed at 8:30 without a fuss and sleeps through the night. My husband's job takes him out of town one or two nights a week. Within the last few months, Brian has had difficulty going to bed by himself when his daddy isn't home.

Instead of going quietly to sleep, he cries and says he wants to sleep with me. I don't feel right about letting him sleep in our bed because I don't want this to become a habit, but I must admit I've given in to him until now. My mother and several friends have told me to let Brian cry it out and never to let him sleep with me. I'm confused.

(A) I have a hard time with words like "never" and "always." More often than not, they're used to transform generally true statements into complete falsehoods.

In this case, the generally true statement is: "Children belong in their own beds." The complete falsehood is: "Children should *never* be allowed to sleep with their parents."

Putting a child in his own bed reaffirms his individuality and defines him as separate from the marriage. It also defines the marriage as a separate entity—part of the family in which the child does not participate, but benefits from nonetheless.

There are, however, rare occasions when allowing a child to sleep with one or both parents is harmless and perhaps even appropriate.

A sick child, for instance, may need the added security and tender loving care of his parents' bed. (I would hesitate to extend this arrangement on a regular basis to a chronically ill child.) Letting a child sleep with his parents the first few nights after a move may help him make the adjustment to new surroundings.

The exception could be invoked during *any* family crisis, especially those involving loss or transition—a death in the family, a parent (or sibling) hospitalized, or a major trauma, such as following a house fire.

There is no harm, either, in letting children climb in the bed with parents in the morning for a few minutes. (I find this particularly stimulating on Mondays. It may have something to do with being kicked repeatedly in the side, but nothing so completely motivates me to leave the bed as a child who has just crawled in with me.)

In Brian's case, I see no reason why he shouldn't be allowed to sleep with his mother when Dad's out of town. Brian is seeking additional closeness with his mother as a way of calming the anxiety over his father's absence. The more reassurance he is given, the easier it will become for Brian to deal with these interruptions in the family routine.

I caution his parents not to extend this practice to nights when Daddy is home. But not necessarily *never.*

Night Terrors vs. Nightmares

(Q) Our four-year-old son did something the other night that literally freaked us out. About one in the morning, we heard him in the den, talking to himself. I got up, went down the hall, and found him on the sofa. When he saw me, he became agitated and acted like he didn't recognize me. I sat down next to him to try and calm him down, but when I put my arm around him he began hitting me and screaming for me to let him go. By this time, his father had joined us and, seeing that Brian was delirious, tried to pick him up and hold him. Instead of relaxing, Brian became stiff, pushed away, and made this absolutely awful face—his teeth were clenched, his eyes were wide open and rolling around, and he was breathing rapidly. Then he started screaming again. This went on for about ten minutes, although it seemed like an hour. Finally, my husband lay down with him and Brian went back to sleep. In the morning, he remembered nothing of the incident. What was that all about?

(A) Brian had what's known as a "night terror," which is different in character from the more common "nightmare." During a nightmare, the child awakens, becomes fully conscious quickly, and is able to remember the context of the bad dream. Nightmares, especially recurrent and/or frequent ones, may be related to emotional stress.

Night terrors are to nightmares what Ghengis Khan was to Al Capone. An episode usually begins suddenly, with the child sitting up and screaming in terror. He is confused, incoherent, disoriented, and possibly hallucinating. Signs of intense physical stress are present, including a rapid heartbeat, sweating, and dilated pupils. During the terror, which may last from ten to thirty minutes, any attempt to console the child will generally fail, and may even elevate his agitation. When the child finally calms down, he'll fall back to sleep quickly. In the morning, he will probably not have any memory of the episode.

Most pediatricians and psychologists agree that night terrors are developmental phenomena, unrelated to stress or trauma in the child's waking life. They occur most often with children between three and eight but may persist into early adolescence.

I conducted extensive research into night terrors for eight years. My protagonist was my daughter, Amy, who had her first night terror at three and her last at eleven. Initially, an episode always began with her sleepwalking into the upstairs bathroom, after which we would find her and the "freak-out" would commence. The first few years, she had one about every four months as well as every time she ran a fever. As time wore on, they occurred less often and she became able to recognize and exercise more conscious control over them. On the last occasion, she just came into our bedroom and announced, "I'm feeling weird," whereupon she got in bed with us until she felt better.

I asked Amy a few questions concerning her feelings and perceptions during an episode. Her description gives some insight into the altered state of consciousness characteristic of a terror:

"When I'm having a freak-out, I feel weird, especially in my stomach. It's like everything gets all crumpled up and then it gets straight and then it gets crumpled up again. When things are crumpled up, I feel crazy and scared and I feel like knocking things over and tearing things up. When they get straight again, I feel O.K. It's kind of like I'm lost in a maze and can't find my way out. I also see things that aren't really there, but I can't describe them. It's more like a feeling than really seeing something. Everything, even stuff I see every day, seems different and scary."

The next time Brian has one, and the likelihood is that he will, hold him on your lap and rock him until he calms down. As you do, talk softly to him. Telling him who you are and that everything's all right. If he suddenly acts rational, but wants to go somewhere, like into another room of the house, be firm but gentle in telling him he has to stay put with you. After the episode is over, remain with him until he's fallen back to sleep.

Night Lights

(Q) Our four-year-old goes to bed easily, but wants us to leave his bedside lamp on until he falls asleep. We've tried making Scott go to sleep with his lamp off, his door open, and the hall light on, but he acts afraid, calls us back into his room repeatedly, and takes much longer to fall asleep. Nine out of ten times, if he has trouble falling asleep, he wakes up in the middle of the night and calls for us. The obvious solution is simply to leave his lamp on, but we're both concerned that Scott may develop the habit of always needing a light on in his room at night. Also, by catering to his fears in this way, won't we be reinforcing them?

(A) To begin with, it's unlikely that Scott will develop a lifelong dependency on bright lights at bedtime just because you let him go to sleep with a lamp on when he's four.

Fears, especially ones associated with the dark, are common to four-year-olds. Imagination, which begins emerging around age three, is in full bloom by this time. Understandably, the child is not in complete control of the imaginative process, and sometimes it "gets away from him." To top it off, preschool children don't understand how a word can exist for something that doesn't. For example, the phrase "witches aren't real" is contradictory to a four-year-old. In his mind, there wouldn't be a word for it if there weren't witches.

One way this age child deals with fears is to form attachments to "transitional objects" like teddy bears and bedside lights. These provide imagined protection against imagined things that go bump in the night. By indulging a child in this respect, you are not catering to the fear, nor will the transitional object become a lifelong fixation. How many adults do you know who still cuddle up with teddy bears?

On his own, Scott has come up with a solution to his fearfulness, a way of controlling it that is, after all, more desirable than screaming or demanding to sleep with you. By allowing him his bedside lamp, you will reinforce not the fear, but his ingenuity, self-sufficiency, independence, and creative intelligence, not to mention his courage. Furthermore, he will go to sleep quickly and quietly, a joy for which many parents would gladly turn on every light in the house.

Monsters in the Closet

(Q) Our five-year-old daughter, who just started kindergarten, is afraid to go upstairs by herself. She will not climb the stairs, day or night, without one of us in front of her, and she demands that we check her bedroom and the closet in particular, for monsters. If we balk or insist she go by herself, she becomes hysterical. I'm afraid this may be the beginning of a serious emotional problem that, handled wrong, could have a permanent effect on her. What should we do? We have another child, who is fourteen months old.

(A) There's a monster in your closet, too. It's the Something-Horrible-Will-Happen-to-My-Child's-Mind-If-I-Do-the-Wrong-Thing Monster.

This foul creature lives in closets wherever there are parents who believe that children are little Humpty Dumptys in life's biggest egg-toss game: one wrong move and they'll be broken forever.

This monster in *our* closet haunts our relationships with our children, jumping out at us when we least expect it, zapping our common sense and paralyzing our spontaneity.

He lurches through our waking nightmares, hissing, "Your children have emotional problems, and it's all because of you."

Well, I'm afraid I bring you bad news. *All* children grow up with emotional problems. Emotions *are* a problem, especially for children. Emotions are powerful, unpredictable, violent, stormy, confusing, and often painful. Most of a person's growing years are spent learning how to tame these beasts within.

For the first twenty years of her life, a human being stumbles through one emotional upheaval after another—birth (the all-time champ), separation, being two, learning to share, going off to school, puberty, sexuality, and leaving home.

Just as one crisis begins to subside, another comes along to knock her over, turn her upside down, and shake all the change out of her pockets. That's enough to put monsters in anybody's closet.

Being a parent, however, can be just as frustrating and confusing and emotionally painful as being a child. The important difference is that, while children have little control over how rough their lives are, parenthood is only as rough as *we* make it. One way of making it rough is to feed the monster that waits in *our* closets.

Most children have monsters of one sort or another lurking about. But the only ones that hang around for long live in homes where the parents have a pet monster too.

By himself, a child's monster is impotent. But put him in league with a parent-monster and pandemonium is guaranteed to break loose.

Banish your monster first. Children aren't fragile little eggs who can't be put together again. If they were, they'd never survive past their third birthdays.

Children are tough, resilient, flexible little people who rebound extremely well from hardship, frustration, trauma, and all the other slings and arrows of their truly outrageous fortunes. With a little support from us, they also do quite well at chasing monsters out of their *own* closets.

Sure, your daughter's fear of monsters is probably an indication that her world is suddenly a bit more scary than it ever was before. She has to go to school all alone and watch all that attention go to baby sister, who is home with Mommy all day long just as big sister used to be. Ah, well, that's life, right?

So get in there and do what you already know you have to do. Refuse to scout the way to her room. Tuck her in as usual at bedtime, and if she screams for you to stay, say, "I'm sorry. I won't stay. *You* put the monster in your *own* closet by pretending him there. Now you must pretend him gone."

Once you chase *your* monster off, hers will waste away in no time. After all, it's lonely being the only monster in the house.

. . . and Other Problems

Food Fights

(Q) We have one child, a two-and-a-half-year-old daughter. She was breast-fed until she was ten months old. When she was five months old, our pediatrician told me to begin giving her solid foods. I was reluctant to do that since she seemed to be getting enough nourishment from me, but he told me bluntly that my attitude was irresponsible. She refused to cooperate with her new diet, spitting out food, turning her head, screaming, and so on. At the pediatrician's insistence, I began virtually force-feeding her. To make a long story short, the same situation exists today. My daughter will not eat anything resembling a meal. She eats cereal and toast in the morning and cheese, potato chips, popcorn, peanut butter and crackers, and celery slices for snacks. Lunch is a sandwich, maybe. Supper always turns into a scene. We have *made* her sit at the table, spanked her, bribed her, and literally forced food into her mouth to make her eat. But if we make her eat something she doesn't like, she throws it up later. As a result, every aspect of our relationship is strained. What can we do?

(A) Food has the potential of acquiring tremendous significance within a family, involving issues completely unrelated to its nutritional value.

The transfer of food from parent to child during the first year of life entails lots of physical closeness and stimulation, so that while the infant is receiving nourishment, she is also being nurtured.

As the child strides into her second year of life, the parents' role of keepers of the cupboard can easily become a central issue in the almost inevitable power struggles that develop as the second birthday approaches.

As the almost-two-year-old grows increasingly verbal, she is likely to begin asserting definite likes and dislikes for particular foods and demand to be fed on a schedule that runs counter to family custom.

In addition, the toddler is no longer wholly dependent on her parents to give her food, and she further flexes her independence by experimenting with ways of obtaining it for herself. She discovers how to climb on the counter, open the refrigerator, and take the lid off the pickle jar.

In short, the giving of food from parent to child can, under certain stressful circumstances, become confused with the quality or quantity of affection in the relationship, the question of who is in control of the family, and how much autonomy the child is permitted.

When food assumes this significance, it begins to "mediate" the relationship. In other words, it becomes the substance through which (or over which) parent and child attempt to resolve certain issues.

Everyone can easily forget that the reason for sitting down to a meal is *not* to consume food. Eating is secondary to the social and ritual aspects of mealtime.

Meals, and the evening meal in particular, bring the family together. They are a setting in which the values of sharing and unity are reaffirmed. It matters little *what* people eat or *how much;* good conversation and the feeling that "we are all of one family" are what count.

So the idea is *not* to persuade your daughter to eat. She is eating enough and her diet is adequately balanced. The goal is to involve her in the ritual of unification at the dinner table.

During the day, you can cater to her preference to a reasonable extent, but retain control over *when* food is served (remember that two-year-olds usually need a midmorning and midafternoon snack).

At the evening meal, prepare your daughter's plate with small portions of the same food that the rest of the family is eating. If she mentions her distaste for any of the items on her plate, ignore the content of her statement, but take the opportunity to involve her in conversation by responding with something like, "Tell Daddy what we did today." Encourage her participation in conversation, although there should be times when the talk between adults does not involve her except as a listener.

Any comments that adults make about the meal should be brief and complimentary. Require her to remain at the table until everyone is excused, but do *not* at any time ask her to eat even a single bite.

Don't serve dessert as an extension of the meal. If something special is on the menu, serve it one or two hours later, before her bedtime perhaps. Don't use dessert as an enticement for eating. Nor should her right to share in late-evening treats be made conditional on how much she eats for supper.

One last word: For your next child, find a pediatrician who is supportive of breast-feeding and more knowledgeable about infant nutritional needs.

(Q) This may sound trivial, but my daughter, who is four, asks for food almost constantly throughout the day. The rule is that she may have one small snack midway through the afternoon, but she can't seem to understand and won't accept that limit. I'm tired of her demands and whining and am counting on you for an idea.

(A) Have I got an idea for you! But first, let's clear up one thing. This is not a trivial question. Any question involving food is important. After all, what's more essential than food?

For that reason, food can acquire potent symbolic character within a family, and disputes regarding *what* people eat, *when*, and *how much* can generate lots of conflict among family members. Food takes on even more significance in the relationship between parent and child.

Certainly one of the strongest and most enduring associations formed during the child's first year is that of food and parent (usually mother). As the child grows, parents retain the role of food givers. From this perspective, it's easy to comprehend why food so often becomes the issue-of-choice in power struggles between parents and children. The conflict can take many forms, but the basic issue remains "who controls the food?" And, in a broader sense, the overriding issue is, "who controls the family?"

Therefore, it is as essential as food itself that parents exercise absolute, unquestionable control of the distribution of food in the family. This is not to say that the system cannot be flexible enough to allow children some freedom to serve themselves, but the final authority must rest with parents.

If parents cannot demonstrate their authority in this area, then how can they claim to be authorities at all?

It is a legitimate and necessary exercise of their responsibility and authority for parents to restrict the "when?" of eating to certain set times of the day. Most children require a midmorning and midafternoon snack, so plan for one or both, depending on the age of the child and the mealtime schedule.

There is a hassle-free, field-tested way of announcing snack time, while at the same time communicating your authority as keeper of the pantry. I assume there is a relatively large clock face somewhere in your house, probably in the kitchen. Take a piece of paper and make an identical clock face, minus the hands. Now, decide when snack time will take place. Then, draw the hands on your paper clock to indicate snack time. Tape the paper clock next to the real clock, call your youngster in, and tell her, "When the hands on the real clock look like the hands on the paper clock, I will give you a snack. Now you can tell when snack time is!"

It is unlikely that any preschooler will grasp the connection immediately, so expect her requests to be off the mark for several days. When they are, simply show her the two clocks, point out that they are not "the same," and reassure her that when they are, she will get her snack as promised. Be sure you remember to show her what you mean by "the same" when the magic time arrives.

Techniques such as this are especially effective when you want to establish routines with a young child. Children often need some visible reminder of rules, times, and other boundaries that are otherwise invisible.

(Q) We have tried various approaches to getting our four-year-old daughter to eat vegetables, but nothing has worked. Do you have a solution?

(A) I might. First, I'll tell you what doesn't work. Young children could care less about the benefits of vitamins. Don't waste your time.

Talking about how wonderful vegetables taste as you shove them in your mouth doesn't work either. It's true that children learn by example. But in this case, your daughter will simply learn never to believe anything you say. In addition, she will begin to suspect your sanity.

Trying to scare the child with stories of malnutrition and rickets won't work either. Not only will she continue to refuse to eat vegetables, but she'll also start having nightmares, which will keep you up all night, every night, eventually making *you* look as if you have some bizarre nutritional deficiency.

Making the child sit at the table until she's eaten her vegetables will only result in a power struggle no one can win. You will lose because getting into power struggles with children indicates to them that you really have very little power. They lose because when children don't have confidence in their parents' power, they feel insecure.

When my daughter, Amy, was four years old, she complained bitterly about the presence of green things on her plate. She not only wouldn't eat them, she didn't even want them there, ruining the presentation and polluting the taste of other foods on the plate.

The first thing we did was make a rule: The same foods will be on everybody's plates. No one in the family will get a special plate. Next, we told Amy she didn't *ever* have to eat green things. We made no attempt to persuade or frighten. We didn't simulate a religious experience when we were eating vegetables, nor did we tell her she would have to sit at the table until she ate her green things.

"But," we said, "you must eat everything on the first plate that we give you in order to receive a second helping of anything on the plate that you particularly like."

From that day forward, we put only slightly more than a tablespoon of each of the foods served at dinner, including a vegetable, on her plate. This virtually guaranteed that after she finished eating those foods that she liked—roast "beast" and mashed potatoes, for example—that she'd still be hungry. At that point, she had a choice: Did she want to go hungry, or did she eat her veggie and receive seconds of the things she liked?

We predicted that, at least initially, Amy would choose not to eat her veggies. She didn't let us down. We allowed her to leave the table whenever she chose, but covered any food remaining on her plate with plastic wrap. If, later in the evening, Amy said she was hungry and requested something to eat, we simply pointed to her dinner plate and said, "We'll be glad to warm the rest of your dinner for you in the microwave. When you're eaten the rest of what's on your plate, you may have just about any snack you want."

She struggled with the dilemma we laid before her for several weeks before she began—grudgingly but without complaint—eating her veggies at first sitting. Not always, mind you, but more often than not.

Amy is now nineteen. Several nights ago, when she left the table, her steamed broccoli was untouched. That hasn't happened in a long time. Could this be the Return of the Veggies from Hell? I love sequels.

(Q) Our seven-year-old will not eat. I don't think he has ever finished a plate of food, regardless of how little it held. I have gone so far as to play "restaurant." No good. His "favorite food" is only his favorite until I put it in front of him. Then come the excuses: "I'm not hungry anymore," "It doesn't taste good," "This isn't the way so-and-so fixes it," "I have a stomachache."

At the evening meal, he dawdles, complains, nibbles, picks—everything except eat. I am nearly out of my mind. We've tried making him eat, taking privileges away, sending him to bed early, even bribing him. No change.

Two hours after the dishes have been done, and my chest pains have nearly stopped, he wants potato chips or popcorn or ice cream because, as he puts it, "I'm hungry now." To keep from wringing his neck, I'm wringing my hands. Help me.

(A) The urgent and anguished tone of your letter moved me to seek the counsel of the famous sage, Juan Hoo Nose, whose ability to sniff out solutions to riddles such as these has become legend. I persuaded him to meditate on your problem.

Here are his remarks:

Tell the belle to stop wringing. Juan Hoo Nose, ta-da, to the rescue. No wonder her son will not eat. She has told him, in effect, that the most wonderful thing he can do for her is eat the food she prepares. When he refuses, her self-esteem suffers more than his belly. Why should he be responsible for making her feel like a good mother?

She hands him a whip and then complains when he uses it. Any child worth his weight in Legos will seize the slightest opportunity to face off with his parents in a power struggle. It's only natural. Unfortunately, there are no winners in such a struggle. In the long run, this mother will feel bad about herself and resentful of her son. In turn, the son will learn distorted and untrue things about women and his ability to establish successful relationships with them will suffer.

Without realizing it, this mother has subscribed to the old adage, "The way to a man's heart is through his stomach." This saying was invented by men who wanted to keep women enslaved in the kitchen. To solve the problem, she must stop basing her opinion of herself on whether or not her child eats and concentrate on improving his manners instead of his appetite.

First, she must never play "restaurant" again, particularly at family meals. His plate should have small amounts of the same foods everyone else is having.

Second, no attempt should be made to persuade or force him to eat. But every attempt must be made to improve his decorum at the table. His parents should tell him that he is not required to eat, but he is required to sit at the table and behave properly. A list of his bad manners should be made, including all the complaints he makes concerning food. If he does or says something on the list, he should be sent from the table to spend the rest of the meal in an isolated part of the house, like the bathroom.

During the meal, parents should make no long conversation about food. Table talk should be about pleasant subjects only. This changes the meal from an exercise in eating to an exercise in togetherness. The child should be encouraged to enter the conversation, but not allowed to dominate it.

If food remains on his plate after he has been excused from the table, it should be covered in plastic wrap and set aside. Later, when he complains of hunger, unwrap the plate and give it to him, saying, "When you finish your supper, you may have potato chips or whatever else you want before bed."

If he yells and screams, send him to his room until he is calm. Parents shouldn't compromise. The child must eat the food on his plate before any other food is given to him, including seconds of any one item.

If this mother wants to be reassured that her son will not waste away because of her stubbornness, she can call her pediatrician. He will appreciate the comic relief.

It may take several weeks or several months before the child regains a normal appetite and begins behaving himself at the table. But it will happen. The Nose knows.

(Q) When we sit down to eat, our ten-year-old complains about the food on her plate. Trying to persuade her to take even one bite of something she doesn't like is worse than pulling teeth. On several occasions, after we insisted that she eat something, she ran to the bathroom and threw up. We have made her sit at the table until she finishes everything on her plate—she sits and sits, but still refuses to eat. I know it's wrong, but guilt-ridden Mom here has sometimes given up and fixed her something she would eat, in the name of peace. Do you have a better way?

(A) Sure. But first, let's untangle the situation. The overriding issue has nothing to do with nutrition. It is a matter of manners and your daughter's proper place in the family.

It is rude to complain about food that someone else has prepared. It is equally rude to refuse to eat it because of some neurotic prejudice. Do you want your daughter going to someone else's home and complaining about food her hosts prepare for her? Then don't allow her to complain about the food you prepare.

With regard to her place in the family, must I remind you that she is a child? By allowing her to disrupt family meals with her complaints, by pleading with her to eat, by fixing her special food, you are, in effect, aiding and abetting her grasp for prominence within the family. As long as she can control the family by whining and complaining at the dinner table, she will.

Stop catering to her!

From now on, serve her plate with ridiculously small portions of the same foods everyone else in the family is eating—two or three forkfuls of each item. As time goes on, and the problem is nearing solution, gradually increase her portions until they are reasonable for her age and appetite.

Inform her that she doesn't have to eat anything that is not to her liking, but that she may not, under any circumstances, complain. If she violates this rule, either verbally or facially, take away whatever privileges she usually enjoys after dinner and move her bedtime up one hour.

Refuse to let her have seconds of anything, or dessert, until she cleans her plate. Do not make any remarks about what she eats or doesn't eat and don't make any attempt to persuade her to eat. In fact, pay no more attention to her than you do to anyone else at the table, and less than you pay to one another. If she eats everything, allow her seconds of anything. If she acts like she's going to throw up after eating something, simply tell her to go to the bathroom. When she returns, inform her that throwing up or acting like she has to is tantamount to a nonverbal complaint and earns the same punishment.

When the meal is over, clear her place along with everyone else's. If any food remains, cover it and set it aside. Later, when she complains of hunger and asks for food, show her her plate and tell her that when she finishes what remains, she may have whatever snacks you normally allow.

If she happens to take you up on your offer, however, and cleans her plate, do not then cook for her or fix her any special foods.

Initially, she will test the new rules. She will complain, she will throw up, she will refuse to eat, and then later she will complain of hunger pains. In other words, you ain't seen nothin' yet.

Take heart! Two or three weeks of hurling herself upon the barricades and she will become convinced and cooperative.

Take your choice: Three weeks or eight more years?

Security Blankets

Big people really don't know much about children. We like to think we know it all, but nothing belies that more quickly than the things we get ourselves upset about.

Take little Sammy, for instance. He's going to be five years old next week and he still carries a blanket with him wherever he goes. At least, that torn, ragged piece of cloth *used* to be a blanket. Once upon a time, it was the blanket that kept him warm in his bassinet. Then it moved with him to his crib, and then to his bed, and then . . . As Sammy goes, so goes the used-to-be-a-blanket.

"What's the matter with Sammy?" ask his parents. Something *must* be wrong because children aren't supposed to carry blankets around for five years. Sure, Linus carries a blanket, but that's just in the funny pages, and so you think Linus is cute. When it's your own little Sammy it's not so funny.

Maybe Sammy is insecure. That means nervous, doesn't it? "Oh my gosh," exclaim his nervous parents, "we must have done something terrible-awful to Sammy to make him so nervous!"

Maybe they took his bottle away too quickly. Or perhaps they toilet trained him too early. The separation . . . yes, that must be it . . . when they had that big argument and separated for three months when Sammy was only twenty months old. . . . He missed his daddy so much. "What have we done? Maybe we should take him to a psychologist!"

Something must be done to make Sammy more secure so that he will give up the blanket. He goes to kindergarten next fall, and his teacher will know what fiends his parents are if he walks in waving that blanket around for the whole world to see.

"C'mon, Sammy, give us the blanket. You're a big boy now. You don't need that smelly old blanket anymore. If you give us the blanket, we will buy you a new bicycle. . . . Why not, Sammy?"

Take the blanket while he's sleeping? Say that Santa Claus took it? How about having the blanket-fairy come and leave him some money for it?

No, we mustn't force it away; that might make him *more* insecure. Then he might start sucking his thumb. On and on go Sammy's parents.

But the problem with Sammy is not Sammy at all. The issue is with his *parents.*

Big people must have answers for everything. The more complicated the answer, the more blind faith we invest in it. In the process of becoming big, many of us forget how simple life can be.

Big people become upset, and even frightened, by things that they do not understand, such as children.

When big people do not understand something, they weave security blankets out of words and call them explanations. Sometimes these explanations get ponderous and cumbersome. When they get sufficiently complicated, they become fantasies.

This is what happened to Sammy's big people. They do not comprehend the insignificance of the blanket, because they no longer see the world in simple terms. They have learned too many words.

They do not understand why Sammy wants his blanket with him wherever he goes, and this is upsetting. The four-year-old down the street doesn't carry a blanket around. Sammy is different. Sammy's parents think that something is wrong, so they invent a fantasy filled with dragons and demons and, in no time, the blanket becomes the most important thing in the house. The issue of the blanket grows to such proportions that it suffocates everyone's common sense.

"Hey, Sammy! Just between you and me, tell me about your blanket."

"I jus' like it."

That sounds simple enough. On the other hand, maybe Sammy *is* a bit insecure. After all, everyone's trying to take his blanket.

Sumbthucking

When she was a child, my daughter, Amy, would park her thumb in her mouth when she was bored, tired, cranky, or just plain laid back. And that was fine with me. She began perfecting her technique the day she was born.

Not everyone feels the way I do. Quite a few people believe that something is wrong with the Amy's of the world.

Thumbsucking defies convention, and this makes adults uncomfortable. As long as adults have "reasons" for things, they feel O.K. So, they have invented some to explain why an occasional thumb is where it shouldn't be. Take your pick:

The "Bad Nerves Theory" says that sumbthucking is a thign of inthecurity. To parents who buy this idea, a thumbsucking child is a constant reminder of what monsters they are. They become especially distraught when their child sucks in public, thus broadcasting her miserable condition to the world.

Another theory, attributed by some to a certain Zigmund Fraud, says that children suck their thumbs because during infancy they experienced some trauma associated with breast- or bottle-feeding. These poor kids grow up sucking on one substitute nipple after another—cigarettes, straws, siphon tubes, Life Savers, anything. As adults, they are the perverts who prefer to drink their beer straight from the bottle.

Sometimes it's easier for little girls to get away with sucking their thumbs than it is for little boys. There are even people who think a girl who sucks her thumb is "cute" (until she goes to school). A thumbsucking boy is in mortal danger of growing up to be effeminate, or so the story goes. The solution? Paint the offending digit with colorless yuk. That'll make a man out of him.

Then there are the horror stories—Bedtime Tales for Thumbsuckers: "There once was a frog-prince who sucked his thumb. When he grew up, his teeth were crooked, his eyes were crossed, his ears stuck out and flapped in the wind, he caught a dread disease, his cheeks dimpled, and the princess would not marry him." The part about the dimples gets 'em every time.

I have my own theory. Because of thumbs, people can build the things they dream of, like rocket ships and time machines. A child who sucks her thumb is saying, "I love my thumb. I love being human." Now isn't that nicer than bad nerves and a face like Alfred E. Newman?

As far as I can tell, children suck their thumbs simply because it feels good. Thumbsucking is calming and relaxing to a child. It is a portable source of pleasure, always right on hand! The answer to why some children suck their thumbs and others don't is simply, "Because." It's no more significant than liking or not liking spinach.

So, the big fuss is over something rather insignificant. A child is not going to stop sucking her thumb because of ridicule, threats, criticism, demands, or punishment. These "persuasive" measures can, in fact, create a problem where there was none to begin with.

A child cannot separate the feelings we communicate to her about thumbsucking from the feelings she has about herself as a little person. If she is harassed about sucking her thumb, it is a good bet she will begin to feel bad about herself. She may withdraw and spend more time alone so she can suck in private or seek relief from her growing insecurity by sucking more and more. Where there was once a healthy child who sucked her thumb for pleasure, there is now a child who sucks to relieve the anxiety and discomfort of feeling that there's something wrong with her.

If your child sucks her thumb, leave her alone. If you must mention it, say something like, "Hey there! I see your thumb in your mouth. I'll bet that feels pretty good. You know something? I love you."

One of these days, when she feels like it, and she has developed other interests, she will stop—but it will be in *her own* time, *not* yours.

Discipline in Public Places

Mommy took me to the store
To shop and spend the day,
But I had other things in mind,
Like, for instance, play!

While she was looking for a dress
I ran away and hid;
I went under a table
And found another kid.

Mom found me in the makeup
Playing with this other child.
Together we were having fun;
Mom said that I was *wild.*

I cried for her to carry me,
I said I hurt my feet.
I cried 'cause I was hungry
And then I wouldn't eat.

I asked for toys but she said, "No!"
And so I threw a fit.
I screamed and kicked and pulled my hair;
When she bought the toy, I quit.

I took my shoes off in the store,
But can't remember where.
Mommy got all red and shook
And bought another pair.

We're home now; Mommy's resting.
I'm playing with her fountain pen.
When she wakes up I'll ask her,
"When can we go again?"

Controlling children in public places is a sticky problem, to be sure. If you scream at them or spank them, everybody looks at you, and you feel lower than a rattlesnake. If you look the other way, children play "Hide and Seek" (guess who does the seeking?), or they break something, or they help themselves to some candy or something horrible like that. If you hold their hands, they fight you. If you don't, they run wild. Shopping can be loads of fun.

Try this. First make a list of rules for public places. It could read something like this:

1. You walk with me and stay with me. I will not hold your hand unless you want me to.

2. You are quiet in the stores. You do not scream, yell, or have a tantrum.

3. You walk. You do not run.

Those three are enough to cover most of the child's favorite public pastimes. Besides, three is probably all the child can remember.

Next, cut some "tickets" out of stiff, colored cardboard. When that's done, you are prepared to meet with your youngster. You are the chairperson (chairparent?) at this conference. Begin by saying, "Moe, you are probably wondering why we are having this little talk, and so I'm going to tell you. We are going to talk about going to the store, Moe, and after we talk about it, we are going to get in the car and go there. When we go to the store, I get mad because you run in the store, and you scream, and you yell, and you throw tantrums when you want toys, and you run away from me. I'm not laughing, Moe.

"I'm going to tell you what the rules are before we go to the store. The first rule is: You will walk with me and stay with me while I am shopping. I am not going to hold your hand unless you want me to. The second rule . . ." and so on.

When you finish going over the rules, pull out the "tickets" and say, "Before we go to the store, I am going to give you these tickets. The tickets are yours, so don't lose them. Every time you break a rule I'm going to take away a ticket. If you lose all of your tickets in the store today, then I will not let you go outside to play after supper (or some such desirable activity). You must have at least *one* ticket in order to play outside tonight. Do you understand? Good. Then let's go practice the rules at the store."

When you get to the store, review the rules in the parking lot, give Moe the tickets, remind her what the deal is, and proceed. If Moe breaks a rule, say, "You were running. The rule says you will walk. Give me a ticket for breaking the rule." If you must take the last ticket, do so without any big fuss, but gently remind Moe what the consequences are, in case she "forgot."

The number of tickets should vary according to the time you expect to be shopping. Start by estimating how many hours you are going to be gone, add one to this number, and give that many tickets. In other words, if you think it's going to be a two hour trip, give three tickets.

Try to remember when you were small and what torture shopping was. When children are bored or tired, they are more likely to misbehave. So don't expect a preschool child to tag along with you cheerfully for more than an hour. Bring a stroller, or take the time to hunt one when you get to the store (many stores provide them).

The deal made with the tickets should involve some privilege that the child would normally look forward to doing at home that same day. Do not offer bribes such as ice cream or minibikes for good behavior.

Credit for this idea goes to Won Sung Lo, of Won Sung Lo's Irish Laundry, who coined the phrase, "No tickee, no washee."

And, as a Last Resort . . .

Several years ago, I was waiting in the customer service area of a large department store when a young couple came in with their son, who was about two-and-a-half. The father held the child as the mother talked with the clerk. But this two-year-old had obviously had enough of being carried, because he immediately began squirming and pushing away from Dad, wanting to get down. Dad held on and tried to distract him, but to no avail.

The child, a typical two-year-old, continued to struggle and protest, becoming increasingly agitated and vocal.

Finally Dad sat him on the counter and said, "Hey, Billy, how about if you and I go look at the toys and pick one out for you to take home, O.K.?" That must have sounded good to Billy, because he stopped crying and, still sniffling, nodded assent. Dad told Mom they'd meet her in the toy department, and off they went.

Billy's parents inevitably wound up paying for that little trip to the toy department for months, maybe years, to come.

For many reasons, children are far more difficult to handle in public places than in the relative quiet and privacy of home.

Anyone looking for a quick and easy way of dispensing forever with public shenanigans is going to be disappointed, however, because there isn't any. There are, however, things parents can do to contain even the worst situation imaginable and gradually bring a child's public behavior under control. A few suggestions are:

- In advance, tell the child the purpose of the outing, so he knows what to expect.
- Do not make promises of "If you're good, we'll buy you a so-and-so." "Deals" like this teach a child to expect compensation for appropriate behavior. A child so taught may never learn that good behavior is its own reward.
- You can save yourself a lot of grief if you do not teach your young'un to expect a goodie every time the family goes shopping. In fact, I advise just the opposite—teach him to expect nothing but basic necessities. Not only will he never acquire the obnoxious habit of constantly pleading for toys, etc., during shopping trips, but he will be surprised and appreciative when you do present him with something special.
- Just before going into the shopping center or restaurant, remind the child of a few simple rules, such as, "Stay in your stroller, talk quietly, and touch things only with your eyes."
- When rules are broken, or need to be created on the spot, take the child immediately aside and either remind or inform.
- Stay away from places where toys or candy are sold. Don't even walk through them, if you can avoid it.
- If the child starts screaming, or acting out of control, take him quickly into a remote area of the store and sit with him until the tantrum subsides or control is reestablished. The quicker you stop the momentum of the child's misbehavior, the better. If things don't improve, you might consider taking the child outside the store for a while or even straight home.

• A spanking administered at the scene rarely accomplishes anything except louder screams and lots of disapproving looks. On those infrequent occasions when I felt spanking was appropriate, I would remove myself and my child to a private place (a corridor, a bathroom, outside) and, with no warning, give the spanking there. Intended only as a slight shock to terminate the tantrum and remind the child of my authority, it was usually effective.

• Abandoning a shopping cart of groceries or a table of restaurant food to reestablish control over a child may seem drastic and self-defeating, but I know from personal experience that it pays off in the long run. I recall, on one occasion, getting up in the midst of a meal, taking my youngest outside, and sitting in the car with her while the rest of the family finished eating. The minor inconvenience was well worth the lesson it taught Amy.

• For extreme emergencies, I recommend that each parent carry a set of fake nose and glasses, so that if all else fails, they can beat a hasty retreat into anonymity.

How to Survive a Trip

A friend of mine has a recurring nightmare in which he is handcuffed to a steeling wheel of a car traveling down a deserted stretch of four-lane highway. There are two young children in the backseat, both gorging on junk food. In his dream, the highway has no exits. The children are bouncing up and down in the backseat, screaming about needing to use the bathroom, fighting over toys, crying, and constantly asking, "When are we going to get there?"

My friend should be thankful this is just a nightmare. I know a lot of parents for whom this nightmare is all too real. Backseats were not designed with children in mind. They are confining and boring, and it's asking much of a child (or any human being) to sit peacefully in one for any extended time.

The mood of an entire vacation is set during the trip, but there is no reason the tone of the ride must be one of anger and frustration. Parents can spare themselves and their children a lot of misery by planning thoughtfully for everyone's needs during the journey.

To begin with, pack a small cooler chock-full of a variety of healthy, sugar-free snacks. These can include raisins, carrot and celery sticks, dry roasted peanuts, crackers, peanut butter sandwiches, fruit, and such good, old-fashioned drinks as apple and orange juice.

Let the children eat freely: just the act of eating will help them stay calm. Keep junk food off the menu. The refined sugar (and often caffeine) in it doses children with an over supply of quick energy, turning a car into a pressure cooker. When you eliminate all sugar-sweetened foods and drinks from the trip menu, the children probably won't have to use the bathroom as often. How about that? Two birds with one stone.

Pack a cloth bag or box with books, coloring books, colored pencils (crayons melt on the back shelf), and other "trip toys" to hold the children's attention and interest. Keep this inventory in the front seat, with an adult acting as "toy librarian." When you sense that a child is losing interest in one toy, take it away and provide another in its place.

It also helps to vary the seating arrangement during the trip. For instance, the adults can switch back and forth between driving and sitting in the back with one of the children. Keeping the children separated in this way, at least part of the time, may be a good idea. An older child can ride in the front with whoever is driving, while another adult keeps younger children occupied in the back by reading stories or carrying on quiet conversation.

Word games are fun, and even the driver can play. Rhyming games (what rhymes with *cat*?), guessing games (I see something that is green. What is it?), and name games (I am an animal with a long neck who eats leaves from trees and . . . Who am I?) are just some ideas for keeping everyone in a positive frame of mind.

Plan regular stops so people can stretch and empty their bladders. Trying to travel more than six or eight hours in a day with children can easily backfire. By leaving in the middle of the night, however, my family has managed to drive a straight twelve hours without turning into a bunch of blithering idiots. Blithering maybe, but not yet to the idiot stage.

There is even a creative answer to the question, "What do we do when they misbehave in the car?" It's a game I call "Tickets." All you need to play are pocket-sized rectangles of colored cardboard.

Before anyone gets into the car, explain to the children the rules governing behavior during the ride. Keep the list brief. Some suggestions might be: (1) seatbelts must be buckled, (2) no fighting or arguing, (3) no yelling or screaming, (4) no throwing, and (5) each child is allowed to ask, "When are we gonna be there?" just once.

Remind the children that they have a special event waiting for them at the end of the trip (swimming, exploring, playing with cousins, for example). Now comes the clincher: "I am giving five tickets to each of you. Each time you break a car rule, I will take a ticket away from you. If you fight, I will take a ticket from each of you, regardless of who started it. When we get to the beach, you must have at least one ticket left to go swimming. If you don't have a ticket, you must sit on the beach with me for thirty minutes."

It works, believe me. Take careful note of the punishment—it is quite enough that you promise to withhold the special event for a brief time. Vacations are not for suffering. Besides, if one suffers, all will suffer. The number of "tickets" can vary with the anticipated length of the trip—one ticket per hour, perhaps, up to a maximum of five or six.

Have an enjoyable vacation. Plan ahead, drive carefully, and don't forget the sunscreen.

Preschool Follies

(Q) My son is four years old. He has never been a perfect child and I don't want him to be, but he has always been easy to raise. He misbehaves sometimes, but my husband and I enforce the rules and nothing ever gets out of hand.

But he gives his teachers at the day-care center a hard time. I don't work, but I put him in a center so he can be with other children. He goes there only in the mornings. Every time I pick him up, his teacher has another story of what he has done. It all seems like such little stuff to us, but she gets upset because it happens so often. For instance, the other day he pulled down his pants on the playground. Last week, he stuck his tongue out at the teacher and then laughed while she chased him around the room.

What I don't understand is why he isn't like this at home. Is he rebelling so he can spend more time with me? Is he not getting enough attention at home? Please tell me what you think I should do.

(A) To begin with, children always manage to get enough attention, wherever they are. Some of the attention is positive (praise, interest, enthusiasm, and encouragement) and some is negative (criticism, punishment, reprimands). Children need more positive strokes than negative, but they will work for whatever kind they can get.

It sounds as though you are sensitive to your child's needs. You put him in day care so he can be with other children, you enforce rules, and so on. I would guess he gets many more positive than negative strokes from you and your husband.

Sometimes, however, it's more *fun* to work for negative strokes. For instance, wouldn't it be fun to drop your pants and listen to everyone howl and scream? And wouldn't it be fun to have the teacher chase you around the room? This doesn't work out well with every grown-up, but some will go for the bait every time. Your son is not doing anything malicious, he isn't hurting anyone, and he's having loads of fun doing what all the other children (and most adults as well) wish they had the nerve to do.

Call it the class clown syndrome. Once the bug strikes, it's almost impossible to cure. In fact, I doubt this is something that we even *want* to cure. The class clown is blessed with an irrepressible sense of humor, a flair for the absurd, and an imagination that defies convention.

What this all adds up to is a happy and extremely creative child. Happy, creative children, if not given enough opportunity to use their talents constructively, will use them any way they can. What is more exciting and creative than to entice a grown-up into your game and then beat her at it? The problem is that some grown-ups can't stand being outdone by a child.

Your son's behavior may be an indication that he is with the wrong age group at the center. Perhaps he would fare better with five-year-olds. Or the program at the center may be too structured for him. Generally speaking, creative children need less structure and more open-ended opportunities to explore, discover, and experiment with the environment. Perhaps a different program is the answer. Shop around and see what other centers have to offer.

Perhaps a day-care program is not the answer to his needs.

Look into other possibilities, such as swimming, dancing, gymnastics (tumbling), or art classes.

There is one small point to consider: dropping your trousers and sticking your tongue out at grown-ups are fun and get everyone's attention; nonetheless, this is not desirable public behavior.

The teacher could ignore the behavior. Unfortunately, ignoring behavior such as this simply doesn't work. There is no way that a classroom of four-year-olds isn't going to laugh and squeal when someone's pants come down. Forget about ignoring.

The teacher could put your son in isolation for five minutes whenever this kind of behavior occurs. In this case, however, I doubt whether this alone will work. If your son is bored, then he needs more stimulation, and the teacher needs to provide it before he provides it for himself by dropping his pants again. If the teacher cannot give him more opportunity to earn positive strokes, then my earlier suggestions about another age group or program should be considered.

If you feel that the program is what you want for him and wish to leave him there, then ask his teacher to give you a brief daily summary of his misbehavior. Take privileges away at home based on the number of incidents which occur at school. For instance, one incident at school and he can't ride his bike that day. Two incidents, and he can't go outside in the afternoon. Three incidents, and he can't play his records in the evening. But whatever you do, don't offer him any special rewards for being "good."

Just hug and kiss him and tell him you're pleased that he's found other ways to have fun. Talk about what those other ways are. After all, what's more special than a parent's love and attention?

School Daze

Several years ago, a second-grade teacher asked my advice about one of her students, a seven-year-old girl who, within six weeks after the beginning of school, had managed to walk away with the "Outstanding Nuisance of the Second Grade Award" by—believe it or not—asking questions.

Indeed, blue-eyed Julie asked, according to the teacher's first estimates, close to a hundred questions a day. This usually patient veteran of thirteen second-grade campaigns was showing unmistakable signs of going "blotto" as we stood talking in the hall. She apologized profusely for taking my time with such trivia ("You must think this is silly"), grinding her teeth, her hands fluttering in and out of the pockets of her smock like a pair of lunatic hummingbirds—showing all the classic symptoms of a sudden midyear retirement.

Just then the classroom door opened and out walked (as I quickly learned) the infamous, blue-eyed Julie herself.

"Mrs. Boulderdam?"

Immediately, hands fluttering madly, Mrs. Boulderdam's eyes darted down the hall, measuring, I'm now sure, the distance between where we stood and the front door. For several moments her eyes jumped back and forth between Julie and freedom, finally coming to rest on the child's upturned face.

"Why, yes, Julie, what do you want?" Her lips were stretched into a tight smile over clenched teeth.

"Is this the way to write my name?"

Mrs. Boulderdam tensed, and I thought I saw her hands fluttering toward the child and then quickly back into her smock, but it happened too fast to be sure.

"Yes, Julie," she stammered, "that's the spell you write—make you name," and then, with great effort, "the way you write your name now go back into the room I'll be there in a minute."

As Julie disappeared through the door, Mrs. Boulderdam looked at me with one of the most pitiful expressions I've ever seen on a grown-up.

"Help," was all she said.

A rough count through the remainder of the day showed Julie was asking between six and ten questions an hour, and her pace never slacked. The really amazing thing was that Mrs. Boulderdam had lasted even six days, much less six weeks.

Almost all of Julie's questions were unnecessary, in that she probably knew the answer or could have figured it out. Intelligence, or the lack of it, was definitely *not* the problem.

Actually, Julie's only question, asked in various ways throughout the day, was, "Will you reassure me that I'm an important person around here?"

The trick was going to involve getting her to ask fewer questions and feel better about herself.

To begin with, I advised Mrs. Boulderdam to draw a large question mark on each of twelve index cards.

Sometime later, she took Julie aside and told her how much she liked her (she really did, too) but that Julie needed to begin thinking through answers to her own questions. Mrs. Boulderdam offered to help Julie practice "thinking without help" by giving her the cards as "reminders."

Every time Julie came to Mrs. Boulderdam with a question, she had to give up one of her cards in exchange for an answer. When Julie's twelve cards were gone, Mrs. Boulderdam would refuse to answer any more of her questions for that day.

Julie started each new day with the twelve cards in her possession. When Julie had a question, Mrs. Boulderdam would ask her, "Have you thought about it, Julie?" and then, "Do you want to give me a card for the answer?"

Julie caught on very quickly. After a week, she was asking fewer than ten questions a day, most of them "necessary."

Julie felt important because Mrs. Boulderdam had done something special—just for her. She also learned something valuable about independence.

Mrs. Boulderdam's hands stopped fluttering, and she finished out the year in fine form.

Madness in the Morning

(Q) I am writing to you out of sheer desperation. My problem may seem trivial, but it is driving me absolutely up a wall. Both my husband and I work and it is necessary that we leave the house by 7:45 every morning. On the way to work, I drop our Jamie, who is four and a half, at his day-care center. The problem is that every morning Jamie plays and stalls and everything else you can think of—except getting dressed.

I lay out his clothes when we all get up at 6:30 and the fight begins. I start by calmly telling him to get dressed, but always end up yelling at him and oftentimes putting the last few pieces on him myself. The only thing he can't do by himself is tie his shoes. We all end up angry and everybody's day begins on this miserable note. The problem is not that Jamie is tired. He goes to bed (no problems here) at 8:30 (after a bedtime story—his favorite thing) and is alert in the mornings. He just finds all kinds of reasons for not putting his clothes on. Can you help us?

(A) Come down off the wall. Your problems are almost over. It's quite clear that Jamie is a clever little fellow. Clever enough to figure out that when Mom and Dad are busy and in a hurry, one surefire way of getting everybody's attention is to *not* cooperate. After all, what's the rush? Who wants to hurry up and be without Mom and Dad all day long?

You made two very important statements. First, Jamie *can* dress himself. Second, Jamie likes being read to in the evening. If you will purchase a kitchen timer (see page 34), we will have all the ingredients for our recipe.

Now, with the timer in hand, Mom and Dad sit down with Jamie and say, "Hey, big guy, we aren't going to yell at you about getting dressed in the morning anymore. Instead, we are going to play a game called Put Your Clothes On. Here's how the game is played. When we wake you up, we will put your clothes on the chair in your room. Then we will set the timer for fifteen minutes and put it on your dresser.

"When we set the timer, it will begin ticking like a clock, and in fifteen minutes, a bell will ring like this (demonstrate the bell ringing). If you have all of your clothes on before the bell rings, then you win the game. The prize for winning is that you get to pick a bedtime story that night. Isn't that exciting?

"If the bell rings and you don't have your clothes on, then Mom and Dad will put them on. But you don't win the game, so you cannot have a bedtime story."

Then, do exactly that. If he wins, make a big deal about it, letting him know how nicely he dresses himself and so on. Read him a short story before school. If he doesn't win the game, dress him yourself. If you have to do this and he protests, simply tell him that those are the rules, and you want him to win tomorrow. He *will* start to win, believe me.

You can gradually shorten the time until he can put his clothes on at a comfortable pace. A "star-chart" taped to the refrigerator is an additional way to reward him when he wins. It's called the no-more-footprints-on-the-wall method of child rearing.

A Cure for the "Sloppies"

(Q) My seven-year-old is the sloppiest child you ever saw. He never puts anything where it belongs. His coat is never hung up, his bike is always parked dead center in the driveway, his dirty clothes are piled where he took them off, his books land on the sofa when he comes home from school . . . need I go on? It seems as though I yell at him all the time, but nothing changes. Help save my hair!

(A) Yelling is a trap fraught with paradox. The more you yell, the less you accomplish. A yell is threatening, and the sheer volume may prompt a child to follow instructions, but once the shock wave passes, it's generally back to business as usual.

Yelling is also a waste of energy. You invest a tremendous amount of yourself and get nothing of lasting value in return. The more you yell, the more of yourself you exhaust, until finally you're bankrupt. And your seven-year-old is ready to cash in all the chips.

A yell is aggressive, but not assertive. It is an expression of frustration and an admission of powerlessness. In fact, the yell transfers control of the issue to the child, who is all too willing to be the center of the storm, in control of the family.

It is essential that you do something more constructive than yelling, before the entire family gets hooked into behaving as though a seven-year-old sits in the driver's seat!

Take a piece of paper and, down the left-hand side, make a list of all the things your son "misplaces"—bicycle, coat, schoolbooks, dirty clothes, shoes, and so on. Be very specific, so there is no room for misunderstandings ("It only says *coat;* I didn't know you meant my *rain*coat too!")

Then, to the right of your first list, make a second which tells *exactly* where each item belongs. Coat . . . on a hanger in the hall closet. Bicycle . . . parked against the side wall of the carport. Dirty clothes . . . in the hamper in the upstairs bathroom.

Find a quiet time to sit down with your son and go over the list of things and places: "You and I have not been working together very well. I have made this list to help both of us know what the rules are for putting things away."

After your discussion, post the list on the refrigerator door or some other equally visible place. Beside it, post a "scorecard"—a sheet with seven boxes in a row, representing seven days.

"For the next seven days, we are going to keep score on how well you are learning the rules. If you leave something out of place, I will call it to your attention. You must mark a check in the box for that day and then put the item where it belongs. In return, I promise *not* to yell."

During the week, monitor his compliance, but don't crowd him. If he refuses to put his own check in the box, make it for him. Be sure to call his attention not only to things *out* of place, but to things that are *in* place as well, letting him know you appreciate his help. As the days go by, discuss his progress, or lack of it, in optimistic, matter-of-fact terms.

Don't offer him any goodies for a certain level of performance, but if you are so moved, you might reward several days of improvement (or a "perfect" day) with some spontaneous show of affection and gratitude: "You have done so well, how would you like to go with me to MacArnold's for a Crabapple Swizzle?"

On the other hand, the week may not produce any measurable change in his willingness to abide by the rules. He may not be quite ready to stop fighting with you. In that case, at the end of the week, be prepared to make him a "deal."

Put up another scorecard. Write a large number "four" at the top. Arrange a second summit conference. Inform him that he will be confined to his room for thirty minutes when he receives his fourth check of the day, and that any additional checks will immediately earn him another thirty minutes apiece.

Then you simply enforce the rules. In the end, it's largely a matter of trust. You trust him to abide by the rules, and he learns to trust that you will enforce them.

By following this plan, or a variation of it, you will make significant changes in the way you handle the situation. You will define the nature of the problem in clear, precise terms. You will give accurate, nonjudgmental feedback on his compliance with the rules. Finally, you will take an authoritative position on the issue, letting your son see you stand firmly, but gently, in one place.

He can be expected to test the system for weaknesses. That is his right! If you hold firm, he will eventually accept that you are no longer willing to participate in a struggle over "where things belong."

Pet Peeves

(Q) Our eighteen-month-old son is forever pulling our cat's tail or picking it up by the neck. Punishing him and talking to him have not worked. How can we teach him not to do this?

(A) At this age, you son is driven to touch, feel, and squeeze everything in sight. Every squeeze, every poke, is a way of asking the question, "What are you, and what do you do?"

Parents should childproof the toddler's environment, so he can interact freely and safely with his surroundings. Childproofing also improves the mental health of the parents, who might otherwise struggle constantly to keep the child out of places where he shouldn't be.

When a pet is part of the child's world, decide how to deal with the child's curiosity about the animal. One way to prevent frustration or harm is to keep the child and the pet completely separated, but this may be incompatible with the place the pet occupies in the family.

Another option is to hold the child's hand and patiently teach him how to stroke and handle the pet. Don't, however, bank on seeing any immediate results. Teaching a toddler restraint, tenderness, and sensitivity requires lots of patience.

Another way of handling the child's interest in the pet is to let them interact freely (which usually means as often as the pet will allow). Personal experience tells me that when the pet is familiar with the child, and the child means no harm, no harm is likely to come to either.

When my son was this age, we had a cat named Roy that Eric would maul every time their paths crossed. At first we were concerned that perhaps Eric was hurting Roy or that Roy might scratch him. Whenever Eric had Roy in his grip, we talked to him about being gentle or became mildly excited and pried them apart. Eventually we noticed that whenever Eric grabbed him, Roy went limp and endured the assault looking like last year's dish rag. After seeing how well Roy handled it, we stopped paying attention to the situation. Roy was obviously surviving the attacks and seemed to "know" that Eric meant no harm.

Lo and behold! After we stopped making it an issue, Eric stopped chasing Roy around the house.

To satisfy my own curiosity, I asked the opinion of several veterinarians. They all said they thought separation was the best solution if the parents were concerned about the child's handling of the pet. However, they knew of few pets injured by toddlers. The smaller the pet (kittens and puppies), the more vulnerable it is to innocent abuse. These veterinarians also thought that the family pet was not likely to retaliate against a child and that the pet could, in most cases, take care of itself.

A supervising emergency room nurse told me that although emergency room personnel see many children who have been hurt by animals, almost all of the injuries involve older children or animals that are either strays or that belong to another family. It is very rare, she said, to see an injury inflicted on a toddler by a family pet. In fact, she was unable to recall any incident of that nature in her many years of experience.

Young children require supervision, pet or no pet. For the sake of the animal, it is probably unwise to raise toddlers and kittens or puppies at the same time. For the child's safety, keep toddlers away from pets with a history of belligerence, strays, and other families' pets that may not be tolerant of strange, probing hands.

All these approaches have drawbacks. If parents choose to take the path of least resistance and let Mother Nature take care of the situation, however, harm is unlikely to come to either child or pet. That the child will ever become intentionally cruel and abusive to animals is even more unlikely. Most important in determining a child's permanent attitude toward animals is the example *we* set.

BB Guns

(Q) My father wants to give my eight-year-old, his grandson, a BB gun for Christmas. I don't like the idea, but Grandpa says Billy is old enough to learn to use a gun and develop respect for it. What's your opinion?

(A) My opinion is that guns are dangerous machines and have no place in the life of a child. A BB shot can seriously injure a human and kill a small animal. This potential disqualifies a BB gun as a toy.

I question the value of teaching a child "respect" for a gun. Respect implies an attitude of reverence and esteem. I don't see how a gun could possibly take on such significance in a child's world. In fact, I think it is impossible to teach respect for *anything* with a gun, unless you are confusing respect with fear.

It doesn't matter what you *intend* to teach a child by giving him lessons with a gun. The actual outcome will by determined as much, if not more, by methods and materials as by intent. The medium is the message and the message is quite dangerous.

Children are impressionable, easily excited, and impulsive, and they demonstrate an unremarkable lack of self-control and foresight. God gives every child a parent so that someone can hold the reins.

And because we hold the reins, children have relatively little control over their own lives. Growth is a product of the dynamic tension generated as a child pulls against the restraints we impose upon him, and this inevitable conflict is also inevitably frustrating.

Children translate this conflict and frustration into play and daydream, both of which are often saturated with themes of power and control. In fantasy, a child can safely pretend that his strength and authority have expanded to fantastic proportions. He *becomes* his favorite superhero, and his need for power finds harmless expression on the magic carpet of imagination.

Put a weapon into that context, and you've added an ingredient that can ignite the whole mixture. The danger is that the child will soon absorb the weapon into his play as a tangible symbol of power. Go one step further, and you've got one child holding a BB gun and another child who just lost an eye.

I have an idea: if you want to give your child something that will help him develop a sharp eye and allow him to shoot animals and even people without any risk . . . buy him a camera.

How to Divide Your Attention

(Q) Being a first-time mother, I have difficulty knowing how much one-to-one attention my three-year-old daughter needs. It seems the more we give, the more she demands. What are some general guidelines? I interact with her all day long during housework and shopping as I answer questions, tie bibs on dolls, and so on. We try to have a story at bedtime and some time during the morning to play as she directs, but it's never enough. Any suggestions?

(A) With the first child, parents are prone to confuse what is actually *needed* with what is simply *wanted.* It's an easy trap to stumble into for several reasons, not the least of which is our anxiety about dealing with a relatively unfamiliar set of demands and responsibilities. Hand in hand goes a desire to do everything just right, which further blurs the already faint line between what is necessary for the child's well-being and those things that are simply whimsy.

Don't count on children to clarify matters. They are just as likely to scream for a toy firetruck as they are for something to eat when they are hungry.

Children *need* nutritious food and water and warmth and room to explore and stimulation and people who talk softly and loving relationships and routines that organize their lives and cuddles and kisses and praise. They need parents who set limits and enforce rules and give lots of warm, accepting strokes.

On the other hand, children *want* parents who will be at their beck and call and solve all their problems and carry them everywhere and make them the center of attention and let them do and have whatever they demand and give lots of warm, accepting strokes.

It's not difficult to see why many children come to believe that parents are for anything and everything. From the moment a child arrives in the world, parents bathe and feed and carry and hold and rock and wait on her hand and foot. From a young child's point of view, parents are servants. Mom is a lady in waiting and Dad is a valet.

Ah, but good domestic help isn't easy to find these days. Sometimes the servants get uppity and refuse to follow instructions. That's usually no problem for a child with a healthy set of lungs. Servants are easily intimidated by tantrums.

Many parents interpret tantrums as screams of genuine pain, a symptom of needs that have gone abused and neglected. So they perform whatever peculiar act the scream demands, and by-and-by, the child learns that tantrums push all the right buttons. In the long run, then, the child gets the lesser part of what she needs and a greater part of what she wants, some of which she doesn't need at all. How confusing!

The solution? The same one that solves most other problems of raising children: establish predictable guidelines, set firm limits, and enforce them consistently. Set aside several times during the day—say, once in the morning, afternoon, and evening—when you will devote thirty minutes to nothing but your child. Give each period a name, such as "playtime," "doll-time" and "story-time." A child of three and a half has no concept of what thirty minutes means, so use a timer. At the beginning of each period, set the timer for thirty minutes and say, "Mommy will read stories until the bell rings, and then I am going to do my own work (be specific)." When the bell rings, you then excuse yourself, saying how much fun you had, and leave the little one with a suggestion for occupying her time.

If you stay with the routine and let her know how determined you are, then things will settle into place quickly.

Children may *want* servants, but they *need* parents.

"Betcha!"

(Q) My son is almost four years old, and he is driving me crazy. He will hardly do anything I ask until I become upset enough to spank him. And this is the child I promised myself I would *never* spank. When I ask him to do something, he gives me this "you gotta be kidding!" look and turns away. It's maddening! Sometimes he just says "No!" as coolly as you please. If he knows he is going to get a spanking (and he almost always does) then why does he do these things?

(A) Your almost-four-year-old is only doing what every young child must eventually do—he is challenging your authority. He demands to know, "By what right do *you* tell *me* what to do?"

As long as the question is unanswered, he is free to engage in a power struggle with you.

After all, no one told him the rules before he got here. It is *your* responsibility to describe the rules to him, not *his* to figure them out. If you aren't clear on what they are, then he is free to make up his own game and his own rules. And he has. It's called "Betcha!"

In Betcha! the parent starts the play by asking the child to perform some task, however small. The child counters by refusing to cooperate. Parent then responds, "Oh yes you will!" The child says, "Betcha!" and the game is on!

Betcha! isn't much fun, however, because no one ever wins. In fact, both people always end up losers. How monotonous! But when it's the only game in town, well . . .

"But he almost always gets a spanking," you say. So what? Who pays *that* price? You do.

The game repeats itself because it has never been resolved. And it will not be resolved until you stop expecting *him* to change. He's not going to stop inviting you to play Betcha! until you stop accepting the invitation. In fact, he doesn't even know *how* to stop.

To begin the end of Betcha! stop *asking* your son for his cooperation and start *telling* him exactly what you want him to do. Begin every "request" with the phrase, "I want you to . . ." and then fill in the blank with a clear, concise description of the task. Stop apologizing for having brought him into a less-than-perfect world.

Here are two of many possible approaches you can take to bring Betcha! to a close. Choose the one that suits you better, or use them as models for devising a solution of your own.

Plan A: Instead of spanking as a *last* resort, spank as a *first* resort. I have no problems with spankings per se, as long as they are used effectively, to accomplish something. Up until now, your spankings have been an expression of frustration and defeat. Use your hand to emphasize your authority and to stop the game before it has a chance to get started.

Tell him what you want from him. If he signals his refusal, immediately reach around and clap him firmly on the rear (*do not* announce what is coming with warnings or threats). Then, face him and repeat what you want. Remember in the movie *The Godfather,* when Marlon Brando made someone an offer he couldn't refuse? Use that tone of voice. If he still refuses (he probably will the first few times), take him to a chair and have him sit until he's ready to comply. Meanwhile, you go some other place and busy yourself.

If that sounds too mean, then try Plan B: Buy a kitchen timer if you don't have one. Sit down with almost-four and say, "Yesterday (all things in the past happened "yesterday" to an almost-four), when I told you to do something (use an example), you said 'No!' I got mad and yelled and spanked. I don't like that. Today, if you say, 'No,' I'm going to put you in your room for five minutes. When I put you in the room, I'll set this timer and when five minutes is over, it will ring, like this. Then you can come out and do what I told you to do. Understand?"

He will nod his head, which means that he doesn't understand, but knows when to nod his head.

You are letting him know that you are changing the game. You must then show him what kind of change you're talking about.

Now, it is *your* move.

"Look at Me!"

(Q) We have a four-and-a-half-year-old daughter, and an eighteen-month-old son. Our problem is other people—neighbors, friends, even grandparents—who pay lots of attention to the baby and very little to the older child, to the point of virtually ignoring her. When other people come over, my daughter begins "performing," interrupting conversations and misbehaving in other ways to get attention. How can I get other people to understand that she needs attention too?

(A) I'm sorry, but your daughter's plight fails to evoke my sympathy. It seems obvious that the *real* problem is her misbehavior when you have guests in your home.

This problem involves other people only to the extent that they have become *her* audience and *your* excuse for failing to control her. You have unintentionally given her permission to misbehave when there is company, and she has seized the opportunity to command as much attention as possible.

I suspect that she would get *more* attention if her behavior was appropriate to her age and the situation. She is probably being ignored *because* of her "performance," not because your guests are insensitive.

One disappointment in being an eldest child occurs when the spotlight takes its turn on the second born. Babies attract lots of attention. That's a fact of life your daughter is capable of living with. But she won't make a comfortable adjustment to her slightly diminished status unless you stop trying to protect her from the hardship of having a younger sibling.

Take a quiet moment to sit and talk with her. Tell her you understand how difficult it is to share things, including attention from other people. Point out that she must nonetheless learn to share and promise to help her.

Make a list of the inappropriate things she does in front of guests—cartwheels, Ed Sullivan impressions, and so on. Make it clear that you will no longer accept this behavior, and let her know how you *do* expect her to act.

When she entertains company with one of the items on the list, put her in Time-Out (see A Matter of Timing, page 36) for five minutes. Make sure you give her a hug and a kiss when she manages to control her enthusiasm in front of visitors.

The world may be a stage, but your daughter is a bit young for a leading role.

Tattletales

"Mrs. Brickyard! Elmo just said a bad word to Angela, and she didn't do anything to him. He's *mean!* Are you gonna paddle him? Are you, huh?"

When children fight, the easiest solution is often to appeal to the nearest adult to come bail them out. Because it is the easiest thing to do, it also takes the least amount of thought and effort on the part of the child or children. Therefore, when we respond to a tattletale, we encourage children not to think.

Webster's Dictionary defines "tattling" as "making idle talk; to chatter or to gossip." It defines "idle" as "something worthless" and "chatter" as "nonsense."

Tattling is senseless and destructive. No only does it often prove unfair to the child who is tattled on, but it is harmful as well to the child who does the tattling. The "tattletale" is usually the child least liked by siblings, shunned by peers and held in disfavor by adults.

We adults inadvertently create the problem. The unfortunate victim of our actions is the "tattletale," because the child who tattles will have trouble being trusted and accepted by peers.

Tattling should be discouraged. When a child comes to you with a tale of woe or wanting to play "informer," do her a favor by saying, "I'm sorry that happened, Ashley, but I will not be able to come and help. This sounds like something you and Johnny can work out peacefully on your own."

If tattling is a habit with the child, be more definite about your feelings: "You are tattling again. You and I have talked about tattling before, and you know that I will not settle your problems for you. You must solve this one for yourself."

Don't make the mistake of saying, "I don't like tattling," and then rushing to the scene anyway. Children learn more by what we *do* than what we say.

If the problem occurs frequently in a certain group of children, take the time to talk to everyone in the group or class about tattling and proper ways of solving problems. Help children make the distinction between what you *want* to know about (cuts, falls, and so on) and what you don't want to hear.

Tattling is the beginning of a long string of yarn that, unless cut early, grows larger and larger, becoming a burden for the child who must carry it around.

Bad Words

"Bad words." We all know what they are. Worse than that, we know what they *mean!* Horrible, unmentionable things, all of them. We don't use them . . . much. Or we at least use them "properly," for pardonable reasons such as, "I was drunk," or "I lost my temper."

In the life of a child, there are three stages in the development of bad words. The first stage occurs when the child first hears the words. Bad words are more likely to attract a child's attention than "good" words. Bad words stand out because of the emphasis we give them in tone and volume.

Take the phrase, "That worthless blankety-blank." Say it out loud, substituting your favorite bad word for "blankety-blank." See what I mean? Any young child, hearing that for the first time, will remember "blankety-blank." The child may also notice, if the "blankety-blank" is a person who is present, how she turns red and begins to act strange. The thing most apparent to the child witnessing such a scene is the power of the words and the attention they command. End Stage One.

Stage Two. The child runs outside where his friends are playing and says, "Hey Timmy, you know what you are? You're a blankety-blank."

Timmy runs to his mother and says, "Matthew called me a blankety-blank."

Timmy's mother calls Matthew's mother, Matthew's mother calls Matthew's father, who beats the blankety-blank out of Matthew. Poor Matthew doesn't even know what blankety-blank means.

That's just one possible scenario. Matthew might wait to let go with blankety-blank at kindergarten. Then the whole world knows.

In any case, when Matthew shows off his new words, people almost always show him, in return, how tremendously significant they are.

Stage Three finds Matthew testing the shock value of his new vocabulary on an assortment of people and finding out what a wide range of reaction they provoke. Grandma faints, Sally runs away, Jeffrey cries, Billy fights, Billy's older brother laughs, and the teacher talks herself blue in the face. What a great time Matthew has—making magical, meaningless sounds.

Actually, a fourth stage will emerge several years later, when Matthew discovers that blankety-blank has a definition, of sorts. At that point, Matthew may begin to use it "properly"—only when he's drunk or angry, for instance. Ain't life amazin'?

There is nothing to be accomplished by trying to prevent Stages One and Two from occurring. All children hear the words from somebody, sometime. And all children use them on somebody, sometime.

Trying to prevent this makes a problem where there was none before. I call it the Magnifying Glass principle. Matthew says a bad word and the adults around him teeter on the verge of hysteria. The exaggerated reactions have the same effect on Matthew's behavior as a magnifying glass seems to have on a butterfly wing.

Matthew's bad language gets a great deal of attention. Isolating his bad word and acting as though it is the most significant aspect of his behavior confirms Matthew's hunch that these are powerful words indeed. Never mind what else Matthew might have learned and accomplished during the day—he said a bad word. That's more important than anything else, isn't it?

When we isolate and overreact to any particular behavior, we hold an invisible magnifying glass up to it, causing that behavior to get bigger and more noticeable.

If you don't want Matthew to use "bad" words, then obviously you shouldn't use them yourself, not even "properly." What you *do* will have more influence on Matthew than what you *say,* especially if the "say" and the "do" don't jibe.

When Matthew says a bad word—and he will—be cool. Say something like, "Listen, Matthew, I know that some people use words like 'blankety-blank' when they talk, but no one in our family uses them and neither will you." That's clear and will make a more positive impression than, say, beating the blankety-blank out of him.

By allowing ourselves to get upset by the small things that children do, we set the stage for repeat performances. Once we set the stage, children play the parts we assign them.

It Takes Two

The storm gathered upstairs while I sat reading the paper. It began as a rumbling confusion of voices, suddenly punctuated by a gruff, insistent, "GET OUTA HERE!" Then came a piercing screech. Another who-done-it was unfolding at the Rosemond's.

"Daddy!" It was Eric, then twelve years old, calling from the top of the stairs. I kept reading.

"DADDY!"

"Eric?" The sound of his name brings him thundering down the stairs, an avalanche of indignation.

"Dad, Wayne and I want to play in my room and Amy won't leave us alone."

"Oh really? I'm reading the paper here on the sofa."

"DAD! She's messing everything up and we can't play!"

"Sounds complicated."

"Will you tell her to leave so Wayne and I can play?"

"No, I won't."

"Why not?"

"You know why not, but if you want to hear it again," deep breath, "I am not a referee. The two of you can work these things out without my help."

"All right then, can I drag her out and lock the door?"

"You know the rule for fighting in our house—nobody gets hurt. And keep Wayne out of it."

"I won't hurt her, but can I lock her out?"

"I'm not going to tell you what to do."

"O.K. I'm gonna ask her one more time, and then I'm throwing her out and locking the door."

"Remember the rule."

Dramatic about-face and exit, stage left. A few moments later, I heard the unmistakable racket of a body being dragged, kicking, across the floor and dumped in the hall. *Slam!* Little fists pummel the door . . . "LET ME IN! I HATE YOU! YOU'RE THE WORST BROTHER IN THE WORLD!" Then, down the stairs she flies, the one-and-only Amy the Screech. "Daddy!"

"Yes, Amos?"

"Eric pushed me out of his room," (here come the crocodile tears) "and LOCKED THE DOOR!"

"Oh really? *I'm* reading the paper."

For years, I gave Eric and Amy that same message—Daddy would not referee their fights or judge who was "right" and who was "wrong."

I never appreciated the meaning of "it takes two to tango" until Eric and Amy began "dancing" with each other. In fact, this particular tango is probably an inevitable consequence of having more than one child in a family.

It takes the better part of childhood for children to learn the art of getting along. While they may need a coach occasionally, it is generally best for adults to maintain a respectable distance from the dance. It takes two to tango and a third to get tangled.

Children have a talent for turning what could have been a simple exercise in learning how to live together into a melodrama, peopled with cardboard characters straight out of *The Perils of Pauline.*

Someone is the villain, heir to the throne of Snideley Whiplash. Someone else is the victim—oppressed, downtrodden, and certain to evoke lots of sympathy. We adults are generally typecast as a cross between the pope and Henry Kissinger. It's a generous offer, which I always refuse. But they keep offering, because as often as they tangle, the trivial becomes the grandiose, and another melodrama begins. It's the alchemy of childhood.

I suppose that transforming real people into two-dimensional stereotypes makes their conflicts seem less threatening, less personal, and therefore less enduring. That may have something to do with the way children are able to forgive and forget so easily.

Ah-ha! The trick of growing up involves learning to keep conflict personal, and *still* being able to forgive and *learn* rather than forget.

I stayed out of their conflicts because I trusted them to work things out for themselves. I stayed out because any solution *they* devised would have been more valuable and enduring than one *I* imposed on them. I stayed out because I didn't want them growing up to believe in melodrama. I stayed out because I wanted them growing *out* of their stereotypes, not *into* them.

Meanwhile, I kept waiting for the last tango.

Twins

If you've been blessed with twins, here are some recommendations—more "don'ts" than "do's."

First of all, don't hang rhyming names on them. It may be cute and all the relatives may expect you to, but it may contribute to problems later.

Identical twins have as much right to separate identities as any other two children. Names like "Fred" and "Ted" obscure the fact that, although they may share identical physical characteristics, they are fundamentally different people.

Rhyming names can also create confusion. Young children have difficulty discriminating between similar sounds. When you ask a two-year-old to "Get the hat," he may walk over and pet the cat! That may be funny, but one problem twins don't need is never being sure what their names are or whose name you called.

Don't *ever* dress them in identical clothes, even for a family portrait. You get more for your money buying two interchangeable outfits father than two matching outfits. When the outfits are interchangeable, each child shares two, and maybe even four, different groupings. When the outfits match, each child has one outfit.

Not only is matching clothing impractical; it's confusing to twins and to other people. Matching clothing encourages the false idea that they are the same person in two bodies.

Don't buy them identical gifts for special occasions. Identical toys may seem fair and impartial, but they will create several problems and solve none. Identical toys, like identical clothes and rhyming names, create turmoil and conflicts. You may know "whose is whose," but young children won't. Besides, it's an extension of the unhealthy "you-are-one-person" idea.

Buying identical toys will not prevent fights, either. Children will fight over toys no matter what you do, until they are old enough to see the value of sharing. This won't happen until they are at least four years old. They will learn the art of sharing much sooner if each has her own unique set of possessions. What's to share if everything is alike?

Several years ago, I talked with the parents of twin girls who were then nine years old. They had rhyming names, wore identical clothing, and had identical possessions. At the time, Sherry had developed an outgoing personality, while Cherry had become quiet, shy, and dependent on her sister to do things for her. I persuaded the parents to refer to Cherry by her middle name, to see that the girls never wore matching outfits, and to purchase no identical things for them. Several weeks later, the parents told me they had seen a great transformation in Cherry, who was now called "Lynn." She had become as independent and outgoing as her sister. When the girls had attending a family reunion, Lynn had run up to a favorite aunt and exclaimed, "Look at me, Aunt Lydia, I'm a brand new person!"

If you have twins, encourage each to develop an individual identity. Appreciate and nurture their separateness. Making them carbon copies of each other will plant the seeds of competition, resentment, or dependence.

PART FOUR

Uncommon Sense

In the original, 1981 version of Parent Power!, *this section was entitled "Sounding Off" because a lot of the views expressed within were highly controversial for that day and time. A lot has changed in ten years, including my opinions about some things. So, this section contains almost all new material, and because I'm no longer "sounding off" in quite as controversial a matter, my editor suggested I retitle it "Uncommon Sense." I thought that was fairly flattering, and I can't resist flattery, so uncommon sense it is.*

As you read, keep in mind that I'm not asking you to agree. I want you to think. Not long ago, another psychologist, in the process of taking issue with my point of view concerning a certain issue, called me an "iconoclast." I thought he was insulting me. When I consulted the dictionary, however, I discovered that an iconoclast is "one who attacks venerated institutions or ideas." So, he really wasn't insulting me at all. In truth, I've never been comfortable with the notion that because most people agree about something, even if they are recognized authorities of one sort or another, that their point of view is necessarily correct. And I've always been outspoken. Those two traits, in combination, make for an iconoclast. So be it.

Television

The average American preschool child spends more time watching television than in any other waking activity. Between her second and sixth birthdays, she watches twenty-five hours a week, or 5,200 hours during four of the most important years of her life. By the time she enters first grade, she will have spent close to one-third of her waking hours in front of a television set.

Since the late 1960s, groups like Boston-based Action for Children's Television (ACT) have fought to improve the quality of children's programs. ACT has succeeded in eliminating vitamin ads aimed at children and commercial pitches by children's program hosts, and in reducing by 40 percent the commercial time on Saturday morning television.

But better television viewing may *not* be what our children need. A growing body of evidence strongly suggests that television's harm to children—to preschoolers in particular—has little, if anything, to do with *what* they watch.

It doesn't matter what's on the screen. The harm is in the very *watching* itself.

When a child watches television, she is inert, physically and mentally. She is passive, disengaged, uninvolved (or involved only momentarily and superficially). She can choose from a small set of programs (often similar in nature), but she cannot determine what she sees, or from what perspective, or in what sequence.

As she watches, her pupils are fixed on one stationary point in the visual field. Instead of scanning, she stares. Most of the time, her hands rest limply in her lap. She is a spectator, a bystander, along for the ride down a one-way street.

In short, watching television is akin to doing nothing. It is perhaps the most democratic technology ever invented. Anyone can watch, and almost everyone does. No prerequisites are necessary—no talent, no prior experience. One working eyeball is all you need.

Even the claims made for such so-called educational programs as "Sesame Street" and "Electric Company" are suspect. A study done by the Russell Sage Foundation and summarized in *Sesame Street Revisited* (Russell Sage Foundation, 1975) determined that regular "Sesame Street" watchers actually made fewer gains in reasoning and problem-solving skills than children who watched only occasionally.

The preschool years are the most critical formative period of a human being's life. In this brief time, a child develops an enduring personal style of relating to the world—socially, emotionally, perceptually, and intellectually. Research has clearly demonstrated the importance of exploration, play, and fantasy to the growing child.

But instead of being a stimulant to intellectual and physical activity, television acts as a narcotic. Dr. T. Berry Brazelton, a Cambridge, Mass., pediatrician and author of *Infants and Mothers,* says television induces a trancelike state in young children. "(It) assaults and overwhelms a child," Brazelton has said. "He can respond to it only by (becoming) more passive."

Children's television advocates disagree. Dr. Edward Palmer, former head of research for the Children's Television Workshop (producers of "Sesame Steet" and "Electric Company"), asserts that watching television is a "remarkable intellectual act."

"All the while kids are watching," Palmer says, "they are making hypotheses, anticipating, generalizing, remembering, and actively relating what they are seeing to their own lives."

But one look at the glazed, vacuous expression on the face of a young child immersed in a program convinces me that watching television is hardly remarkable, barely intellectual, and in no way an act.

Contrary to what children's television proponents would have us believe, television is not, and can never be, a child's best friend. It is, instead, one of his worst enemies. A child's time is better spent doing just about anything other than watching television.

Since 1955, the number of hours preschool children spend watching television has more than tripled. During these same years, academic achievement scores have declined steadily, the national literacy level has deteriorated, and public schools have been beset by an epidemic of young children who have difficulty learning to read.

A recent study of a half-million California schoolchildren concluded that the more television children watched on school nights, the lower their achievement test scores. Wilson Riles, former California superintendent of public instruction, said the results show a link between television watching and poor achievement that, up till now, educators have only "suspected . . . and talked about."

Watching television is not in any way comparable to reading. You don't *learn* to watch television—you just do it. Reading requires involvement—a quality noticeably absent from the television experience. Reading is an active, problem-solving exercise—a two-way street. You cannot "watch" a book.

We have evolved a brain ideally suited to this challenge. But the brain of a six-year-old who comes to school with six thousand hours of television under her eyelids is potentially in big trouble. Unless some drastic changes are made, she may not be willing or able to alter the habit of being a passive "watcher."

Researchers at the National Institute of Mental Health have found evidence that brain cells grow in response to intellectual exercise and stimulation (much as muscle cells respond to physical stimulation) and atrophy, or weaken, for the lack of it.

That research raises the possibility that many "learning disabled" children are just average video kids whose brains, weakened from too many hours of watching television, cannot rise to the challenge of learning to read.

Recent research on children who can't read also indicates that watching television trains their eyes to stare instead of scan. Dr. Edgar Gording, a remedial reading expert, says many of the nonreaders he works with have never learned to move their eyes from left to right. That basic visual skill would presumably have developed had these children spent less time during their preschool years staring at a television screen and more in play and other active pursuits.

Equally frightening is the addictive quality of television. The more children watch, the more they want to watch. If they are prevented from watching, they often go through a period of emotional withdrawal that's stressful not only to them, but to their parents as well. They become sullen, moody, and irritable. They become obsessed with the television and make repeated attempts to "connect" with it. They become aggressive, unruly, and anxious. Their frustration and anxiety build, choking off their ability to engage in constructive behavior.

When addicted children aren't plugged into the television

set, they will probably plug themselves into one or both of their parents, hassling and whining, "Do for me! Do for me!"

After reaching the limits of tolerance, parents are likely to put them back in front of the tube, hoping to buy a moment's peace. They don't realize that their children's inability to occupy themselves is partly a result of the time they spend glued to the tube. Television drains children of initiative, motivation, and autonomy and weakens their tolerance for stress.

But why is television addictive while radio, for instance, is not? It's a matter of different technologies. Typically, live or filmed television productions are shot using several cameras, each watching the action from a different angle.

The networks have found that viewers will watch the screen longer when the scene shifts from one camera to the next. So shift it does, at three-second intervals, on the average.

This is why small children will sit for long periods, transfixed by programs they cannot possibly comprehend. The incessant shifting of reference point overrides the need for understanding. It does not interest the child—it mesmerizes her.

Paradoxically, a child who sits staring at a television screen for several hours is learning how *not* to pay attention. She is adapting to an attention span of a few seconds.

After six thousand hours of this insidious training, the child arrives in a public school classroom where her teacher discovers that she cannot concentrate.

Since watching television has never required anything of her, she doesn't finish anything she starts. She doesn't know why she can't sit still, can't pay attention or can't finish her work—she just knows she *can't*. And so, "I can't" becomes more and more a part of her self-image.

Veteran teachers have remarked to me that, as a group, children today are far less imaginative and resourceful than children were a generation ago, when childhood television viewing was less than half what it is today. This observation is hardly surprising. The explicit nature of the television experience leaves little to a child's imagination. In fact, it subtly discourages children from exercising their creative resources.

Over the past thirty years, we have allowed the television networks to create their own myths; among them are the terms "children's program," "family program," and "educational program."

Presumably, programs like "Captain Kangaroo" and "Sesame Street" are "children's programs." But television watching is not an appropriate pastime for children, preschoolers in particular. Television is a handicap to childhood, not a help. There really are no children's programs. The so-called children's program exists and thrives because of *parents,* not children. These shows keep children "occupied," but, contrary to what their producers would have parents believe, they offer nothing of value. There are no programs for families either. The terms *family* and *program* are incompatible, because the moment a group of people calling themselves a family sits down to watch television, the family process stops.

The terms *watch* and *together* are also incompatible. You don't watch television together. You watch alone. Regardless of how many people are in the same room watching the same television, each has retired into a solitary audio-visual tunnel.

Television may not actually be spawning communication problems, but it certainly becomes an excuse for maintaining them. The more people in a family drift apart, the more watching television becomes a convenient means of dutifully enduring each other's presence while simultaneously avoiding acknowledgment of it—all under the pretense that watching television is a "family affair."

"All television is educational," said Nicholas Johnson, former member of the Federal Communications Commission. "The question is—What's being learned?"

On the surface, a child watching a Saturday morning cartoon and a child watching "Wild Kingdom" are viewing entirely different kinds of programs—one pure entertainment, the other supposedly educational. But there are no programs that earn, more than any others, rights to the term "educational." A child watching a cartoon and a child watching "Wild Kingdom" are both exposed to the same educational message: *You can get something for nothing.*

Children are impressionable little people. They have no way of evaluating, and therefore resisting, television's insidious message.

They accept. They absorb. They adapt. And they become whatever they are massaged into becoming by whatever influences prevail in their environments.

Video Nothings

The March 3, 1990, issue of *TV Guide* carried an article on video games which quoted Patricia Marks Greenfield, professor of psychology at UCLA and author of *Mind and Media: The Effects of Television, Video Games, and Computers,* as saying, "Video games develop a whole bunch of intellectual abilities, like problem-solving and visual/spatial skills."

Greenfield also pooh-poohed the notion that children can become addicted to video games. Commenting on the observation that some children seem to become obsessed with them, she said, "Of course, kids are going to want to play till they've mastered a game, but I would call that mastery motivation rather than addiction."

Professor Greenfield needs to come down from her ivory tower and talk to people like Ken and Kathy Kelly of Charlotte, N.C. After determining that they would never purchase a video game unit for their five-year-old son, Kenny, they finally relented and bought him a Nintendo system in January, 1990. Here's what the Kellys had to say about their decision:

"We had two rules: Kenny was to share with his sister, and they could play for forty minutes a day. After just a few days, we began seeing changes in Kenny's behavior. He became irritable and bossy. He would get very upset—crying, stomping his feet—when he wouldn't get to the next level in Super Mario. He constantly tried to sneak additional time, and there were several nights when we awakened at three o'clock in the morning to find him playing Nintendo.

"Kenny also began to balk at going to school. When we dropped him off, he would start crying and screaming. On several occasions, his teachers had to help peel him out of the car. He also started fighting with his classmates and sassing his teachers. He was sassy and belligerent with us and our baby-sitter.

"We couldn't figure out what was the matter. We were almost at the end of our rope when I read about a situation in your book,

John Rosemond's Six-Point Plan for Raising Happy, Healthy Children, that was very similar to our own.

"So, we removed the Nintendo from the house and told Kenny it was broken. Within a few days, Kenny was back. No more tantrums, no more belligerent, sassy behavior, and he started happily going to school.

"Needless to say, the unit will never be 'fixed,' and we'll happily go back to being the only house in the neighborhood without one."

The Kellys' experience could be dismissed if it were an isolated one, but it isn't. Over the past few years, several hundred (no exaggeration) parents have written me concerning similar video-game-related horror stories. These tales don't sound like descriptions of mere "mastery motivation" to me. I've been around enough addicts and enough highly motivated people to know the difference.

As I've said before, video games are not really games at all. They provoke high levels of stress and are, indeed, addictive in the sense that many children become obsessed with constantly increasing their scores (or "skill levels" as they are deceptively termed). Compared to the harm that they are obviously capable of causing, the contention that video games improve certain problem-solving and visual/perceptual skills rates a big "so what?"

Unfortunately, it's what many parents want to hear.

Toys

I've been trying to remember what toys I played with when I was four or five years old, but the only one that comes to mind is an electric train Uncle Ned gave me for Christmas in 1952.

I must be getting senile. Surely I had more toys than that! After all, I was a child, and children have lots of toys. Therefore, I had lots of toys!

What were they?

This is driving me crazy. I'm going to call my mother.

"Listen, Ma, I was sittin' here tryin' to remember my toys. You know, the stuff I played with when we lived in Charleston, and . . ."

"Toys? We didn't buy toys for you."

"No toys? None?"

"Well, let's see. Come to think of it, Ned gave you an electric train one Christmas and you had some lead cavalry and a set of Lincoln Logs. But those were rainy day things for you."

"So what did I do when it wasn't raining?"

"You played outside. Lizard hunts and other great adventures. You were never at a loss for things to do. I could hardly ever find you. I remember one day . . ."

Lizard hunts. Great adventures. Gone all afternoon. What a life! I remember now. My toys were things of the earth. Stones and puddles and sticks and stuff. I was never bored. I didn't know *how* to get bored.

Is it my imagination, or do lots of children today have trouble getting un-bored?

How many times have you heard a child say, "I've got nothin' to do!"

Today's children expect, and even demand, to be entertained, because they've *been* entertained. Every day, in every conceivably irrelevant way. They are, by and large, a stubbornly inert generation.

Parents who give their children too much of their time, too much television, and a roomful of toys: These are the environmental afflictions of today's children. These are the things that stand in the way of their learning to occupy themselves creatively. They are barriers to the free outpouring of intelligence.

Paradoxically, children quickly become dependent on these obstructions—unwitting participants in their own undoing.

Take toys, for instance. Today's child is, generally speaking, a toy addict. He's gotta have 'em. New ones. All the time.

He lives in a clutter of toys. They're everywhere. Bits and pieces of broken toys sift to the bottom of an oversized toybox. His shelves are stacked with them, his closet and cabinets are packed with them, his floor is strewn with them. Every time his grandparents come for a visit, they bring him more obligatory toys. Every time his parents go shopping, he gets a toy.

Yet he says, "I've got nothin' to do!"

He is almost right! The choices are too overwhelmingly many. The clutter fogs his imagination, obstructs his vision, and frustrates his growing. He avoids the frustration by avoiding the clutter. The only thing he knows to do is to compulsively add to it. Translated, "I've got nothin' to do" means, "I forget how to do for myself."

The more toys he has, the more he depends on them and the more he wants. Ultimately, the toys themselves have no value whatsoever. He ignores them. He doesn't take care of them. That's what happens when supply outstrips need. The ritual trip to the toy store becomes an end in itself: his fix.

The more toys he has, the more he expects of *things* and the less he expects of himself. He acts helpless, and we continue to feed his helplessness, slowly but surely strengthening an overall "I can't" attitude toward the challenges of living.

Here are a few of my thoughts on toys:

- The best toy is one the child creates. Take your child outside and show him how to build forts out of sticks, to dig moats with an old soup spoon, to make boats out of folded paper, to build walls out of stones, to fashion trees out of pinecones—the possibilities are infinite!
- The best commercial toys are flexible (they can be combined in lots of different ways) and encourage imaginative play. Small, doll-like figures and other true-to-life miniatures are fine. So are simple building sets, clay, crayons, water colors, finger paints, and so on.
- For the most part, steer clear of so-called educational toys. Generally they have little, if anything, in common with a child's developmental needs. Their "problems" are largely irrelevant and tend to inhibit, rather than encourage, creative thinking.
- Instead of buying toys that "do"—toys that perform—give children a few, basic things they can manipulate. Let the children's imaginations do the "doing."
- Don't limit children to toys traditionally considered appropriate to only one sex. If a boy wants to play with dolls, buy him dolls. If a girl wants to play baseball, buy her a bat and ball. The freer they are to explore the possibilities of living, the better choice-makers they will become.

In the final analysis, *less* is *more.*

The Push for Preschool Literacy

Several years ago I came across a story about a Miami woman who was developing and preparing to market a series of teaching toys for tots. She said parents could use her toy designs to teach basic academic skills to preschoolers.

Her ideas evolved from work she did with her own child who, at the age of two, knew all the letters of the alphabet and had a reading vocabulary of one hundred words. She was quick to point out that her daughter is not a prodigy and says every two-year-old has the same potential.

She is correct, and *that* is the problem.

Think of the world as a vast warehouse stocked with all the many things that make up the known universe. In one area are rocks, another is full of ferns, and so on.

When a child enters through the main gate, she is assigned a couple of guides whose job it is to provide whatever assistance she needs to become learned in the ways of the warehouse. When they do their job properly, the guides simply support the child's inborn desire to become competent.

Teaching a preschool child to read is equivalent to leading her into one area—the "Reading Section"—and saying, "This is the most important place in the warehouse. We want you to spend lots of time here."

Instead of enhancing a preschool child's relationship with the world, teaching her to read actually *restricts* the flow of information available to her, narrows her environmental experience, and is contrary to the most basic principles of human growth and development.

A child who is trained to pay disproportionate attention to any *one* aspect of her environment will pay insufficient attention to other, equally relevant, aspects. To say it is more important for a child of four to learn to read than to collect leaves, splash through puddles, or play with the family dog is extremely prejudicial. To discriminate in this fashion against certain elements of the environment, or to arbitrarily and artificially enhance certain others, ultimately distorts the child's perception of the universe, and, therefore, her sense of "place" within it.

Indeed it *is* possible, using certain enticements, to teach very young children to read. The question is not "Can it be done?" but "Should it be done?"

A growing number of developmental theorists, including Hans G. Furth, who has written several books on intelligence in children, insist that teaching a preschool child to read seriously impairs her intellectual growth for at least several years thereafter.

Joseph C. Pearce, author of *Magical Child,* says that reading requires the preschool child to begin dealing with abstractions before she has finished building a coherent understanding of the tangible universe. Premature literacy, he says, disrupts the growth of intelligence in much the same way premature birth disrupts physical and neurological growth.

If the child does not benefit from this early training, who does? Quite obviously, her parents, who can take pride in having the "fastest child on the block"—almost as satisfying as sporting a new Mercedes.

An unfortunate, but not surprising, finding is that, in most cases, the preschool reader's early lead completely evaporates by the second or third grade. The closer one looks at the push for early literacy, the more it takes on the character of a monstrous practical joke.

If a preschool child learns to read on her own (as many do), that is a creative expression of *her* initiative and takes its place as part of her overall inquiry into the world and its tickings.

That many children learn to read spontaneously, without ever being taught in any formal sense, is a testament to the amazing nature of human intelligence.

On the other hand, teaching a young child to read, before she is sufficiently prepared to take full advantage of the instruction, is nothing more than an abuse of her creative and intellectual potential.

(Q) We have an eighteen-month-old daughter. She is our first, and perhaps our only, child. We are already looking ahead, as I suppose many parents do, to the time when she goes off to school. Several of our friends teach, and they tell us stories about children who have a very painful and frustrating time learning how to read. Are there things we should be doing between now and then to prevent reading problems later? When should we begin teaching her the alphabet and her numbers, and how far should we go with this?

(A) Don't go anywhere with it. If you want your daughter to be a successful reader, read to her. Nothing you can do will contribute more toward her desire to read and her lifelong enjoyment of reading.

In fact, there may be nothing else so completely enriching as those tender and expressive moments. The time you spend reading to her is alive and flowing with love and trusting wonder.

Nestled safely in your arms, watching and listening as new worlds unfold, stretching the limits of her understanding and her imagination—she will learn that reading feels good. This is the most valuable gift you can give her.

The rest of my advice is all *don'ts,* beginning with television.

A growing body of evidence strongly and convincingly suggests that one big reason Johnny has trouble learning to read is because Johnny spent more time during his preschool years glued to the tube than in any other single activity.

Actually, watching the flicker of a television can hardly be called an "activity," and this is precisely why it constitutes a serious threat to a child's developmental vitality.

"Sesame Street" and other "new breed" children's programs, because they strive so hard and successfully to hook the preschool viewer, are, in my estimation, the chief culprits.

So what if children learn their ABC's and other academic tidbits by watching "Sesame Street"? What's the rush?

"Oh, but John, if a child goes to school today without knowing at least her ABC's and her numbers, she'll be lost from day one," you may be thinking.

Bullfrogs! I am unimpressed by preschoolers who can perform the alphabet, count to one hundred, add one-digit numbers, and so on. That's not readiness. That's trivia!

The developmental needs of a preschool child have *nothing whatsoever* to do with learning these nonsensical mnemonic games. These recitations benefit parents, *not* children.

Preschool children need to play, to explore, to imagine, to create, to do. They need to learn how to share and take turns. They need to learn that their independence is not threatened by obedience to authority. They *don't* need to learn the ABC's—unless they ask. If their *own* searching brings them to the questions, they need answers. But, by all means, keep the "lessons" informal and low-key.

Let the child initiate the games. Let the search belong to *her.*

(Q) Two years ago, my daughter, now four and a half, could recite her ABC's and numbers through ten. She has been printing her name since she was three and correctly identifies every letter of the alphabet. Now I am having a problem with her and don't know what to make of it. Every day,we sit down for at least thirty minutes and work on her letters, name, and so on. For the past few months, however, she either refuses to work with me, complains that it's too hard, or acts as though she has forgotten much of what I taught her. I am becoming quite frustrated. Could she really be forgetting? What do you think?

(A) I think she is trying to tell you something. The games she once enjoyed playing with you have ceased to be fun. Something about the way Mom plays the game has changed. The rules are different.

As that first day of school inches steadily closer, you have become increasingly determined to insure that, when the dash to the head of the class begins, she will be in the pole position.

And she, in turn, has grown increasingly confused and uncomfortable with the expectations. This is no longer a game—this is serious business, the make-it-or-break-it stuff of real life. What began as a playful adventure two years ago has evolved into a repetitiously boring demand that shouldn't be made on a child of four and a half.

Where on earth did you get the idea that knowing letters and numbers is essential for a four-and-a-half-year-old? Never mind, I know the answer. I've been there too.

Parenthood is an uncertain undertaking. No one comes around saying, "Good job, Mom!" The standards are vague and indefinite, making it virtually impossible to assess how well you are doing.

Somewhere along the line we begin measuring our own adequacy against how well, or quickly, our children "perform" the normal process of growth and development. Christy, who talked at twelve months, is "smarter" than sixteen-month-old Jody, who still says "goo-gaa." Therefore, Christy's parents must be creating a better environment than Jody's parents.

This absurd concern with who has the most advanced kid on the block is all too common. Whose lives are our children living? Theirs or ours?

Any developmentally healthy child can be taught to recite and even recognize the letters of the alphabet by the age of four. The same is true for numbers. But it doesn't mean a thing. Learning how to say "ef" when shown this shape—F—is no more outstanding an accomplishment than learning to say "dog," when a furry, four-legged creature runs up and licks your face. The crucial difference, however, is that the meaning of "dog" can be experienced directly, while the meaning of "ef" is completely abstract. It doesn't mean a *thing* to a four-year-old.

Furthermore, the head start you hope to provide your daughter is unlikely to give her any enduring advantage. The child who enters school already armed with her ABC's (and so on) may enjoy a brief stint as valedictorian of her kindergarten or first grade, but within two years she will, in all likelihood, be performing at about the same level she would have been without the push.

Take the cue and stop working so hard. You aren't a teacher, you're her mother—remember? And she's just four and a half. If she has what it takes to excel, all she needs from you is the opportunity, and your support and confidence in her.

Instead of the daily "drill," take a walk together around the neighborhood. Go to a park. Feed the ducks. She's only four and a half once—for a very short time.

How to Make a Kid Hate Piano (or anything else for that matter)

Several years ago, I received a letter from a mother whose daughter wanted to quit piano lessons after only six months. I ran her letter and my answer—"If your daughter has discovered that she doesn't enjoy piano, let her quit"—in my syndicated newspaper column. That didn't sit well with a number of piano teachers.

One, who identified herself as a "University of Southern California graduate in piano performance, a performing artist and piano teacher of twenty years, and a parent of two daughters studying piano" chastised my irresponsible, culturally destructive position.

"We have a nation plagued with people running from anything that is a struggle, such as higher education, marriage, employment, etc. The child should be encouraged to commit to the instrument for at least one full year—preferably three."

She went on to talk about how learning to play piano instills self-discipline, a sense of accomplishment, and respect for the great musical artists of the world.

A school orchestra director from the Chicago area, calling my answer "cavalier," insisted that parents should not only make the decision for the child, but should also "state firmly and unwaveringly that practice will occur at a certain time of the day. . . ."

She included a position paper by a big-shot professor of music (since he didn't write me personally, I'll keep his name out of it) in which he says, "When parents decide a child should learn to play an instrument . . . they are on trial, not the child." From the first, says the good doctor, parents must make the child understand that their decision is permanent and he/she "will continue in the program regardless of progress."

No wonder so many kids hate piano lessons. This sounds like a screenplay for *Piano Teachers From Hell.*

What's this stuff about parents being on trial, anyway? So if parents like me don't force their children to practice piano every day, we're a bunch of irresponsible slugs, or what? I can't help but think the professor doesn't really like children.

His "position," which I take is the gospel for many music teachers, feeds the myth that parents are only as good as their children's grades, behavior, and accomplishments. In effect, children aren't responsible for what they do—parents are. So when a child misbehaves or fails at something, parents should feel guilty. That's the kind of mumbo jumbo that makes people miserable, sick, and/or crazy.

But wait! If the child, who had no say in the decision, says he wants out, he's to be told, "Sorry, kid, but I'm on trial here, and I'll be damned if I'm going to be found guilty. You're going to take lessons and practice, like it or not."

Hey! Lighten up!

These folks need to get over the idea that quitting is equivalent to failure. Quitting one thing simply makes room for another, hopefully better. And the only way the "hopefully" is going to happen is if the child isn't made to feel guilty about his likes and dislikes. Take me, for example. If, as a kid, I hadn't been allowed to quit trombone lessons, I'd have never become the great blues harmonica player I am today.

As for the idea that training on any instrument instills appreciation for the musical giants of history, I took formal music lessons for less than a year, and yet I have deep respect and appreciation for the world's great composers: Jimi Hendrix, Brian Wilson of the Beach Boys, and Van Morrison, for instance.

(Q) My eight-year-old son, Smitty, has been enrolled in Suzuki violin lessons since kindergarten. He likes his teacher, the opportunities for performance, and seems to take pride in playing well. What he doesn't like is practice. He hates it, and has from day one. From reading your book, I know how you approached the piano practice problem with your daughter, Amy. I'm unwilling to take that path because to my way of thinking, a music education is not optional. Suzuki method stresses parent participation. Consequently, I supervise Smitty's practice, during which he unfailingly acts cross and ugly. In response, I feel angry and resentful, and practice becomes an ordeal for us both. I've tried various rewards and punishments, including having him pay for his own lessons, to encourage a better attitude on his part, but nothing has worked. What I need from you is some way to help Smitty be more pleasant, so I can be pleasant, and we can enjoy this thirty or so minutes together.

(A) Since receiving your letter, I've talked to several other parents whose children are enrolled in Suzuki violin, as well as a former Suzuki teacher. The parents all confirmed that, yes, parents are all but required to supervise practice. The former teacher, however, shook her head in dismay and told me that parent involvement was not as stressed when the Suzuki method was first introduced to this country.

Who made the decision that Smitty should take violin? If it was you, then why should Smitty take responsibility for that decision? If it was Smitty, and he likes his lessons, and likes his teacher, then why not let the teacher deal with whether he practices or not? I suspect that if you weren't involved, and Smitty could approach his practice with complete autonomy, he would practice somewhat less, but enjoy it more. In the long run, he would probably make more progress. In the event he decided he didn't want to practice, and the teacher wouldn't continue with him unless he did, then one could only conclude that the violin was not for Smitty. Maybe he's destined to become a rock 'n' roll star.

The tone of your letter says you've made this violin practice thing some sort of test. Of your authority? Of your parenting skills, perhaps? If so, then you're bound to lose, sooner or later. I guarantee that with enough strategically applied force you can push violin practice down Smitty's throat. I also guarantee that should you succeed, you'd better prepare yourself for future power struggles that are even bigger, and far more disruptive, than this one.

If I were you, I'd stop being my own worst enemy. This Suzuki violin thing, in the grander scheme of a lifetime, just isn't worth it. I'd tell Smitty that learning an instrument is part of his education, but that whether he does his homework or not is his business, to be dealt with by his teacher. If he decides to practice, fine. If not, so be it. If he decides to practice and needs your help, let him ask for it. If he asks for it and then seems to resent it, get the message and get going.

Divorce

Even though America's rate of divorce has slowed within recent years, it's estimated that nearly 40 percent of all children born in the 1980s will spend some time in a single-parent household. Early research into the effects of divorce on children tended to characterize them as victims of "broken homes." It was taken for granted that these children would suffer psychologically.

Recent research has shed new light on the impact of divorce on children. We now know that the divorce experience is profoundly different from one child to another and is influenced by such things as age, gender, birth order and socioeconomic status.

Looking closely at the various stresses affecting divorced families, researchers now conclude that the risk to children stems more from stressful family situations than the act of divorce. They find that the level of discord between parents is a more accurate predictor of later problems than the separation itself.

Although divorce is almost always painful for children, it creates fewer problems than does continuing to live in the midst of a bad marriage. It's been shown that the lower the level of parental conflict before and after a separation, the better the children's overall adjustment. When conflict continues following a separation, it's almost inevitable that children will become embroiled, if not as pawns, then as mediators. Either of these roles puts a child's emotional health at great risk.

Regarding the often hotly contested issue of custody, children whose parents perpetuate bitter conflict after a divorce are probably not going to benefit psychologically from joint custody. Not surprisingly, children whose parents work out a relatively amicable divorce are relatively unaffected by the specifics of the custody arrangement.

In cases where one parent has primary custody (usually the mother), the child's successful adjustment is very much a function of how successfully the custodial parent adjusts.

In general, however, boys have greater difficulty adjusting to divorce than do girls. In particular, boys are more likely than girls to react to the stresses of divorce with inappropriate social behavior and/or depressed school performance.

Since only 10 percent of children in single-parent households live primarily with their fathers, many psychologists believe that boys have more problems because they lack the consistent influence of a male role model. This explanation is supported by the finding that girls living primarily with their fathers tend to experience comparable adjustment difficulties.

These gender-specific findings have caused psychologists to question the traditional assumption that mothers should be given the benefit of the doubt where custody is concerned. It appears that the standard arrangement wherein mothers retain primary custody may not be generally best for boys, but more research is needed to determine whether this is more of a factor at certain ages than at others.

Speaking of age, divorce tends to be hardest on kids between the ages of seven and thirteen. Some researchers think this is because young school-age children are old enough to understand the concept of divorce, but not old enough to understand and deal with the emotional issues involved. In addition, a preschool child tends to invest security in the primary caregiver, usually his or her mother, whereas an older child's security is more invested in the family as a unit. For both of these reasons, young school-age children are more vulnerable to the stresses of divorce.

It's interesting to note, however, that teens in single-parent households often show more independence, responsibility, and maturity than their peers. It appears that divorce can, in some cases, be a strengthening experience for a child, especially if the child can make a successful adjustment to adolescence.

In summary, the evidence overwhelmingly suggests that divorcing parents should avoid prolonged legal battles, and make every effort to resolve their anger and establish reasonably good communication with one another. Otherwise, a complicated and stressful time in a child's life will be even more difficult.

(Q) My wife and I have decided to separate and divorce. What's the best way to tell the kids, ages seven and five?

(A) Telling children that you've decided to separate is never easy, and reaching agreement on what to tell them can be especially difficult when you haven't been able to agree on much of anything lately. Nevertheless, this is a time for parents to set their animosities aside and work together. It's one of the most important conversations parents can ever have with children, so it's vital that it be done properly.

With that in mind, here are some guidelines for parents to follow when telling children about the decision to separate or divorce:

• Tell them together. Neither parent should be excused or excluded from this important conversation. Even if it wasn't exactly a joint decision, you should inform the children jointly.

• Don't inform the children until your decision is final. Telling children "We're thinking of separating," or words to that effect, will only upset them and make them tremendously anxious. Don't ask the children their opinions about the decision, either. Inform, don't ask permission.

• Wait until a day or two before the actual separation to tell the children. Make your decision, make your arrangements, then tell the children and go through with it. The more time there is between breaking the news to the kids and the separation, the harder they will work to try to keep the two of you together.

• Ideally, the day you tell them should be a nonschool day,

but if that's not possible or convenient, then keep them out of school. One of the worst things you can do is tell the children and then send them off to worry for the rest of the day at school or day care.

• Don't improvise! Decide beforehand exactly what you're going to tell the children and stick to the program. The more you stumble over or surprise one another, the more confused and upset both you and the children will become. It's a good idea to outline the conversation. Decide what topics you're going to cover, what you're going to say, and who's going to say it. After preparing your outline, rehearse the conversation. This minimizes the likelihood of surprises.

• Anticipate what questions the kids may ask and have your answers already prepared. Careful planning of this sort demonstrates to the children that you're confident of the decision, and helps them feel more secure about it as well.

• Keep the actual conversation short and to the point. There's really no reason to let it last longer than a few minutes, five at most. And no speeches, please! As Detective Joe Friday of "Dragnet" used to say, "Just the facts, ma'am." Give the children time to ask questions, but don't hesitate to call "time" if their questions become repetitive or too personal.

• Don't editorialize. Tell the children "what," but keep your explanations simple and brief. The best explanation of all is simply, "Things haven't worked out the way we planned, and we think it's best we no longer live together." The children should also hear that you believe it's a good decision that will, in the long run, work out well for everyone. Under no circumstances should you say things like, "We don't love each other anymore." Nor should one parent make the other out to be the villain, as in, "Your mother has decided she doesn't love me anymore and wants me to move out."

• Be prepared for the worst possible reaction. Sometimes children take these things well, sometimes they don't. If a child becomes hysterical, you must be prepared to step in with authority and restore control.

• Reassure the children that nothing has changed about your love for them. In this time of upheaval, it's important for children to know that certain things aren't changing and never will. In other words, help them understand that even though you are no longer going to be husband and wife, you're still going to be Mom and Dad.

• Let them know what custody and visitation arrangements you've decided upon. This is one area where the children may want to have some input. Regardless, this is neither the time nor the place for a discussion of such a sensitive subject. Later, when things have calmed down, you can solicit their opinions about custody and visitation issues, but this is the wrong time to let them have the floor where such things are concerned. The children should also know that although the parent with primary custody is going to be making the everyday decisions, that major decisions will still be made jointly.

(Q) After twelve years of marriage, my husband and I are separating with every intention of making it final. We bear no ill will toward one another, however, and want to do what's best for our two boys, ages seven and four. Since both of us will continue to live in the same town, and since the kids have good relationships with both of us, we have talked about joint custody. Neither of us feels comfortable with depriving the other of time with the children, so we will probably settle upon an arrangement that gives us both equal time with the children. We want your advice on how to split the kids' time as well as how visitation should be handled.
(A) You're probably going to regret asking me, because I am generally opposed to custody arrangements of the type you two are considering.

The matter of child custody is one that should be resolved solely in terms of the best interests of the children. Split custody agreements, however, are usually drawn with the interests of the parents uppermost in mind.

In my experience, the parents are wanting to either (1) be "fair" to one another, (2) avoid conflict over the issue of custody, or (3) minimize feelings of guilt over having broken up the family. From this perspective, split custody is mistakenly viewed as the most rational and democratic of all custody options when, in fact, it is potentially the most unstable and disruptive.

A broken home is an imperfect solution to an imperfect situation. Likewise, there are no perfect custody arrangements, but some are better than others.

Before I proceed any further, I should say that I'm sure there are some split custody situations out there that are the best of all possible imperfect worlds for the people, and especially the children, involved. But show me one that was arrived at by putting children's interests first, and I'll show you ten that were arrived at by parents seeking to protect their own interests.

I must also acknowledge the danger inherent to speaking in generalities. In the final analysis, the answer to "What's the best custody arrangement for us, and especially the children?" is an individual matter. What's best for the Smiths may not be best for the Joneses. So, when I say that in general, split custody is not a desirable situation, I mean exactly that—in general.

What's so undesirable about it? More often than not, split custody agreements interfere with the formation of stable peer relationships, reduce discretionary time, disrupt academics, and result in a lack of continuity with respect to discipline, routines, and responsibilities. As such, they are destabilizing, stressful, and diminish a child's sense of security. I call it the "Suitcase Kid" syndrome.

In short, divorce is unsettling and uprooting enough for a child without the additional uprootedness of split custody. The alternative is a traditional custody arrangement, involving a primary parent and a primary place of residence. As for visitation with the noncustodial parent, it should be regular and predictable.

When your children are old enough to participate in and accept responsibility for a decision to split custody, discuss the option among yourselves. Until then, I encourage you to put the children's interests before your own when deciding the terms of their custody.

(Q) My husband and I separated several months ago. Ever since then, our usually outgoing, happy, four-year-old daughter has been clinging and whiny. She wants to be with me all the time, which can be extremely annoying, but if I tell her to stop following me around, she begins to cry. Almost every day, she asks if her daddy is coming back. He's not, and that's my choice, but I'm worried that the truth will upset her even more. What should I be doing to help her through this crisis?

(A) Following a separation, young children will often cling almost desperately to the remaining parent. Preschoolers—boys as well as girls—tend to be more dependent upon their mothers than their fathers. Nevertheless, your husband's presence in the home was essential to your daughter's "picture" of the family as a constant, unchanging unit. Her father's departure altered this picture, disrupting her sense of how the world works. To reduce her anxiety, she clings to you, her remaining parent, as if to say, "Don't you leave me, too!"

This is no doubt an extremely vulnerable time for you, as well. Your security has been turned upside down, and your emotional resources are stretched to their limits. Under the circumstances, it may be difficult for you to respond patiently to your daughter's intense, often overpowering need for reassurance. So, if it hasn't already, a vicious cycle may be developing: The more anxious you are, the more anxious your daughter becomes. The more insecure she acts, the more anxious you become, and so on.

If you feel yourself to be caught up in this cycle, it may be wise for you to see an experienced family counselor of one sort or another. A competent professional can help you restabilize your new family situation.

Under the circumstances, it isn't unusual for a child to regress to behaviors typical of earlier stages of growth—behaviors associated with safety and security. Your daughter's clinging is one example of this. She's asking for reassurance that you alone are capable of meeting her needs. And whether you realize it or not, you are.

Let your daughter know that there are times for closeness and times when both of you need to be in different places, doing different things. If you don't want her sitting on your lap or following you around, be clear and firm about that. If she cries, just give her a comfortable place to do her crying in. Giving her unlimited access to you, while it's what she wants, isn't what she needs and will only make matters worse.

Answer her questions clearly and honestly. By no means should you editorialize about the separation. Just stick to the facts. Tell her that Daddy isn't coming back to live with you, but make no attempt to explain the reasons behind that to her. Tell her what role her daddy will continue to play in her life, and remember that he will continue to play a role in your life as well. In the long run, the best thing for your daughter is two parents who do their best to put aside the animosities that contributed to their breakup and make every effort to communicate often and well.

(Q) Three years ago, my husband and I divorced. Our son, six, sees his daddy two weekends a month and during holidays. The problem is that whenever I discipline Jimmy or tell him he can't have something he wants, he becomes furious with me. He tells me he hates me and wants to live with his daddy. Several friends have said this is just a manipulation and not to let it bother me, but I don't understand why he says it so much.

(A) He says it because you believe it. When you stop believing a six-year-old knows which parent is best suited to meeting his needs, he will stop saying it.

Relax. Nearly all children say things of this sort sometime. In my years on the front lines, I've heard them all, ranging from that timeless standard, "I Hate You!" (played in the key of screech) to the slightly more uptempo "You're the meanest Daddy in the World (Sho-Bop-Sho-Bop)." So what? Nothing, that's what.

Children are masters of exaggeration. Under the influence of frustration, they can blow the most insignificant of events completely out of proportion.

Why take "I hate you" any more seriously than "I hate Rusty!" ("He pushed me!")? What makes the former more final, more meaningful, than the latter?

Children are mountain-makers. They can't control their emotions any better than they can control their lives. And for these reasons, they need parents in control of their *own* emotions and circumstances.

The mountains children build crumble quickly—unless adults act impressed by them, that is. You're making too much of Jimmy's threats. Your anxiety has put power in his hands—too much power for a six-year-old to handle.

Far from manipulating *you,* you are inadvertently manipulating *him* into believing he really would rather be with his daddy. If the words are powerful enough to make Mom cringe, then perhaps they *are* true.

The next time Jimmy says he wants to live with his daddy, look him in the eye and say, "You live with *me,* and you will do what I tell you to do."

If he persists in his fury, send him to his room immediately, with instructions not to come out until he's calm and ready to cooperate.

Parenthood is not a popularity contest.

(Q) I am a divorced father and have visitation with my six-year-old daughter every other weekend. For the first year or so after her mother and I separated, Angie always seemed excited to see me when I picked her up. During our time together, she usually stayed close to me, wanting and giving lots of affection. Within the last few months, however, she seems to want more attention from women we're around than from me. If we're over at my parents' house, for instance, Angie sticks close to her grandmother and wants to be included in everything she's doing. If she has a hurt or needs help with something, to Grandmother she goes. She's much the same way if we're with my girlfriend. This probably sounds ridiculous, and I feel ridiculous about it, but I'm jealous. Is Angie's behavior normal or does it mean I'm doing something wrong? If I am, how can I correct it?

(A) You're not doing anything wrong.

Sometime around age three or four, children realize that boys and girls are different. A year or so later, they further realize that boys grow up to be men and girls grow up to be women. These revelations define a new stage in the development of self-concept for a child, because implicit in all of this learning is the understanding that boys and girls not only look differently, but *act* differently as well.

Consequently boys begin looking more toward their fathers and other men for tips on proper "boy behavior," and girls to their mothers and other women for tips on proper "girl behavior." Previously, the amount of attention a child gives to and wants from any particular parent was defined by a number of factors, including the time that parent spends in the home and whether the child perceives that parent as primarily nurturing or punitive. Now, however, children clearly begin expressing more interest in the same-sex parent.

This process is known as *identification* and lasts for upward of two years. During this time, children pay close attention to the parent who is more "like" them. In addition, this age boy will be more interested in men in general, and this age girl will be more interested in women.

So, Angie is nothing but normal. If anything, she must feel very secure in her relationship with you to be able to give attention freely to other adults in your presence.

My advice is to let the situation run its course, as it will in a couple of years time. If you express your jealousy, it will only confuse her and make it difficult for her to be open with and close to you. As Angie nears adolescence, she will begin seeking more attention from you as a means of "testing" her newly acquired femininity.

Having a daughter who went through these stages, I can assure you that it's well worth the wait.

(Q) I have been divorced from my ex-husband for nearly ten years. We've both remarried but I have custody of our son, who is now thirteen. His visits with his dad, which occur fairly often, are like a vacation. He has very few responsibilities, and because there are no other children by his father's second marriage, he is treated like royalty by father and stepmother alike. Now he tells me he wants to go live with his father, which like a slap in the face after ten years of being the responsible parent. Sooner or later, he's bound to become disillusioned at discovering some of his father's faults, which include a bad temper and a tendency to blame the closest person when something goes wrong. Both my mother and my husband say I should let him go, but I'm not so sure. What do you say?

(A) I'm not going to attempt to tell you what to do, because I don't know enough of the facts to arrive at even an opinion. But I'll tell you a story, for what it's worth.

Once upon a time, there was a boy who parents were divorced when he was four years old. When he was six, his mother remarried and they moved to a big city more than a thousand miles away from his father, who had also remarried.

From that time on, until he was fourteen, his only visits with his father occurred during the summer. Compared with living with his mother and stepfather, his visits with his father were like heaven. He did pretty much what he pleased, and his father bought him just about anything he wanted. The older he got, the more he believed that his father could do no wrong and that all of his problems would be solved if he could only live with him all the time.

You see, at his mother's, there were rules and he had lots of chores and he didn't get but a little of what he wanted. Besides all that, he didn't get along with his stepfather well at all. He began to think of himself as a boy Cinderella—"Cinder-fella" if you will. The more he thought about it, life with Mom looked worse and worse while his imagined life with Dad got better and better.

When he was fourteen and at his father's for the summer, the boy told his dad he wanted to live with him all the time. His dad said that was O.K. with him. Whoopee! Now all the boy's troubles were over!

He wrote his mom a letter, telling her of his decision. He expected her to call out the National Guard to try and get him back. Instead, he got a letter from her that said:

"Dear Son: I think I can understand why you've decided to live with your father. I'm not mad and I don't think you're making a mistake. In fact, I think you're at the age when you need to spend more time with your father. We will all miss you and we hope you will come visit us during the summer, but if you don't want to for a while, that's all right. We love you and want you to know that if you ever want to come home, you can, no questions asked. Be good. Love, Mom."

To make a long story short, the year the boy lived with his dad was not all he had imagined it would be. Things were different, but when everything was tallied, no better. At the end of the year, the boy decided that it would be best if he went back to live with his mother and stepfather. Just like they promised, they asked him no questions, which was probably best, because he wouldn't have known the answers.

The boy in the story was yours truly. I didn't know it then, but I do now that letting me go was the hardest thing my mother ever did. Of all the sacrifices she made for me, that was the biggest and the one for which I respect her the most. Had she not been so understanding, had she let go with anger instead of love, I would never have been able to change my mind and go back home.

You obviously harbor animosity toward your ex-husband, perhaps for good reason, but the fact that you don't like him doesn't mean he isn't or won't be a good parent. Given your son's intense desire to go live with his dad, it may be best for all concerned if you don't stand in his way. Letting go will be one of the most difficult things you've ever done. If you do it like a winner, however, no one will lose, and *that's* what's really important.

(Q) I am the divorced and remarried mother of a five-year-old boy who spends every other weekend with his father. Until recently, Billy has looked forward to these visits. Lately, though, he's been telling us he doesn't want to go and has thrown extremely dramatic temper tantrums when we have forced him.

According to his father, however, Billy stops crying shortly after they pull away from the house and is acting his normal, happy self by the time they get on the road.

When he returns, he seems fine, although he doesn't volunteer much information about the visit or seem eager to talk about it. What little he does say tells us that the visits are not very exciting—most of the weekend is spent watching television, with an occasional trip to the park.

Asked why he doesn't want to go, Billy just shrugs and says, "I just don't want to." We are certain that nothing inappropriate is happening during the visits, but are worried that we may be damaging him psychologically by forcing him to go.

Should we continue to force, or should we let him make this decision? If he's not old enough to decide, then please tell us how to handle his resistance. You probably need to know that Billy has formed an excellent relationship with my new husband and seems to be growing increasingly attached to him.

(A) If there were any indication that Billy was being subjected to anything inappropriate during his visits, I would advise you to suspend them until you could look more closely at the situation. In this case, that doesn't sound necessary.

The explanation for Billy's behavior is probably as simple as this: His visits with Dad are boring. Increasingly, your new husband is meeting Billy's need for a male role model and father figure.

And so, given the choice between staying where his heart is, as opposed to going where the action isn't, Billy makes the logical one. He can't articulate his feelings, he just doesn't want to go. When you won't let him have his way, he becomes upset. In turn, you become unsure of yourself and begin to waver. Billy senses your indecision, and his tantrum escalates, which is what tantrums do when they are not handled firmly.

No, you should not allow Billy the privilege of this decision. He is hardly old enough to appreciate the importance of spending time with his father on a regular basis.

In advance of his next visit with his dad, sit down with Billy and say words to this effect: "Billy, you have been telling us you don't want to go with your dad. When we make you go, you throw a tantrum. We think it's important for you to spend time with your dad, and the decision of whether you go or stay is up to us. We have decided that you must visit with him. If there is something you don't like about the visits, you can tell us and we will talk about it. But you are going with your dad, whether you throw a tantrum or not." Short, direct, and authoritative, which is just what Billy needs, no more and no less.

When Dad comes to get him, if Billy starts to complain, remind him of the conversation and tell him firmly that he must go, no matter what. Then follow through, even if that means carrying him kicking and screaming to the car. I believe his tantrums will stop as soon as you take the bull by the horns.

I don't think your role should stop there, however. Someone needs to tell Billy's father that the visits are probably boring and give him guidance concerning his responsibilities. Maybe he doesn't know what Billy likes and doesn't like and needs you to tell him.

In other words, the father/son relationship needs a little shove, and it sounds like you're in the best position to give it.

(Q) I am a divorced, single mother. My daughter is fourteen years old. Occasionally things come up with which I feel I need my ex-husband's support.

In the past, when I have felt she needed discipline from him, I have called and asked him to incorporate that into one of their visitation weekends.

This has happened several times. The last time I asked him for his support, he refused, saying he wasn't going to be the "heavy" anymore.

He feels that when a discipline problem comes up in my

home, I should handle it. Likewise, when a discipline problem comes up in his home, he said he would handle it.

I disagreed with him, pointing out that she is just as much his daughter as mine, but I couldn't change his mind.

What is your opinion?

(A) I agree with each of you to a certain extent. For the most part, you should each handle the day-to-day discipline of your daughter in your own homes.

There will also be times, however, when you should both be involved in whatever discipline the situation demands. But when those occasions arise, I agree with your ex-husband that you shouldn't ask him to play the "heavy."

It's completely appropriate for you to request his support (and vice versa) when you feel your daughter needs to be confronted by both of you. After all, you're no longer husband and wife, but you're still her father and mother.

Even though you don't live together, you should still work together where your daughter's upbringing is concerned. This is especially necessary when major decisions need to be made, including major decisions concerning discipline.

The more your daughter sees the two of you working together, the more secure she'll feel and the less chance there will be of her trying to work both sides of the fence to her advantage.

When a serious situation arises concerning her behavior, instead of asking your ex-husband to handle it during his next visitation, request that he join you in confronting your daughter with the problem.

Arrange a time when just the two of you can get together to discuss the problem, either face-to-face or over the phone.

Once you've decided how you're going to handle it, then arrange a second time when the two of you can discuss the situation with your daughter.

Let her see that where discipline is concerned, the two of you are on the same wavelength. This approach provides you with the support you will sometimes need from your ex-husband, but relieves him of having to play the "heavy."

(Q) After twelve years of marriage, we have decided to get a divorce. We recently read an article that said that children from broken homes are at great risk for developing emotional problems. Now we're not so sure about our plans. Even though we both know we would be happier apart than living together, we aren't willing to do anything for ourselves that would permanently damage our children, ages ten, seven, and four. Can you help us solve our dilemma?

(A) What you read is true, as far as it goes. Children of divorce are at increased risk for emotional, social, and academic difficulties. Two of your children are within the range of highest risk, which lies between seven and thirteen.

What the research doesn't tell us, however, and—in fact—will never be able to tell us, is how these children would have fared had their parents stayed together. That's the "children of parents who probably should have gotten a divorce but didn't" group. Although we will never be certain how these kids fare, we can base a certain amount of speculation on the findings of research into the lives of adults who, as children, grew up in dysfunctional families. This includes adult children of alcoholics.

The preliminary findings suggest that, as adults, these kids do even less well than children whose parents divorced. They are likely to enter into codependent relationships themselves, and it is highly likely that they will develop emotional problems. In this way, the seeds of dysfunctionality get handed down from generation to generation.

Keep in mind that for a given individual, research can never tell us what *will* happen. It can only tell us what *has* happened. Whether "might" becomes fact depends on the interplay of more variables than researchers will ever be able to identify, much less allow for as control factors.

Research also generates dilemmas of its own. For example, it finds that boys generally do better academically and otherwise in the custody of their fathers. However, to routinely give fathers custody of their male children would mean, in many cases, that male and female siblings would be separated. While this might solve one problem, it would create a host of others.

I have always maintained that what is in the best interest of parents is also most likely in the best interest of the children. My parents divorced when I was four years old. Both parents remarried, and with the exception of one year during high school spent with my father, I lived with my mother and stepfather. As a child, I was never aware of suffering as the result of my parents' decision, and as an adult, I am absolutely certain they did the right thing for themselves and that I was better off for it.

This is certain: The negative effects of divorce are significantly mitigated when (a) children have regular contact with the noncustodial parent, and (b) parents continue to communicate well concerning the children. While there are no guarantees, the fact that you were concerned enough by what you read to reconsider your decision, that you took the time to seek a professional opinion, and that you were willing to make a personal sacrifice suggests that if you go ahead with your original plans, your children will be fine.

(Q) I am divorced and the mother of a five-year-old girl. My ex-husband sees our daughter every other weekend. He has money to do things for her that I simply can't afford, so her time with Daddy is generally very exciting, which, in turn, means that I have problems settling her down after every visit. For a day or two, she is moody, irritable, very active, and wants to talk constantly about what "she and Daddy did," which is the last thing I want to hear. She has recently started screaming things like, "I like my daddy better'n you!" and "I wanta live with my daddy!" when she's upset with me. This tears me up, and I don't know how to handle her at these times. I've tried talking calmly, but she can probably tell I'm upset. What can you suggest?

(A) The problems and frustrations you describe are all part of what I call "single-mother syndrome."

You resent the freedom and the range of options your ex-husband enjoys in his relationship with your daughter. You resent the fact that he can afford to fill their time together with goodies, but doesn't have to invest any of his time toward the day-to-day responsibilities required of a full-time parent. The arrangement seems to guarantee that you get all the work while he gets most of the rewards.

So, naturally, the last thing you want to hear from your daughter is what a funtastic time she has with Daddy. But you will hear it anyway, because she comes back with her batteries fully charged, already looking forward to next time. You may feel like somebody who just fills the gaps between one "holiday" and the next.

It would help if you developed more understanding of your daughter's point of view. It is, for instance, common for a child whose parents are divorced to put the absent parent (usually the father) on a pedestal. In the child's eyes, Daddy becomes a heroic figure without fault or blemish. The ideal quickly becomes a substitute for the real. The child appoints herself Keeper of the Image, which she polishes and keeps spotless from one visit to the next.

This hero worship is quite enough to push any single mother's tolerance over the line. After all, you probably remember Daddy as a genuine unmentionable.

Unfortunately, the more irritated you are with the talk about Daddy and the marvelous things he does, the more defensive and protective your daughter will become about her relationship with him. Furthermore, she will sense the power which Daddy's name commands in her behalf. When things don't go her way, she will let fly with, "I like my daddy better'n you!"

The best thing you could do for yourself is *listen* when your daughter wants to describe her adventures in pater-dise. In fact, don't just listen—ask questions and probe for details. Take control of the conversation so you will be in a position to say, after an appropriate length of time, "Well, that's all very exciting to talk about, and I'm glad you have fun with your daddy. Mommy is going to stop talking now and go finish my magazine, and I want you to go play in your room." In this way, you begin to redefine the terms of your relationship as soon as she comes home.

Accept that she has a glorious time with Daddy. That's the way it *should* be. You wouldn't wish her a rotten time every two weeks, would you? Furthermore, Dad has a right to take her higher than a kite every time he sees her. Her joy and enthusiasm make being a once-every-two-weeks daddy *almost* meaningful for him.

The trouble you have managing her after she comes home is not Dad's fault. Your resentment is your own undoing. It incapacitates your authority, drives a wedge between the two of you, and sets up confrontations.

Everything rests on your willingness to lay down the sword and listen. By listening (and talking), you invite her to become reinvolved with you and make it less likely that she will carry Daddy's banner around the house.

The more interest you show in her, the easier it will be to reestablish control and the more she will appreciate and look forward to the low-key, secure predictability of home. After all, there really is no place like home, and she knows it.

(Q) My husband and I separated about three months ago, but have remained on fairly good terms. The oldest of our two children, ages eight and four, recently started complaining of things that make us worry that he might be depressed.

Every so often, for instance, he tells us he thinks "bad thoughts" about one of us getting hurt. He says these thoughts just "pop into his head" without warning. Other than this, he's shown no sign that anything's wrong. He's a very active, imaginative child who does well in school.

Both he and his brother, who seems oblivious to our separation, spend plenty of time with each of us. Can you give us some idea of what's going on and what we can do to help him?

(A) To begin with, there's a distinct difference between an adjustment reaction and depression. When parents separate, children are likely to experience a temporary loss of security.

In this case, your son is probably experiencing fears and anxieties around the issues of loss and abandonment.

He may not be able to put his feelings into words, so they take the form of "bad thoughts" that may seem to him almost nightmarish in terms of both content and his inability to control them.

They may indicate a need for him to do more talking about the separation, if not with you, then perhaps with a professional counselor. Up to this point, however, we're talking about an adjustment reaction.

Depression presents a far more serious clinical picture. Typically, a depressed child will exhibit one or more of the following symptoms:

- Deteriorating school performance.
- A dramatic personality change, usually marked by moodiness, irritability, fatigue and/or withdrawal.
- A retreat from social activities.

• The relatively sudden onset of provocative, attention-seeking behaviors.

• Prolonged loss of appetite or sleeplessness.

It's impossible, of course, for me to make a diagnosis, but the information provided leads me to believe your son probably isn't depressed.

If you have any doubts, however, you should seek a formal evaluation from a psychologist or psychiatrist who specializes in children's mental health issues.

There are two reasons why your eight-year-old has reacted more dramatically to the separation than your four-year-old:

First, the oldest child in a family is almost always the one hardest hit by separation and divorce. This is the child who feels the greatest sense of responsibility for the overall well-being of the family.

In this regard, it may be helpful, if you haven't done so already, to reassure your son that he had nothing to do with the decision to separate and that he couldn't have done anything to prevent it.

Second, a four-year-old child usually attaches more security to one parent than the other. If that parent is available and meeting the child's security needs in an adequate manner, a four-year-old may not experience any significant loss of security when parents separate.

By age six or seven, however, a child will have attached a great deal of security to the fact of parents being together. For this reason, a separation is more likely to hit this age child harder than it would have when he was younger.

Adoption

In the years since *Parent Power!* was first published, I've become extremely interested in adoption issues. My interest was first piqued by a mid-1980s *Charlotte Observer* feature story about a woman who had found the child she'd given up for adoption some twenty years earlier. The story gushed about how wonderful it was that these two people had finally been reunited, that their lives were now truly complete, and so on. Little was made of the fact that the birth mother had hired a "search consultant" (a.k.a. private detective) to find her child and, that accomplished, simply called him one day to announce, "Hi. I'm your mother." This was, I felt, completely irresponsible. I also felt that the manner in which the story was written cast birth mother and long-since-adopted son as victims of an insensitive system that conspired to keep them apart from one another.

I began asking questions and discovered that there is a movement afoot to reunite birth parents with their adopted children; that the organizations behind this movement are lobbying for legislation that would force all adoptions to be "open"—meaning that the birth parent(s) know the adoptive parents' identities and vice versa; that these organizations are encouraging birth parents to believe and act as if their "rights" supersede those of the child's legal parents. The media is giving these folks a platform and treating them as victims. Both Phil Donahue and Oprah Winfrey have staged tearful "reunions" on their shows, to the tearful applause of their studio audiences. As a result, adoptive parents are beginning to feel as if they are under siege, that their privacy is threatened, that their children may someday be "claimed" by someone else and that the courts may support the claim.

I wrote a series of articles attacking the philosophy, practices, and motives of the birth-parent movement. As a result, my name showed up on a "hit list" published by a group that calls itself Concerned United Birth parents. I am, they assert, one of a number of scoundrels who are in need of "education." They are, I assert, in need of lessons in manners, respect, and reality. The children they are so bold as to call "theirs" are not theirs at all. Whatever the circumstances, they gave those children up for adoption, thus relinquishing all parental rights. Those children have but one set of parents—the people who raised them.

(Q) My husband and I have been married for seven years and have a five-year-old daughter. Our original plan was to have two children, but physical problems are going to prevent my getting pregnant again.

We are thinking about adopting an older, hard-to-place child, perhaps as old as ten. Our reasons for wanting an older child include not only wanting to provide one of these kids with a much-needed home, but also the fact that the waiting period is considerably shorter, by as much as several years.

If we didn't have anyone else to think of but ourselves, we would adopt as soon as possible, but we are somewhat concerned about how this might affect our daughter. She is extremely well-adjusted, and we wouldn't want to do anything at this point that would jeopardize her self-esteem.

We have talked with her about it, and she has expressed excitement at the idea, but we aren't convinced that she knows what all would be involved. We would appreciate any advice you can give us.

(A) I see no problem with the idea of adopting a second child. However, I would definitely advise against adopting a child older than your daughter.

One can't help but appreciate your reasons for wanting an older child, but I think things would work out much better in the long run if you "bit the bullet" and put yourselves on the waiting list for an infant or toddler.

Bringing an older child into your family would, in effect, displace your daughter's status as firstborn. This displacement could be potentially devastating to her security and self-esteem.

A child's personality and self-concept develop, to a significant degree, in response to his or her birth order. In fact, it's possible to make predictions about personality characteristics on the basis of birth order.

Firstborn children, for instance, tend to be more responsible and achievement-oriented than children born second or third in the family.

In turn, a child's sense of security is firmly rooted in his or her perception of self and the world, which we've established is intimately related to the child's birth order. So, to tamper with a child's position in the family is also to tamper with that child's personality, self-concept, and security.

Since a child's self-concept is fairly well established between ages three and four, I would recommend to parents who are considering adopting an older child that they not do so if an already existing child is four or older.

You're right in saying that your daughter cannot possibly understand the consequences to her of suddenly having an older sibling. To her, the idea of having a brother or sister, regardless of age, sounds wonderful.

Little does she realize how important being the first and forever oldest child in the family is to her security and self-esteem.

The consequences to the older adopted child would not be desirable, either. If the adoption proved disruptive to the life of the family, the adopted child might very well feel responsible for that disruption. In that case, which is quite likely, the adopted child's self-esteem would also suffer.

Please don't misunderstand me, I'm not saying people shouldn't adopt older children, but simply that before doing so, they carefully consider not only the needs of existing children in the family but also the needs of the to-be-adopted child.

(Q) We recently adopted a baby boy. The social worker at the agency told us we should make this adoption part of "normal everyday conversation" from day one. She said we should talk to him about adoption long before he understands what it means, so that it won't come as a shock later. She insisted this approach will prevent problems, but common sense tells us to be more low-key. What's your opinion?

(A) Chalk another one up for common sense. The social worker's advice is considered "conventional wisdom" among adoption professionals. For example, an adoption professional recently told me that from infancy onward, parents should frequently insert the word "adopted" into bedtime stories and make up songs and nursery rhymes about adoption.

This philosophy springs from a 1964 study done by sociologist H. David Kirk, the author of *Shared Fate* (Ben-Simon), a book on adoptive relationships. Kirk identified two approaches used by adoptive parents—"acknowledgment of differences" and "rejection of differences." His support of the "acknowledgment" style led to a simplistic belief in the adoption field that adoptive parents who do not regularly proclaim the differences between adoptive and biological parenting are in a perpetual state of denial and inadvertently are hurting their children.

A 1988 study by family therapist Dr. Kenneth Kaye of Northwestern University Medical School offers refreshingly sensible advice to parents of adoptive chidren—take a relaxed, middle-of-the-road approach to the adoption issue. Kaye concluded that too much acknowledgment could cause as many problems as rejection. He also found that overacknowledgment can result in the child eventually feeling "too different" and therefore inferior.

Granted, parents should tell the child he's adopted. The best time to introduce the subject is between ages four and five. This is when children begin to realize that life has a definite beginning and a definite end. As a result, they begin asking questions about where babies come from. This age child is not only curious, but also intellectually capable of understanding the difference between being born into a family and being adopted.

Talking about the adoption nearly every day and incorporating the word into story and song is as unnecessary as making a daily effort to remind a child that you are his birth parents. Making a mountain out of the adoption molehill also enlarges the possibility of what I term "The Adoption Myth"—the mistaken belief that all problems that arise in the parent/child relationship are related in some way to the adoption.

Several years ago, I saw an adoptive family in which a young teenage girl was having conflict with her parents. Although the problems were typical of the girl's age, her parents were convinced they were due to "unresolved anger" concerning the adoption. They wanted me to talk with their daughter and help her "work through her feelings."

Although fairly certain the girl was not in need of counseling, I did have one talk with her. I discovered that while she wasn't angry at having been adopted, she was tired of her parents' constant references to it.

"They want to talk about it all the time," she said, "like it's something weird, you know? Adopted, adopted, adopted! It's all I've heard ever since I can remember. I'm so sick of hearing it I could scream!"

Her parents later told me they were only following advice given them by the adoption agency caseworkers.

"Well, you're lucky," I told them.

"How's that?" they asked.

"Because," I said, "despite the fact that you were encouraged to blow the adoption out of proportion, your daughter has managed to keep straight in her own mind that it really isn't any big deal at all."

(Q) Seven years ago, I became pregnant out of wedlock and gave birth to a son. When he was fifteen months old, I married a wonderful man who adopted my son and has a fantastic relationship with him. We now have another son who is three years old. We have not yet told the oldest boy the facts of his birth, but feel that he ought to know. However, several people (friends and relatives) have advised us against telling him, saying it will hurt him or he's still too young. We want to be honest with him, but we're confused. What is your opinion?

(A) He needs to know, he has a right to know, he needs to hear it from you before he figures it out or hears it from someone else, and now is an excellent time to tell him.

A seven-year-old will be able to grasp the subtle complexities of the situation. A child this age can think more flexibly than a child even two years younger; therefore, he stands less of a chance of becoming confused.

A seven-year-old's emotional character is more clearly established and less vulnerable than a younger child's. He is more capable of dealing successfully with emotional conflicts that might temporarily surface when the circumstances of his background are presented to him.

An excellent case can be made for not waiting any longer. Unless old power struggles are still begging for resolution, the early elementary years are relatively calm. There is, however, an upsurge in rebelliousness beginning at nine or ten and building to a peak sometime during early adolescence.

A child's reaction to finding out that he was adopted by one (or both) of his parents is likely to be more extreme if the parents wait until the rebellious period to tell him. He could interpret their delay as an indication of a lack of trust in the relationship. That might be all the excuse he would need to escalate his rebelliousness to an inappropriate, and perhaps even deviant, extent.

So, having established this as an opportune time to give him the information, I have a few suggestions which might help prevent everyone's going into a tailspin:

- Make sure your son understands the basic facts of conception, pregnancy, and birth and that he knows what "adoption" means. If he isn't clear on these concepts, you need to give him a mini-course in sex education, with an explanation of the different kinds of families (natural, single-parent, blended) and the difference between natural, step, and adoptive parents. Give him examples of people he knows to bring all this into sharper focus and allow several weeks for it to sink in.

• Anticipate that he may react by becoming temporarily sullen and withdrawn. There's also a chance that he will exhibit mood swings in which he becomes suddenly angry, accusatory, and more easily frustrated.

It's a good bet that he will throw a few curves into the system to test how well it holds up under any stress he might apply to it.

To him it may seem that a lot has changed, including his definition of who he is and how he "fits" into the family. The news may create some temporary disruptions. If so, you must, acting through the strength and solidarity of your marriage, demonstrate to him that nothing has changed. He is the *same* person, in the *same* family, living by the *same* rules, sharing the *same* love as before.

• Schedule a family vacation to begin several days after you explain things to him. Use this time together to reaffirm your bonds. The vacation will make it possible for both parents to be available to each other at nearly all times, thus preventing the child from "cornering" either of you. Any clarifying, disciplining, comforting, and so on which needs to be done can be handled immediately by both of you.

• He may have questions about his biological father, including "When can I meet him?" Answer everything in a straightforward and honest way. It is not wise to allow the child to meet the third party immediately. Explain that his biological father has a life, and perhaps even a family, of his own, and that uninvited contacts would invade his privacy.

If the child persists, assure him that you will share the identity of the biological parent later, perhaps after he graduates from high school. By then, he will be old enough to make a reasonably well-thought-out decision about using that information.

Above all else, let him know that *you* are his real parents, *both* of you. And remember, almost anyone can be a mother or father, but only very special people can be mommies and daddies.

"Ask Not What Your Country Can Do for You, But . . ."

In a 1987 column, William F. Buckley, Jr., bemoaned the "extraordinary ignorance of the younger generation." He cited numerous examples, from Phi Beta Kappan Donna Rice not knowing that Gary Hart was a presidential candidate to college students not knowing the name of the country immediately south of our border.

Buckley blames this epidemic of ignorance on lazy kids, lazy parents, and lazy schools. The latter, he says, have "abandoned their most essential function, which is the transmission of national culture."

As a cure, Buckley suggests that every teenager be required to pass an "Information IQ Test" as part of the requirements for a driver's license.

If the states were to take this bold step, says Buckley, who used the driver's-licence-as-carrot approach to get his son to stop smoking, "what a rush you would see to the books, beginning at approximately age fourteen."

Buckley's column reminded me of two questionnaires I gave several years ago to a group of about fifty private-school twelfth graders, all of whom were college bound.

The first asked questions about pop music, television programs, and contemporary movies (e.g. "Who is the lead singer for the Rolling Stones?" "Name three characters from 'General Hospital' "). The average student scored about 75 percent.

The second pertained to American history and current events (e.g. "From what country did America become independent in 1776?" "Name three American presidents since 1950"). The average student scored less than 40 percent.

No doubt about it, our teens are a generally uninformed lot, cultural bozos who are more likely to have memorized the words to all the songs on the latest Van Halen album than to know the names of all fifty states. Buckley is right; something needs to be done before our cultural traditions, our democratic society and our civil liberties begin falling like dominoes into an irreversible state of disrepair.

But his logic escapes me. There's no connection whatsoever between being well informed and the ability to drive a car. If teens were required to pass a cultural information test before getting their driver's license, they'd be very motivated to pass the test, nothing more. They'd prepare for it by using a study guide published by some enterprising company. In the process, they'd absorb a random set of facts, but would still be ignorant of the concepts that tie those facts together. In short, they, and therefore we, would be no better off than before.

I have a better idea: Begin by raising the voting age back to twenty-one, where it belongs. This is because there is a connection between being well-informed and one's ability to understand and participate responsibly in the democratic process. Theoretically, twenty-one-year-olds know more than eighteen-year-olds, but not sufficiently more to stop at simply that.

Next, require every teen, at high school graduation or age eighteen, to spend a year in some form of service to the nation. In addition to the military, other options could include work among the poor, in national parks, in veterans' hospitals, and so on. A truly universal draft would go a long way toward making responsible men and women out of boys and girls.

Most important, the year spent investing in our society would also instill great appreciation for our democratic traditions and values.

The point has been made that when Nixon did away with the draft, he did away with whatever motivation there was for our nation's youth to inform themselves. In other words, a generation who is not asked to do for their country is a generation who has no reason to discover what the country's all about in the first place.

Buckley's right: The problem comes down to a generation of generally overindulged, lazy kids who have been given too much of what they want and not enough of what they need.

So let's get our youth off their duffs and give them reason to care about this precious and fragile privilege called democracy. After all, the danger to our society of uninformed voters going to the ballot box is infinitely greater than that of uninformed drivers going on the roads.

Junior High School

I don't like junior high school. Never have, never will. The virtual extinction of the neighborhood elementary school containing grades one through eight is one of the prices we've had to pay as school districts everywhere undergo consolidation.

The problem, to begin with, is that junior high school requires more independence, initiative, and responsibility than many children that age may have. Many a child of junior high age, although smart enough to do the work, lacks the maturity to do it in that setting.

The junior high child is dangerously "on his own," a problem compounded by the fact junior high teachers are generally more subject than student oriented. Not only is a junior high teacher less likely than her elementary school counterpart to respond individually to a student who may be having academic problems, but communication from teacher to parent is also less likely to take place.

I risk sounding like I'm down on junior high teachers, but I'm not. It's not their fault; it's the system. These are caring people who do the best job they can within the limitations of a situation that imposes distance between themselves and their students.

That's the academic side of the issue, but the problems spawned by the lessening of structure and supervision don't stop there. There are behavioral and social consequences, as well. As the physical and psychological distance between home and school increase, so do the odds students will begin acting as though they are ready, even entitled to, complete independence from parental authority.

The move from elementary to junior high school creates the dangerous and completely false illusion in many children that they no longer need supervision and structure, that they are capable of managing their lives without interference from adults. It's a rite of passage that occurs two years earlier than it did for children of my generation, and rebellion is the logical outcome.

More than several times have I heard the parents of a junior high student lament: "Everything was fine until she got to seventh grade. Then, all hell broke loose. She began concealing things from us, demanding more freedom, and disobeying us at every turn."

One day, as I sat waiting for my daughter to come out of the junior high she then attended, I marveled at the parade of children trying not to look or act like children: Girls wearing heavy make-up and sexually provocative clothing, boys strutting their comically macho stuff, girls getting into cars with older boys, members of both sexes smoking and cursing. I love a charade.

God bless the "immature" children of the world. Those who are without pretension to be more than just children. The ones who molt their innocence prematurely don't know what they're missing—but they'll miss it for the rest of their lives.

Granted, junior high school isn't the only reason young people stray in such great numbers these days. The media's glorification of youth and sexuality hasn't helped either. Nor has the fact that in many families, children don't have a parent at home after school. Nor has the divorce rate. The difference is that our school systems are a public trust, supposedly responsive to the needs of children. It's unfortunate that none of the many experiments in education that have taken place since the early 1950s—open schools, junior high, the "new" math and reading—have proven worthy. Even the lunches are worse.

Encouraging is the fact that a number of school systems around the country have realized the folly of junior high and are converting to middle schools housing grades six, seven, and eight. Whereas junior high, as the name implies, is a step toward high school, middle school is an extension of the elementary grades.

It's a step in the right direction, and if parents put enough pressure on school boards, it doesn't have to be the last.

Afterword

Having begun this book by talking about my children, I think it appropriate to end that way, too.

As I write these final paragraphs, Eric, now twenty-two, is in his third year at North Carolina State University in Raleigh. (I distinguish that, by the way, from his *junior* year.) Although he's studying economics and business administration, and doing quite well, he has every intention of someday flying for a major airline. Last year, he took a semester off from college and completed the study and training necessary to become both a commercial pilot and certified flight instructor. Over the summer, before returning to school, he worked at a local airport, teaching other people how to fly. He's well on his way to accomplishing his career objectives.

Amy, nineteen, is a freshman at the University of North Carolina at Chapel Hill, where she intends to pursue a degree in television and film production. She graduated from high school with honors and a good-looking boyfriend. Is she still Daddy's girl? Sometimes I almost think so, but she'll never tell.

At the risk of seeming to brag, I'm going to brag. Eric and Amy are Super-Deluxe-A-Number-One-Prime children. They are intelligent, polite, well-mannered, sensitive, outgoing, creative, and inquisitive. But best of all, they are happy people.

Twenty-two years ago no one could possibly have predicted that things would turn out so well. When Willie and I learned that Amy was on her way, life with Eric was still unsettled (see Introduction). He was in the thirty-third month of the "Terrible Twos," which were virtually congenital with him. We lived in fear of his next tantrum, ready to do just about anything to prevent or extinguish it. He still did not sleep through the night, but he seemed immune to fatigue, a condition his parents had become accustomed to. So, what happened?

Willie and I made several fundamental changes in our thinking, that's what happened.

For starters, instead of racking and wrecking our brains trying to figure out how to keep Eric happy, we started asking ourselves, "What do *we* want?" and *making* it happen.

We stopped beating around the bush and began saying "No" when that was what our instincts (or inclinations) led us to say. We soon discovered that, after an initial protest, Eric seemed more comfortable with a firm "No" than with a prolonged bush beating from Mom and Dad.

We swallowed a few "I told you so's" and added "Because I say so" to our vocabularies. To those who say, "There's a reason for everything," my reply is, "Yep, and sometimes the reason is 'because I say so.' "

We decided it is all right for children to cry and for parents to let them. We identified two cries. One occurred when Eric was hurt or sad. In that case, we comforted him. The other occurred when the world did not turn according to Eric's whim. In that case, we let him cry, sometimes sending him to his room until he finished. Lo and behold! He began crying less and coping with minor slings and arrows a lot better.

We stopped using his unpredictable moods to determine the state of our well-being. We stopped worrying about him and started taking care of present business. We stopped flogging ourselves over mistakes, though we continued to make them.

We began paying more attention to one another than we paid to Eric. We restored the equilibrium of our family by planting our marriage at its center. We gave ourselves permission to be inconsistent, to spank in anger as a first resort, and to be "unfair." And that has made all the difference.

I hope I've accomplished what I set out to do with *Parent Power!*—shaken up your thinking a tad, liberated it from the permissive labyrinth it may have been wandering in, and helped make your family life more rewarding and enjoyable.

I have two final thoughts to pass along.

First, raise your children *your* way. Understand that people who write books, articles, and newspaper columns about raising children have suggestions and ideas but *not* the Final Word. If you disagree with them, give *yourself* the benefit of the doubt.

Last, but by no means least, something we all tend to lose sight of when the milk is spilled and the children are urging us up the wall . . .

Enjoy!

About the Author

Family psychologist John Rosemond is director of the Center for Affirmative Parenting (CAP), headquartered in Gastonia, North Carolina. CAP is a national parent resource center whose primary activity is that of providing workshops and other educational presentations for parents and professionals who work with children and families. CAP also provides print and audio materials on parenting and child development.

Since 1978, John has written a nationally syndicated parenting column which currently appears in close to one hundred newspapers across the United States and Canada. He is also the regularly featured parenting columnist for *Better Homes and Gardens* and *HealthFirst* magazines.

Parent Power! is John's third book for Andrews and McMeel. His first, *John Rosemond's Six-Point Plan for Raising Happy, Healthy Children* (1989), which *Esquire* magazine called "refreshingly reactionary," became a best-seller in 1990. *Ending the Homework Hassle* (1990) followed to equally good sales and reviews.

In 1981, John was selected "Professional of the Year" by the Mecklenburg County Mental Health Association of Charlotte, North Carolina. In 1986, he was presented with the Alumni Achievement Award by his alma mater, Western Illinois University.

Throughout the year, John is in considerable demand as a public speaker. His parenting presentations and workshops have drawn high marks from parent and professional groups all over the country.

Last, but by no means least, John is husband to Willie and father to Eric, twenty-two, and Amy, nineteen.

Anyone interested in contacting John may do so by writing him at The Center for Affirmative Parenting, P.O. Box 4124, Gastonia, North Carolina, 28053, or calling him at (704) 864–1012.

If you found this book useful, you'll be happy to know there are more from John Rosemond, America's most widely read parenting authority.

Rosemond is the author of a series of parenting books from Andrews and McMeel. In addition to ***Parent Power!,*** two more books are available at your local bookseller:

John Rosemond's Six-Point Plan for Raising Happy, Healthy Children

Rosemond's critically acclaimed bestseller is a guide for creating a family that brings out the best in every family member. The book is an affirmation of common sense that will free parents from the child-centeredness that is undermining today's family.

The Six-Point Plan is also available as a three-hour audio-cassette tape series (not a reading of the book), and is an excellent tool for stimulating family and group discussions (this book serves as the leader's guide).

Ending the Homework Hassle: Understanding, Preventing, and Solving School Performance Problems

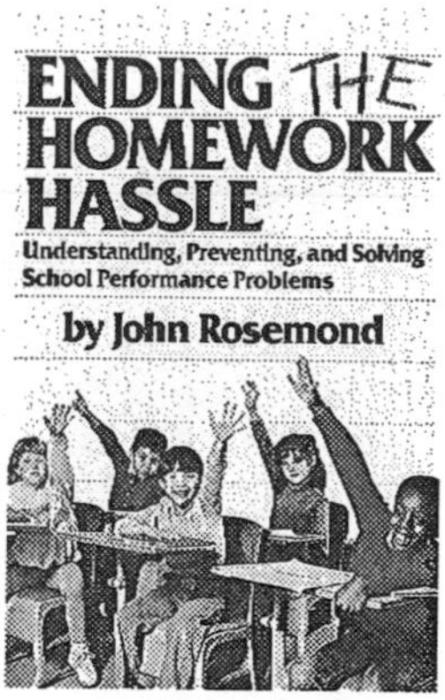

Homework. It's one of the most time-consuming and frustrating of all childrearing issues. But it doesn't have to be.

In *Ending the Homework Hassle*, Rosemond guides parents through a practical, time-saving program that will put an end to their overinvolvement in what should be — needs to be — a child's primary responsibility.

But that's not all! Rosemond addresses just about every school performance problem imaginable. He discusses when and how to retain a child, when to seek remedial help (and how to choose the right help), how to motivate the underachiever, and what you should know about Attention Deficit Disorder — a syndrome that prevents tens of thousands of American children from doing their best in school.

Other books on homework encourage lots of parental involvement. Not this one. Rosemond's approach will help parents disengage from homework hassles as they manage their children toward even greater success in school.